应用型高等院校改革创新示范教材（汽车类专业）

汽车文化（双语版）

主 编 李清民 王万振

副主编 赵培全 范圣旺 黄 健 王 洁 张红卫

中国水利水电出版社
www.waterpub.com.cn
·北京·

内 容 提 要

本书是中英双语教材，共 10 章。第 1 章主要讲述汽车作为现代交通重要的运输工具对社会发展产生的重大影响以及汽车优缺点。第 2 章主要讲述传统内燃机车辆从汽车诞生、汽车初期发展到汽车工业成熟的发展历程，以及新能源汽车发展历史。第 3 章主要讲述大众、福特、通用、宝马和丰田等汽车公司发展历史，推动公司发展的关键性人物，公司主要品牌以及公司世界排名。第 4 章主要讲述戴姆勒、卡尔·本茨、福特等汽车名人对汽车工业发展做出的巨大贡献。第 5 章主要讲述汽车标志蕴含的意义、演变过程等。第 6 章主要讲述汽车发动机分类、工作原理和总体结构。第 7 章主要讲述汽车底盘各组成结构和工作原理。第 8 章主要讲述汽车电气设备各系统组成，主要部件结构及工作原理。第 9 章主要讲述新能源汽车优缺点，纯电动汽车、混合动力电动汽车结构及工作原理。第 10 章主要讲述汽车智能控制、新材料和新概念汽车。

本书在编写过程中紧密结合中国共产党第二十次全国代表大会上的报告精神，基于培养大国工匠精神，激励学生自信自强、守正创新、踔厉奋发、勇毅前行。在知识面上理论性和应用性兼顾，每章都有适量习题，便于读者学习和掌握。

图书在版编目（CIP）数据

汽车文化：汉文、英文 / 李清民，王万振主编. --
北京：中国水利水电出版社，2023.5
应用型高等院校改革创新示范教材. 汽车类专业
ISBN 978-7-5226-1529-5

Ⅰ. ①汽… Ⅱ. ①李… ②王… Ⅲ. ①汽车－文化－
高等学校－教材－汉、英 Ⅳ. ①U46-05

中国国家版本馆CIP数据核字(2023)第086999号

策划编辑：杜 威　责任编辑：赵佳琦　加工编辑：鞠向超　封面设计：梁 燕

书　　名	应用型高等院校改革创新示范教材（汽车类专业） 汽车文化（双语版） QICHE WENHUA (SHUANGYU BAN)
作　　者	主　编　李清民　王万振 副主编　赵培全　范圣旺　黄　健　王　洁　张红卫
出版发行	中国水利水电出版社 （北京市海淀区玉渊潭南路 1 号 D 座　100038） 网址：www.waterpub.com.cn E-mail: mchannel@263.net（答疑） 　　　　sales@mwr.gov.cn 电话：（010）68545888（营销中心）、82562819（组稿）
经　　售	北京科水图书销售有限公司 电话：（010）68545874、63202643 全国各地新华书店和相关出版物销售网点
排　　版	北京万水电子信息有限公司
印　　刷	三河市鑫金马印装有限公司
规　　格	184mm×260mm　16 开本　11.5 印张　287 千字
版　　次	2023 年 5 月第 1 版　2023 年 5 月第 1 次印刷
印　　数	0001—3000 册
定　　价	35.00 元

凡购买我社图书，如有缺页、倒页、脱页的，本社营销中心负责调换

版权所有·侵权必究

前　言

汽车对人类社会的发展做出了巨大贡献。汽车诞生于第二次工业革命期间，历经三个重要时代：蒸汽机时代、内燃机时代、新能源时代。19 世纪末到 20 世纪初，工业革命带来动力装置技术改进，促使汽车成为工业时代最具代表性的产品。当下，汽车给我们的社会生产、个人生活带来诸多便利。随着城市规模不断扩大，生产力快速提高，运输需求急速扩大，交通运输业空前发展，汽车需求呈现旺势。在汽车发展的一百多年时间里，涌现出很多世界知名汽车制造商，如大众、通用、福特、丰田等，同时涌现出一众具有汽车文化气息的世界知名城市，如斯图加特、都灵、底特律等。另一方面，汽车普及给人类生活带来诸多困扰，交通运输压力增大，交通堵塞问题严重，同时汽车在使用中排放大量有害物质，严重影响人类生存环境。内燃机车辆还造成世界范围内能源危机。就目前看，环境污染和能源危机限制了传统内燃机车辆进一步发展，新能源汽车获得巨大的发展良机。

无论如何，汽车是现代社会不可或缺的代步工具和运输工具，同时体现了现代高度发达的技术成就，并造就当今社会的汽车文化和时尚。汽车技术主要包含汽车结构及工作原理、汽车设计、汽车制造、汽车营销、汽车驾驶和汽车维修等。汽车文化主要包含汽车发展史、汽车品牌、汽车标志、名人轶事和超豪华车等。2021 年，《汽车百年》纪录片问世，完美阐释汽车文化内容。本教材重点讲述汽车文化和汽车构造方面的内容。

汽车相关专业中，大多设有汽车文化或汽车概论课程。多位教师对多年授课过程中使用的教学材料加以整理和补充，完成本教材编写。考虑到部分院校要求使用中英文双语教学，本教材采用中英文编写。

本书共 10 章，每段中文内容对应有英文翻译。第 1 章汽车工业发展对人类社会产生的影响，主要讲述汽车作为现代交通重要的运输工具对社会发展产生的重大影响以及汽车优缺点。第 2 章汽车发展历史，主要讲述传统内燃机车辆从汽车诞生、汽车初期发展到汽车工业成熟的发展历程，以及新能源汽车发展历史。第 3 章世界著名汽车公司，主要讲述大众、福特、通用、宝马和丰田等汽车公司发展历史，推动公司发展的关键性人物，公司主要品牌以及公司世界排名。第 4 章汽车技术先锋，主要讲述戴姆勒、卡尔·本茨、福特等汽车名人对汽车工业发展做出的巨大贡献。第 5 章汽车标志和超豪华轿车，主要讲述汽车标志蕴含的意义、演变过程等。第 6 章发动机构造与原理，主要讲述汽车发动机分类、工作原理和总体结构。第 7 章底盘的结构与原理，主要讲述汽车底盘各组成结构和工作原理。第 8 章汽车电气设备，主要讲述汽车电气设备各系统组成，主要部件结构及工作原理。第 9 章新能源汽车，主要讲述新能源汽车优缺点，纯电动汽车、混合动力电动汽车结构及工作原理。第 10 章未来汽车技术，主要讲述汽车智能控制、新材料和新概念汽车。

书中汉语和英语内容是按段落对应的，适合该课程中文或英文教学以及双语教学。双语授课时可用多媒体投放汉语材料，主要用英语授课。这对教师准备授课材料和完成授课任务及学生学习该课程有很大帮助。本书可作为本科院校和高职院校汽车相关专业的教材，也可作为从事汽车行业技能培训或相关领域的工程技术人员、管理人员的参考书。

本书由李清民、王万振担任主编，赵培全、范圣旺、黄健、王洁、张红卫担任副主编，由赵培全担任主审。本书在编写过程中，参考并引用了国内外诸多著作成果，在此，谨向有关学者和专家表示真诚的感谢。

由于编者水平和条件有限，在编写过程中虽认真谨慎，纰漏与不当之处仍在所难免，恳请读者批评指正。意见和建议请发往：2556317330@qq.com。

编　者
2022 年 10 月

目 录

前言

第1章 汽车工业发展对人类社会产生的影响 The impact of automobile development on society 1
  1.1 汽车发展概述 Introduction to automobile development 1
  1.2 内燃机车辆的优缺点 Advantages and disadvantages of internal combustion (IC) engine vehicles 2
    1.2.1 内燃机车辆的优点 Advantages of internal combustion (IC) engine vehicles 2
    1.2.2 内燃机车辆的缺点 Disadvantages of internal combustion (IC) engine vehicles 2
  1.3 内燃机车辆应用困境 Troubles of internal combustion engine vehicles in application 3
  1.4 应对石油短缺的交通运输发展策略 Transportation development strategies to oil shortage 8
  习题 10

第2章 汽车发展历史 Development history of the automobile 12
  2.1 传统内燃机车辆发展历史 Development history of traditional internal combustion engine vehicles 12
  2.2 新能源汽车发展历史 Development history of new energy vehicles 19
    2.2.1 纯电动汽车发展历史 History of pure electric vehicles 19
    2.2.2 混合动力电动汽车发展历史 History of HEVs 22
    2.2.3 燃料电池车发展历史 History of fuel cell vehicles 27
  习题 28

第3章 世界著名汽车公司 Famous companies over the world 30
  3.1 大众汽车公司 Volkswagen Motor Company 30
  3.2 福特汽车公司 Ford Motor Company 33
  3.3 通用汽车公司 General Motors Company 36
  3.4 宝马汽车公司 Bavarian Motor Works（BMW） 39
  3.5 丰田汽车公司 Toyota Motor Corporation 41
  3.6 兰博基尼 Lamborghini 43
  习题 45

第4章 汽车技术先锋 Pioneers of automotive technology 47
  习题 55

第5章 汽车标志和超豪华轿车 Car logo and ultra luxurious car 57
  5.1 汽车标志简述 Introduction to automobile logo 57
  5.2 不同国家汽车品牌 Automobile brands from different countries 65
  5.3 超豪华轿车 Ultra luxurious car 68
  习题 73

第6章 发动机的构造与原理 Construction and operating principle of engine 75
  6.1 发动机的分类 Engine classification 75
  6.2 发动机基本术语 Engine terms 78

6.3 四冲程汽油机工作原理　Operating principles of four-stroke petrol engine ... 80
6.4 发动机总体结构　Engine overall structure ... 82
 6.4.1 曲柄连杆机构　Crank-connecting rods and valve mechanism ... 83
 6.4.2 配气机构　The valve operating mechanism ... 87
 6.4.3 电子燃油喷射系统　Electronic fuel injection system ... 89
 6.4.4 润滑系统　The lubrication system ... 93
 6.4.5 冷却系统　The cooling system ... 95
习题 ... 97

第7章 底盘的结构与原理　Structure and principle of chassis ... 99
7.1 传动系统　Power train ... 100
7.2 车身悬架系统　Frame and suspension system ... 115
7.3 转向系统　Steering system ... 117
7.4 制动系统　Brake system ... 119
习题 ... 121

第8章 汽车电气设备　Electric equipments ... 123
8.1 充电系统　Charging system ... 123
8.2 起动系统　Starting system ... 128
8.3 点火系统　Ignition system ... 129
8.4 照明系统　Lighting system ... 134
习题 ... 138

第9章 新能源汽车　New energy vehicles ... 140
9.1 新能源汽车优缺点　Advantages and disadvantages of new energy vehicles ... 140
9.2 纯电动汽车构造及工作原理　Structure and operation control principle of pure electric vehicles ... 141
9.3 混合动力电动汽车构造及工作原理　Structure and operation control principle of HEVs ... 143
9.4 插电式汽车基本工作原理　General operation principle of plug-in hybrid electric vehicle ... 148
9.5 燃料电池汽车　Fuel cell electric vehicles (FCEVs) ... 148
习题 ... 149

第10章 未来汽车技术　Future car technologies ... 151
习题 ... 156

附录 生词与短语　New words and expressions ... 157

参考文献 ... 176

第1章　汽车工业发展对人类社会产生的影响
The impact of automobile development on society

1.1　汽车发展概述
Introduction to automobile development

汽车尤其是内燃机车辆是现代技术最重大的成就之一。汽车已经为现代社会的发展做出了重大贡献。汽车工业不同于其他工业，其迅速发展促使了人类由早期社会到高度发达的工业社会的进步。汽车工业和其他工业一起构成了世界经济的支柱，并提供了雇佣劳动群体最大的份额。

The automobiles, especially the internal combustion (IC) engine vehicle, is one of the greatest achievements of modern technology. The automobiles have made great contribution to the growth of modern society. The rapid development of the automotive industry, unlike that of any other industry, has prompted the progress of human beings from an early society to a highly developed industrial one. The automobile industry and other industries constitute the backbone of the world's economy and employ the greatest share of the working population.

然而全世界大量汽车的应用已经产生并正在持续引发严重的环境与人类生存问题。大气污染、全球变暖以及地球石油资源的迅速枯竭成为当前人们首要关注的问题。

However, the large number of automobiles in use around the world has caused and continues to cause serious problems for environment and human life. Air pollution, global warming, and the rapid depletion of the Earth's petroleum resources are problems of people's prime concern now.

近几十年来，在与交通运输相关的研究领域，人们致力于发展高效、清洁、安全的交通运输。电动汽车、混合动力电动汽车和燃料电池车已被提议为日后用以替代传统车辆的运输工具。

In recent decades, in the research field related to transportation, people have devoted themselves to the development of high-efficiency, clean, and safe transportation. Electric vehicles (EVs), hybrid electric vehicles (HEVs), and fuel cell vehicles have been proposed to replace conventional vehicles in the future.

1.2　内燃机车辆的优缺点
Advantages and disadvantages of internal combustion (IC) engine vehicles

1.2.1　内燃机车辆的优点
Advantages of internal combustion (IC) engine vehicles

（1）出行便利。在古代，人们出行靠马车或步行。如遇紧急情况路途又远，很难及时赶到。但现在我们有了汽车，无论想做什么都能很快赶到。

Convenient transportation. In ancient times, people travel only by carriage, even on foot. If there is something urgent, and the distance is much longer, it is difficult to get there in time. But now, there are cars, we can go wherever we want and get there quickly.

（2）诱发各种活动。汽车产业诱发出很多活动，如：周末假期旅行；可移动的汽车银行，便利人们进行银行业务；还有可移动的汽车餐厅、汽车理发店和汽车厕所等；参加车展，挑选你中意的车。如果幸运，你还可能成为车模。

Induce various actions. There are many induced actions by the automotive industry. For example, a family makes a car travel on weekend, a removable bank automobile is convenient for people doing bank business as well as removable a restaurant, hair-cut shop, and automobile toilet. Take part in an auto show to choose your favorite car. Just suppose, you are lucky to become a car model.

（3）促进国民经济发展。在主要发达国家，如美国、德国、日本，汽车产业是现代产业的重要组成部分，是国民经济的支柱产业，是衡量地区经济发展的重要指标。

Promote the growth of the national economy. The automobile industry is an important part of modern industry in the major industrialized countries, such as America, Germany, and Japan in which the automobile industry is the pillar of the national economy. The car industry is an important index to measure the development of a regional economy.

（4）解决就业问题。汽车产业在促进其他产业发展中起到重要作用，如石油产业、钢铁产业、公路建设等。所有这些产业都提供了巨大的就业机会。

Solve the problem of employment. Automobile industry play a great role in promoting the development of other industries, such as the petroleum industry, the iron and steel industry, road construction, etc. All these industries provide huge employment opportunities.

（5）汽车是一种文化象征。作为一种文化，汽车已改变了人们生活、工作、思维模式、社会地位、文化生活等各个方面。

Car is a kind of cultural symbol. As a kind of culture, it has changed people's living, working and mode of thinking, social status, and cultural life.

1.2.2　内燃机车辆的缺点
Disadvantages of internal combustion (IC) engine vehicles

内燃机车辆的缺点主要是引发环境污染和能源危机，这也是目前人们首要关注的问题。

Disadvantages of internal combustion engine vehicles are mainly cause environmental pollution and energy crisis which are now the people's primary concern.

1.3 内燃机车辆应用困境

Troubles of internal combustion engine vehicles in application

1. 大气污染

    Air pollution

目前所有内燃机车辆均依靠碳氢化合物类燃料的燃烧以获得所需的能量。燃料燃烧是碳氢化合物与空气之间的反应，它释放出热量和燃烧生成物。热量经发动机转换为机械功率，而燃烧生成物则排入大气。碳氢化合物是由碳、氢原子组成的化学化合物。理想情况下碳氢化合物的燃烧仅生成二氧化碳和水，不会损害环境。绿色植物通过光合作用"消化"二氧化碳，二氧化碳是植物生存中必需的组成部分。动物不会因呼吸二氧化碳而受到损害，除非空气中二氧化碳的浓度增加到使氧气几乎消失的程度。

At present, all vehicles rely on the combustion of hydrocarbon (HC) fuels to derive the energy necessary for their propulsion. Combustion is a reaction between the fuel and the air that releases heat and combustion products. The heat is converted to mechanical power by an engine and the combustion products are released in to the atmosphere. An HC is a chemical compound with carbon and hydrogen atoms. Ideally, the combustion of an HC yields only carbon dioxide and water, which do not harm the environment. Indeed, green plants "digest" carbon dioxide by photosynthesis. Carbon dioxide is a necessary component in life. Animals do not suffer from breathing carbon dioxide unless its concentration in the air is such that oxygen is almost absent.

事实上，在发动机内碳氢化合物类燃料的燃烧绝非是理想化的。燃烧除生成二氧化碳和水之外，燃烧生成物还含有一定量的氮氧化合物（NO_X）、一氧化碳（CO）和未完全燃烧的碳氢化合物（HC），所有这些生成物对人的健康都是有害的。

Actually, the combustion of HC fuel in combustion engines is never ideal. Besides carbon dioxide and water, the combustion products contain a certain amount of nitrogen oxides (NO_X), carbon monoxides (CO), and unburned HC, all of which are harmful to human health.

（1）氮氧化合物。氮氧化合物（NO_X）起因于空气中氮和氧之间的反应。理论上氮是一种惰性气体。然而在发动机内，高温和高压对氮氧化合物的形成创造了有利条件。在氮氧化合物形成中，温度显然是最重要的参数。最常见的氮氧化合物是一氧化氮（NO）。一旦NO排放在空气中，它与空气中的水反应生成硝酸（HNO_3）。硝酸在雨中稀释，被称为"酸雨"。在工业化国家，大量酸雨导致森林破坏、土地硬化、历史遗迹侵蚀等。

Nitrogen oxides. Nitrogen oxides (NO_X) result from the reaction between nitrogen and oxygen in the air. Theoretically, nitrogen is an inert gas. However, the high temperatures and pressures in engines create favorable conditions for the formation of nitrogen oxides. Temperature is by far the most important parameter in nitrogen oxide formation. The most commonly found nitrogen oxide is nitric oxide (NO). It reacts with atmospheric water to form nitric acid (HNO_3), which dilutes in rain.

This phenomenon is referred to as "acid rain". In industrialized countries, a large amount of acid rain results in the destruction of forests, and also harden the lands, and erodes historical monuments.

（2）一氧化碳。碳氢化合物因缺氧导致不完全燃烧，其结果是一氧化碳。对人和动物而言，吸入一氧化碳即意味着中毒。一旦一氧化碳到达血细胞，它替代氧附着于血红蛋白，这样就减少了到达器官的氧供给量，并降低了生命体的体力和智力。

Carbon monoxide. Incomplete combustion of hydrocarbons due to lack of oxygen, and it results in carbon monoxide. It is a poison to human beings and animals who inhale/breathe it. Once carbon monoxide reaches the blood cells, it fixes to the hemoglobin in place of oxygen, thus diminishing the quantity of oxygen that reaches the organs and reducing the physical and mental abilities of affected living beings.

（3）未完全燃烧的碳氢化合物。未完全燃烧的碳氢化合物对生命体是有害的，其中有些成分是直接的毒物或致癌的化学制品，如颗粒状物、苯或其余的物质。同样未完全燃烧的碳氢化合物是烟雾的成因。烟雾能刺激人的眼睛并造成呼吸系统疾病。

Incompletely burned HC. Incompletely burned HCs are harmful to live beings. Some of the components in these unburned HC may be direct poisons or carcinogenic chemical such as particulates, benzene or others. Unburned HC are also responsible for smog. Smog may sting human eyes and cause breath system disease.

（4）其他的污染物质。燃料的杂质导致排放中含有污染物质。燃料中主要杂质是硫，它存在于汽油和天然气中。硫（或硫的化合物，如硫化氢）同氧一起燃烧将生成氧化硫化合物（SO_X）。二氧化硫（SO_2）是其中的主要生成物，当其与空气接触时将产生三氧化硫（SO_3），随后它和水反应生成硫酸，成为酸雨的主要成分。

Other pollutants. Impurities in fuels result in pollutants in the emission. The major impurity is sulfur mostly found in gasoline and natural gas. The combustion of sulfur (or sulfur compounds such as hydrogen sulfide) with oxygen releases sulfur oxides (SO_X). Sulfur dioxide (SO_2) is the major product of this combustion. In contact with air, it forms sulfur trioxide (SO_3), which later reacts with water to form sulfuric acid, a major component of acid rain.

为提升发动机的性能或寿命，石油公司在其燃料产品中添加了化学化合物。铅化合物被用于改善汽油的抗爆性，因此得以有更好的发动机性能。然而这一化合物的燃烧析出铅金属，而铅导致神经性疾病。目前在大多数发达国家中已禁用铅化合物，已被其他化学化合物替代。

Petroleum companies add chemical compounds to their fuels to improve the performance or lifetime of engines. Lead compounds was used to improve the knock resistance of gasoline and therefore the engine gets better performance. However, the combustion of this chemical releases leads metal, which is responsible for neurological disease. Its use is now forbidden in most developed countries and it has been replaced by other chemicals.

2. 全球变暖

Global warming

全球变暖是"温室效应"的结果。"温室效应"系由二氧化碳和其他气体（如大气中的甲烷）所引发。这些气体截获了由地面反射的日光红外线，因而在大气中截留了能量并使之升温。

地球温度的升高导致生态系统破坏，并引发诸多自然灾害，影响人类生存。

Global warming is a result of the "greenhouse effect". The "greenhouse effect" is caused by the presence of carbon dioxide and other gases (such as methane in the atmosphere). These gases trap the Sun's infrared radiation reflected by the ground, thus retaining the energy in the atmosphere and increasing the temperature. An increased Earth temperature results in major ecological damages and in many natural disasters that affect human populations.

例如全球变暖被认为诱发了"厄尔尼诺"现象，该现象干扰了南太平洋区域，并定期地引发洪水和干旱。另外全球变暖导致极地冰盖融化，它提升了海平面，而且引发沿海区域持久的洪水。

For example, global warming is believed to have induced the "El Nino" phenomenon, which disturbs the South Pacific region and regularly causes inundations and dryness. The melting of the polar ice caps, another major result of global warming, raises the sea level and can cause the permanent inundation of coastal regions.

二氧化碳是碳氢化合物和煤燃烧的生成物。运输车辆对二氧化碳的排放占有大量的份额。二氧化碳排放量的分布如图1.1所示。

Carbon dioxide is the result of the combustion of HCs and coal. Transportation accounts for a large share of carbon dioxide emissions. The distribution of carbon dioxide emissions is shown in Fig.1.1.

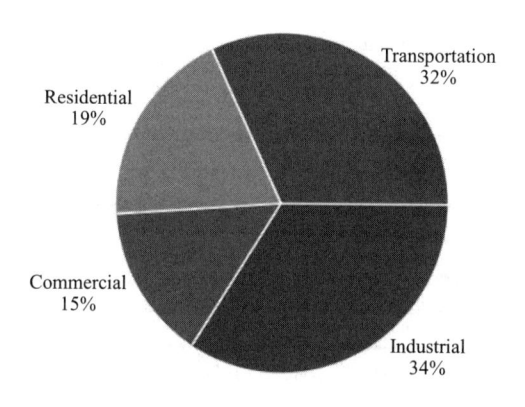

图1.1　二氧化碳排放量分布

Fig.1.1　Carbon dioxide emission distribution

图1.2表明了二氧化碳排放量的变化过程。显然，目前运输车辆是二氧化碳排放的主要来源。除此之外，应该注意到，发展中国家正在迅速增加运输车辆的总量。

Fig.1.2 shows the trend in carbon dioxide emissions. The transportation sector is clearly now the major contributor to carbon dioxide emissions. Besides, it should be noted that developing countries are rapidly increasing their transportation sector.

近几十年的观测表明，地面温度的升高基本上起因于人类活动在大气中释放的大量二氧化碳（图1.3）。部分二氧化碳确实能被植物消化，然而这些自然的消化过程是有限的，它不可能消化所有排放的二氧化碳，其结果是二氧化碳在大气中大量累积。

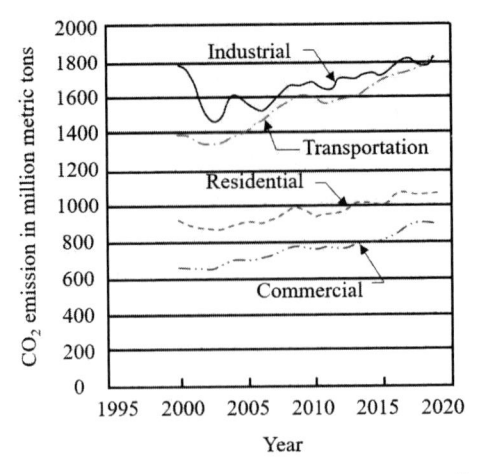

图1.2 二氧化碳排放量变化过程（百万公吨 CO_2 排放量）

Fig.1.2　Evolution of CO_2 emission

The large amounts of carbon dioxide released into the atmosphere by human activities are believed to be largely responsible for the increase in the Earth's temperature observed during the last decades (Fig.1.3). It is important to note that carbon dioxide is indeed digested by plants. However, the natural digesting processes are limited and cannot digest all of the emitted carbon dioxides, resulting in an accumulation of carbon dioxide in the atmosphere.

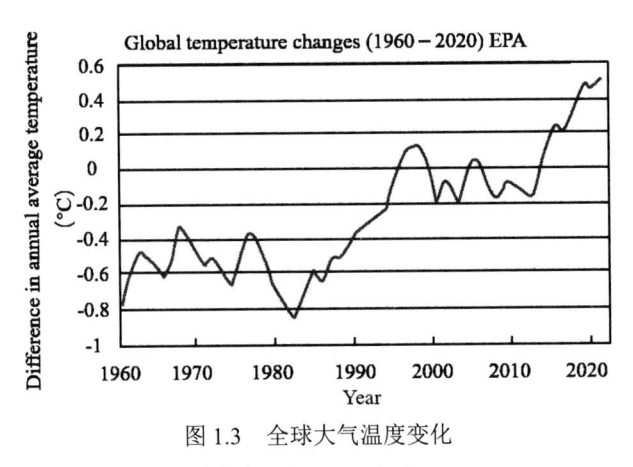

图1.3　全球大气温度变化

Fig.1.3　Global earth atmospheric temperature

3. 石油资源

Petroleum resources

大多数运输车辆使用液态燃料，这种液态燃料来源于石油。石油是一种化石燃料，是活性物质分解物。这些物质几百万年前被埋藏在地质层中。石油生成过程大致如下。活性物质（主要是植物）死亡并慢慢地被沉积物所覆盖。经过很长时间，这些累积的沉积物转化成岩石。活性物质就被截获在一个密闭的空间内，在该处高压和高温作用下被缓慢地变换为碳氢化合物或煤。该过程经百万年才完成。这正是造成地球上化石油资源有限的原因。

The vast majority of fuels for transportation are liquid fuels originating from petroleum. Petroleum is a fossil fuel, resulting from the decomposition of living matter that was imprisoned millions of years ago in geological layers. The process is roughly the following: living matters (mostly plants) die and are slowly covered by sediments. Over time, these accumulating sediments transform to rock. The living matter are trapped in a closed space, where they encounter high pressures and temperatures and slowly transforms into either HCs or coal. This process takes millions of years to accomplish. This is what makes the Earth's resources in fossil fuels finite.

维持石油供应的年限完全取决于新储油地的发现以及累积的成品油存量（同样也取决于渐增的石油消耗量）。历史数据表明，新储油地的发现进程缓慢，而石油消耗量则呈现如图1.4所示的高增长率。假若石油的新发现及其消耗量遵循现在的趋势，则全世界石油资源将在未来几十年被耗尽。

The number of years that oil resources of the Earth can support our oil supply completely depends on the new discovery of oil reserves and cumulative oil production (as well as cumulative oil consumption). Historical data show that the new discovery of oil reserves grows slowly. On the other hand, consumption shows a high growth rate, as shown in Fig.1.4. If oil discovery and consumption follow the current trends, the world oil resource will be used up in the future decades.

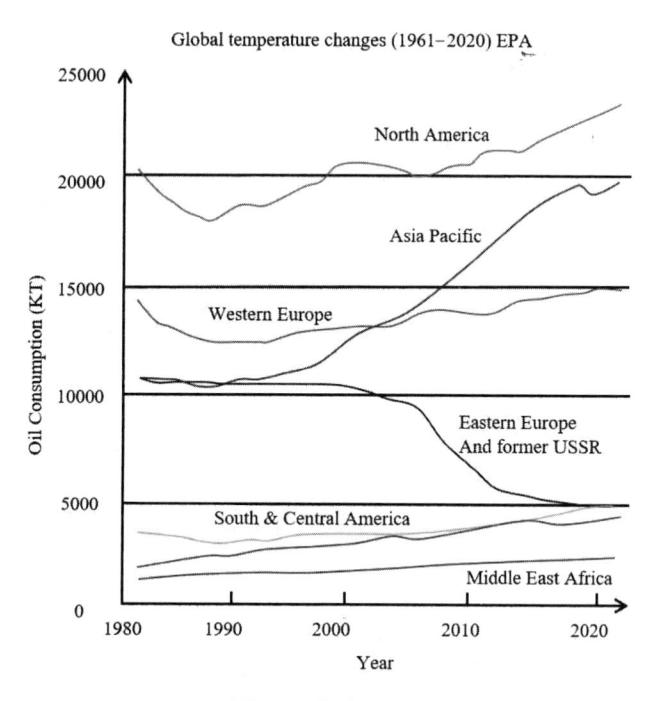

图 1.4　各地区石油消耗

Fig.1.4　Oil consumption per region

4. 引发的代价

Costs

化石燃料过度消耗带来许多问题，其中包括污染、全球变暖以及可预见的资源枯竭等。与之相关的代价难以估量，但其损失是庞大的，且可以是资金上的、人类本身或两者共有的代价。

The excessive combustion of fossil fuels is bringing many questions: pollution, global warming, and foreseeable exhaustion of resources, among others. Although difficult to estimate, the costs associated with these problems are huge and may be financial, human, or both.

由污染引发的代价并非仅限于健康上的花费，它还包括森林毁坏以及历史遗迹侵蚀等。然而健康花费是其中最大的部分，尤其是对享有公费医疗制度和健康保障的居民所在的发达国家。

Costs caused by pollution include, but are not limited to health expenses, the cost of forest destruction, and the cost of monument corrosion. Health expenses probably represent the largest share of these costs, especially in developed countries with free medical service or health-insured populations.

与全球变暖相联系的代价是难以确定的。它包括因龙卷风造成的破坏、由于干旱毁损的庄稼、因洪水招致的资产毁坏，以及为救济受害居民而实施国际援助等，各方面的潜在代价总量可能是巨大的。

Costs associated with global warming are difficult to assess. They may include the cost of the damages caused by hurricanes, lost crops due to dryness, damaged properties due to floods, and international aid to relieve the affected populations. The amount is potentially huge.

1.4 应对石油短缺的交通运输发展策略
Transportation development strategies to oil shortage

改进车辆的燃油经济性对缓解石油短缺有决定性的影响。迄今为止最有前途的技术应用是发展混合动力电动汽车和燃料电池车。混合动力电动汽车采用当前的内燃机为主要动力源，以蓄电池和电动机提供电动能源。它比单独由内燃机提供动力的车辆具有更高的运行效率。目前电动汽车技术发展已相当成熟。另一方面，燃料电池车与混合动力电动汽车相比，潜在的效率更高且更为清洁，现该车仍处于实验室研究阶段，尚需长时间解决其商业化面临的相应技术难题。

Improving the fuel economy of vehicles has a crucial impact on the oil supply. So far, the most promising technologies are HEVs and fuel-cell vehicles. Hybrid vehicles, using current IC engines as their primary power source and batteries/electric motor as the power source, have a much higher operating efficiency than those powered by IC engines alone. The hardware and software of this technology are almost ready for industrial manufacturing. On the other hand, fuel cell vehicles, which are potentially more efficient and cleaner than HEVs, are still in the laboratory stage and it will take a long time to overcome technical hurdles for commercialization.

图1.5描绘了不同发展策略下新型车辆对应的年度燃油消耗量比较。

Fig.1.5 shows the generalized annual fuel consumption of different development strategies of next-generation vehicles.

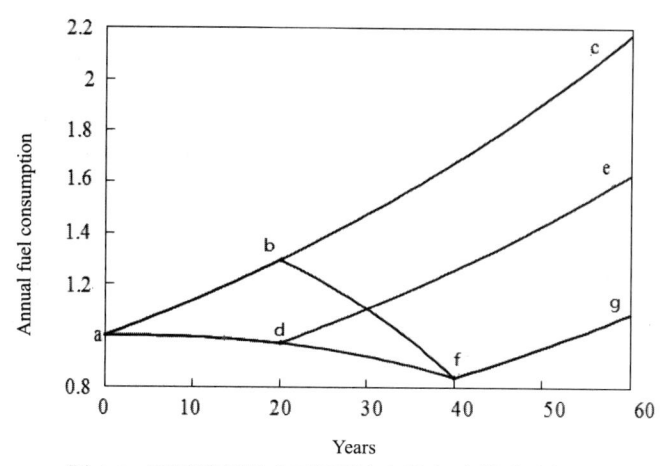

图 1.5　不同发展策略下新型车辆的年度燃油消耗量比较

Fig.1.5　The generalized annual fuel consumption of different development strategies of next-generation vehicles

曲线 a-b-c 描绘了目前车辆年燃油消耗量的发展趋势，其中假设有 1.3%的年增长率，该年增长率即可视为总车辆数的年增长率。

Curve a-b-c represents the annual fuel consumption trend of current vehicles, which is assumed to have a 1.3% annual growth rate. This annual growth rate is assumed to be the annual growth rate of the total vehicle number.

曲线 a-d-e 描绘了混合动力电动汽车的发展策略。在第一个 20 年期间传统车辆逐渐变为混合动力电动汽车；而再经 20 年后则全部车辆均将成为混合动力电动汽车。在该发展策略下，假定混合动力电动汽车比目前传统车辆更为有效（前者燃油消耗量较后者少 25%）。

Curve a-d-e represents a development strategy in which conventional vehicles gradually become hybrid vehicles during the first 20 years, and after 20 years all the vehicles will be hybrid. In this strategy, it is assumed that the hybrid vehicle is 25% more efficient than a current conventional vehicle (25% less fuel consumption).

曲线 a-b-f-g 描绘了燃料电池车的发展策略。在第一个 20 年期间燃料电池车处于发展阶段而传统车辆仍主导市场；在第二个 20 年间燃料电池车将逐渐进入市场，从点 b 出发到达全部为燃料电池车的点 f。在该发展策略中，假定燃料电池车比目前传统车辆在燃油消耗量上少 50%。

Curve a-b-f-g represents a strategy in which, in the first 20 years, fuel cell vehicles are in a developing stage while current conventional vehicles are still on the market. In the second 20 years, the fuel cell vehicles will gradually be put into market, starting from point b and becoming totally fuel cell powered at point f. In this strategy, it is assumed that 50% less fuel will be consumed by fuel cell vehicles than by current conventional vehicles.

曲线 a-d-f-g 描绘了在第一个 20 年间传统车辆变为混合动力电动汽车，而在第二个 20 年间则由燃料电池车取代传统车辆的发展策略。

Curve a-d-f-g represents the strategy that the vehicles become hybrid in the first 20 years and fuel cell powered in the second 20 years.

图 1.6 描述了对应于上述不同发展策略下新型车辆的累积燃油消耗量增长情况。虽然燃料电池车比混合动力电动汽车有更高的效率，但在 50 年内受到时间影响，策略 a-b-f-g（按第二个 20 年间的燃料电池车）的燃油消耗量比策略 a-d-e 高。根据图 1.5 判断，显然可见策略 a-d-f-g（按第一个 20 年间的混合动力电动汽车和按第二个 20 年间的燃料电池车）是最佳的。图 1.6 展现了另一个重要事实：考虑到未来 50 年后石油供应的困境，燃料电池车不应依赖于石油产品。因此下一代运输车辆的最佳发展策略理应立即采用商业化的混合动力电动汽车，而在同时尽最大努力及早实现商业化的、不使用石油的燃料电池车。

Fig.1.6 shows the scenario of generalized cumulative oil consumption of the development strategies mentioned above. Although fuel cell vehicles are more efficient than hybrid vehicles, the cumulative fuel consumption by strategy a-b-f-g (a fuel cell vehicle in the second 20 years) is higher than the strategy a-d-e (a hybrid vehicle in the first 20 years) within 50 years, due to the time effect. From Fig.1.5, it is clear that strategy a-d-f-g (a hybrid vehicle in the first 20 years and a fuel cell vehicle in the second 20 years) is the best. Fig.1.6 reveal another important fact: fuel cell vehicles should not rely on oil products because of the difficulty of future oil supply 50 years later. Thus, the best development strategy for next-generation transportation would be to commercialize HEVs immediately and at the same time do the best to commercialize nonpetroleum fuel cell vehicles as soon as possible.

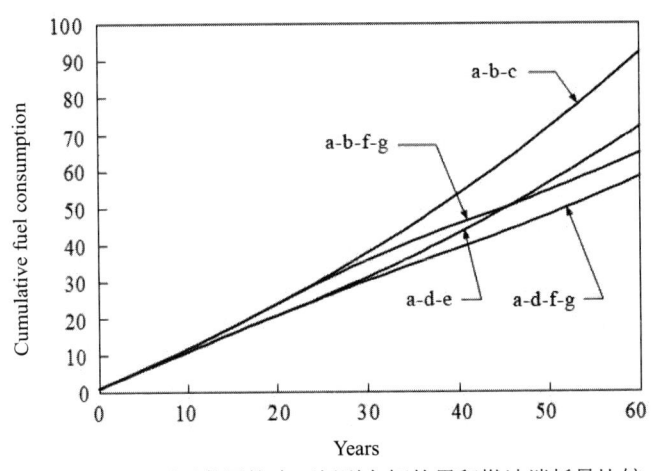

图 1.6　不同发展策略下新型车辆的累积燃油消耗量比较

Fig.1.6　The generalized cumulative fuel consumption of different development strategies of next-generation vehicles

习　　题

一、选择题

1. 目前所有内燃机车辆依靠（　　）类燃料的燃烧以获得所需的能量。
　　A．沼气　　　　　　B．氢气　　　　　C．碳氢化合物　　D．氮氧化合物

2．温室效应由（　　）和其他气体（如大气中的甲烷）所引发。
　　A．一氧化碳　　　　B．二氧化碳　　　C．碳氢化合物　　D．氮氧化合物
3．目前（　　）是二氧化碳排放的主要来源。
　　A．工业生产　　　　B．住宅区　　　　C．商业经营　　　D．运输车辆
4．全球变暖是由（　　）造成的。
　　A．太阳辐射　　　　B．温室效应　　　C．汽油内热　　　D．煤燃烧
5．传统内燃机车辆发展前景是（　　）。
　　A．迅速被新能源汽车取代　　　　　　B．逐渐被新能源汽车取代
　　C．与新能源汽车并行　　　　　　　　D．取代新能源汽车

二、简答题

1．简述内燃机车辆的优缺点。
2．简述氮氧化合物对环境造成的危害。
3．简述一氧化碳对人身健康造成的危害。
4．简述石油资源过度消耗引发的问题。
5．简述应对石油短缺的交通运输发展策略。

第2章 汽车发展历史

Development history of the automobile

2.1 传统内燃机车辆发展历史
Development history of traditional internal combustion engine vehicles

1. 技术背景

    Technical background

汽车出现之前，马车是人们路面上的最好的交通工具，如图 2.1 所示。

Before the automobile came out, the carriage was the best land-based human transport (Fig.2.1).

图 2.1 马车

Fig.2.1 Carriage

2. 汽车的诞生

    The birthday of automobile

在人类发展历程中，人的活动地点变化是重要的组成部分。几乎在每一个时期，人们都希望尽快地把人或货物送到很远的地方，因此促进了内燃机的诞生。发动机借助液体燃料提供动力，驱动"马车"前行。这种自我驱动的"马车"被称为"汽车"。

Mobility has always played a crucial role in the course of human development. In almost every era, man has attempted to find the means to allow him to transport people or cargo over long distances at the highest possible speed. It took the birthday of reliable internal-combustion engines. Engines were operated on liquid fuels to create power that propels the carriage to move forwards.

This kind of self-propelling carriage was called "automobile".

很难想象现代生活中没有机动车是什么样子。汽车要发展，需要满足很多条件，关于这一点，汽车的发展标志有必要明示。这些标志代表对汽车发展所做的必要贡献。

It would be hard to imagine life in our modern day without the motor car. Its emergence required the existence of many conditions. At this point, some development landmarks may be worthy of note. They represent an essential contribution to the development of the automobile:

大约公元前 3500 年，闪族人发明了轮盘；
大约公元 1300 年，更多的改进出现在马车上，比如转向，车轮上的弹簧悬架；
1770 年，约瑟夫·屈尼奥发明了蒸汽机车；
1801 年，雷诺发明了燃气机；
1870 年，尼古拉斯·奥托制造了第一台四冲程内燃机。

About 3500 B.C. The development of the wheel is attributed to the Sumerians;
About 1300 Further refinement of the carriage with elements such as steering, wheel suspension and carriage springs;
1770 Steam buggy by Joseph Cugnot;
1801 Étienne Lenoir develops the gas engine;
1870 Nikolaus Otto builds the first four-stroke internal-combustion engine.

约瑟夫·屈尼奥首次发明了由发动机驱动的车辆（1770 年）。瓦特发明蒸汽机之后，法国军事工程师屈尼奥制造了蒸汽驱动的三轮车，如图 2.2 所示。他的汽车用一满箱水可以行驶 12 分钟。

The first journey with an engine-powered vehicle is attributed to Joseph Cugnot (in 1770). After Watt invented the steam engine, French Army Engineer Cugnot created a steam-powered tricycle (Fig.2.2). His vehicle was able to travel for all 12 minutes on a single tankful of water.

图 2.2　蒸汽驱动的三轮车

Fig.2.2　Steam-powered tricycle

卡尔·本茨于 1886 年 1 月 29 日获得世界上第一个汽车专利，这辆车不是马车改装的，而是全新的、单独的结构，如图 2.3 所示。

The patent issued to Carl Benz on January 29, 1886, was not based on a converted carriage. Instead, it was a totally new, independent construction (Fig.2.3).

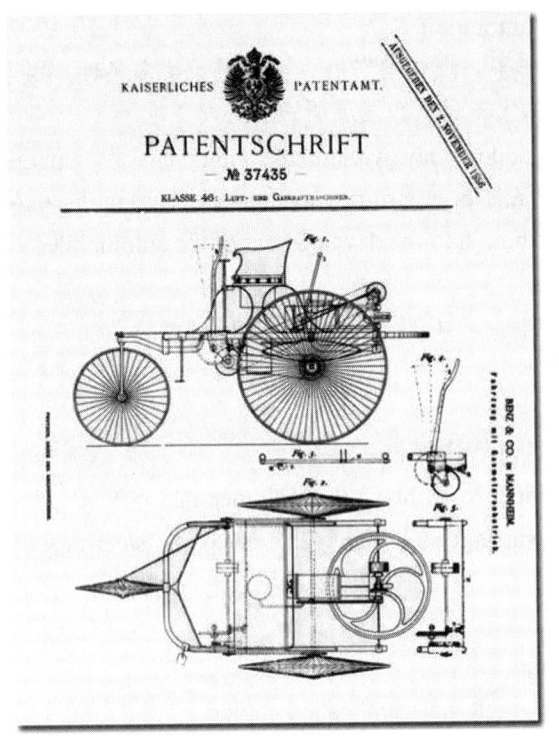

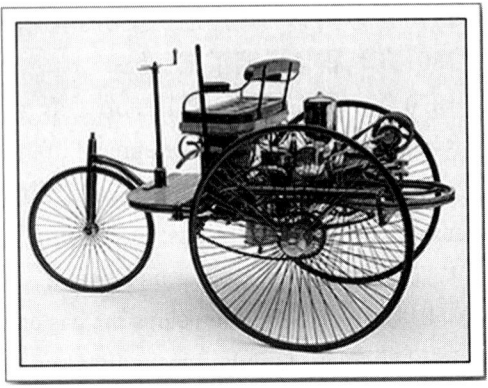

图 2.3　本茨于 1886 年 1 月 29 日获得的专利

Fig.2.3　The patent issued to Benz on January 29, 1886

  1885 年，卡尔·本茨作为汽车的发明者载入了汽车发展年史。他的专利标志着由内燃机驱动的汽车诞生并快速发展。然而，当时公众舆论出现分歧。因灰尘、噪声、危险事故和驾驶员不顾他人随意驾驶引起越来越多的烦恼，多数人提出抗议。尽管如此，汽车发展势不可挡。刚开始，拥有一辆汽车意味着巨大的烦恼，没有路网，不知修理厂在哪里，药店里卖燃油，配件是当地铁匠自主制作的。盛况出现在 1888 年，伯莎·本茨第一次驾车实现长途旅行，这是一个惊人的成绩。她被形容成机动车轮子后面的第一个女人。她还展示了在德国西南的曼海姆和普福尔茨海姆两地 100 多千米（约 60 英里）的超长距离行驶时的汽车稳定性。

  In 1885, Carl Benz enters the annals of history as the inventor of the first automobile. His patent marks the beginning of the rapid development of the automobile powered by the internal combustion engine. Public opinion remained divided, however. The majority of the population protested against the increasing annoyances of dust, noise, accident hazard, and inconsiderate motorists. Despite all of this, the progress of the automobile proved unstoppable. In the beginning, the acquisition of an automobile represented a serious challenge. A road network was virtually nonexistent. Repair shops were unknown, fuel was purchased at the drugstore, and spare parts were produced on demand by the local blacksmith. The prevailing circumstances made the first long-distance journey by Bertha Benz in 1888 an even more astonishing accomplishment. She is thought to have been the first woman behind the wheel of a motorized vehicle. She also demonstrated the reliability of the automobile by journeying the enormous distance of more than 100 kilometers (about 60 miles) between Mannheim and Pforzheim in south western Germany.

3. 汽车的发展

Development of automobile

早期很少有企业创办人——除了本茨——感受到发动机驱动交通工具在世界范围内的重大意义。正是法国人使汽车走向光明。潘哈德和勒瓦瑟利用戴姆勒发动机的营业执照制造出自己的汽车。潘哈德首创了有特色的结构，如转向轮、倾斜转向柱、离合器踏板、充气轮胎以及管状散热器。随后几年，伴随着一些公司如标志、雪铁龙、菲亚特、福特、劳斯莱斯等品牌出现，汽车产业兴盛起来。戴姆勒在全世界销售他的发动机并产生了巨大的影响，极大地推动了汽车的发展。

In the early days, few entrepreneurs—except for Benz—considered the significance of the engine-powered vehicle on a worldwide scale. It was the French who were to help the automobile to greatness. Panhard & Levassor used licenses for Daimler engines to build their own automobiles. Panhard pioneered construction features such as the steering wheel, inclined steering column, clutch pedal, pneumatic tires, and tube-type radiator. In the years that followed, the industry mushroomed with the arrival of companies such as Peugeot, Citroën, Fiat, Ford, Rolls-Royce, and others. The influence of Gottlieb Daimler, who was selling his engines almost all over the world, added significant impetus to these developments.

机动车原有的车身结构简单，逐渐演变成现在我们看到的汽车模样。然而，值得一提的是，那时每辆车都是纯手工制品。1913 年，亨利·福特推出的流水线对汽车行业产生了重大影响。随着 T 型车问世，如图 2.4 所示，他掀起了美国汽车工业的革命。正是在这个时间节点，汽车不再是奢侈品。通过量产的汽车，汽车的价格降到普通民众都可以接受的水平。尽管雪铁龙和欧宝是首批在欧洲推出流水线的车企，但直到 20 世纪 20 年代中期才被认可。

Taking their original design from coach building, the motor cars of the time would soon evolve into the automobiles as we know them today. However, it should be noted that each automobile was an individual product of purely manual labor. A fundamental change came with the introduction of the assembly line by Henry Ford in 1913. With the Model T, he revolutionized the automobile industry in the United States (Fig.2.4). It was exactly at this juncture that the automobile ceased to be an article of luxury. By producing large numbers of automobiles, the price of an automobile dropped to such a level that it became accessible to the general public for the first time. Although Citroën and Opel were among the first to bring the assembly line to Europe, it would gain acceptance only in the mid1920s.

汽车制造商很快认识到，要想在营销市场获得成功，他们必须顺从消费者的愿望。伴随着曾经领先的车速记录，职业赛车手在观众心目中留下永恒的记忆，也记住了他们爱驾的品牌。而且，生产线也在不断扩张，随后的几十年，受追逐流行样式以及经济和政策影响，出现了各种样式的汽车。

Automobile manufacturers were quick to realize that, in order to be successful in the marketplace, they had to accommodate the wishes of their customers. With ever-advancing speed records, professional race drivers left permanent impressions of themselves and the brand names of their automobiles in the minds of spectators. In addition, efforts were made to broaden the product line. As a result, the following decades produced a variety of automobile designs based on the prevailing fashion, as well as the economic and political influences of the day.

图 2.4　T 型轿车

Fig.2.4　Model T car

第二次世界大战对小轿车产生了重大影响。众所周知的"甲壳虫"大众牌轿车由费迪南德·保时捷设计，于沃尔夫斯堡制造，如图 2.5 所示。

WWII had a significant influence on the development of smaller cars. The Volkswagen model that came to be known as the "Beetle" was designed by Ferdinand Porsche and was manufactured in Wolfsburg (Fig.2.5).

图 2.5　甲壳虫轿车

Fig.2.5　Beetle model car

第二次世界大战末期，体型小巧、相对便宜的轿车盛行。为适应这一需求，生产商制造了诸如雪铁龙 2CV，特拉贝特轿车和菲亚特 500C 轿车（意大利语：小松鼠），如图 2.6 所示。汽车制造厂开始演变新的思路：更加突出技术和配件集成化；拥有合理的性价比成为首选。

At the end of the war, the demand for cars that were small and affordable was prevalent. Responding to this demand, manufacturers produced automobiles such as Citroën 2CV, Trabant, and the Fiat 500C (Italian name: little mouse) (Fig.2.6). The manufacture of automobiles began to evolve new standards: there was a greater emphasis on technology and integrated accessories, with a reasonable price/performance ratio as a major consideration.

图 2.6　菲亚特 500C

Fig.2.6　The Fiat 500C

4. 轿车车身的演变

　　Evolution of car body

轿车车身的演变总共有六个阶段，即平板型、箱型、甲壳虫型、船型、鱼型和楔型。

There are all six stages of the evolution of car body which are cart type, box type, beetle type, ship type, fish type and wedge type.

（1）平板型。开始时，汽车是由马车演变的，形状很简单，如图 2.7 所示。

Cart type. In the beginning, the automobiles evolved from carriages, so the car body is simple (Fig.2.7).

图 2.7　平板车

Fig.2.7　Cart type

（2）箱型。1913 年，福特汽车公司设计并生产了新的车身，外形像一个箱子，如图 2.8 所示，它还有另外一个名字：T 型车身。随着轿车的广泛应用，该车实现批量生产。

Box type. In 1913, Ford motor company designed and produced a new kind of car body that looks like a big box (Fig.2.8). It has another name: Model T which was mass produced with cars becoming widely used.

（3）甲壳虫型。保时捷博士发现，小昆虫甲壳虫既能在地上爬，又能在空中飞，它的空气阻力很小。保时捷把甲壳虫的外形引用到轿车车身上，如图 2.9 所示。

Beetle type. Dr. Porsche found a small insect named beetle which not only can climb on the ground but also can fly in the air. Its air resistance is very small. Dr. Porsche used the beetle's appearance to car modelling (Fig.2.9).

图 2.8　箱型轿车（T 型）

Fig.2.8　Box type (Model T)

图 2.9　甲壳虫型轿车

Fig.2.9　Beetle type

（4）船型。1949 年，福特汽车公司设计了新款车身，外形看起来像条船。其成功之处不仅在外形上，还应用了人体工程学理论，如图 2.10 所示。

Ship type. In 1949, Ford motor company designed a new type that looks like a boat. Its success is not only in appearance design but also in applying the theory of human body engineering (Fig.2.10).

图 2.10　船型轿车

Fig.2.10　Ship type

（5）鱼型。该款式轿车车身有较长的尾部，用以减小车身尾部气流。它保留了船型车身的优点，如图 2.11 所示。

Fish type. This type has a longer tail to decrease the air current. It retains the advantage of ship type (Fig.2.11).

图 2.11　鱼型轿车

Fig.2.11　Fish type

（6）楔型。人们发现楔型车身（前端低而后端高）能够克服较大升力，这就很符合现代轿车车身外形，如图 2.12 所示。

Wedge type. People find a new type named wedge type（lower in the front and higher in the rear） to overcome the strong lift. It fits the appearance of modern cars (Fig.2.12).

图 2.12　楔型轿车

Fig.2.12　Wedge type

2.2　新能源汽车发展历史

Development history of new energy vehicles

2.2.1　纯电动汽车发展历史

History of pure electric vehicles

1881 年，第一辆电动汽车由法国人古斯塔夫·特鲁夫制造，它是一辆三轮电动汽车，采用铅酸蓄电池供电、由 0.1hp（马力）(1hp=0.735kW) 的直流电动机驱动，整车及其驾驶员的重量约 160kg。两位英国教授在 1883 年制成了相似的电动汽车。当时该技术尚未成熟到足以与马车竞争，速度为 15km/h、续驶里程为 16km 的电动汽车不足以激发潜在用户的兴趣，所以这些早期结构并没有引起公众关注。1864 年巴黎—雷恩车赛完全改变了这一切：电动汽车以平均 23.3km/h 的速度，在 48h53min 内行驶了 1135km，该速度远胜于马车的速度。公众开始对无马车或如今所称的汽车感兴趣。

The first EV was built by Frenchman Gustave Trouvé in 1881. It was a tricycle powered by a 0.1hp DC motor fed by lead-acid batteries. The whole vehicle and its driver weighed approximately 160kg. A vehicle similar to this was built in 1883 by two British professors. These early realizations did not attract much attention from the public because the technology was not mature enough to compete with horse carriages. Speeds of 15km/h and a range of 16km were nothing exciting for potential customers. The 1864 Paris to Rouen race changed it all: the 1135km were run in 48h53min at an average speed of 23.3km/h. This speed was by far superior to that possible with horse-drawn carriages. The general public became interested in horseless carriages or automobiles as these vehicles were now called.

随后的 20 年是一个电动汽车与汽油车竞争的年代。这在美国特别真实，美国有些城市外围并没有过多道路，这对行程有限的电动汽车不成问题。然而在欧洲迅速延伸的道路要求更高的行驶里程，这就促进了汽油车的发展。

The following 20 years were an era during which EVs competed with their gasoline counterparts. This was particularly true in America, where there were not many roads outside a few cities. The limited range of EVs was not a problem. However, in Europe, the rapidly increasing number of roads called for extended ranges, thus favoring gasoline vehicles.

第一辆商品化的电动汽车是由莫里斯和所罗门制作的电动舟。这辆电动汽车由其发明者所创建的公司在纽约以出租车的方式运营。电动汽车被证明是比出租马车更有应用价值的运载工具，尽管其购买价格较高（约为 3000 美元，对比 1200 美元来讲较高）。该车装有两台 1.5hp 的电动机，最高车速可达 32km/h，其续驶里程为 40km。

The first commercial EV was the Morris and Salom's Electroboat. This vehicle was operated as a taxi in New York City by a company created by its inventors. The Electroboat proved to be more profitable than horse cabs despite a higher purchase price (around $3000 vs. $1200). It was powered by two 1.5hp motors that allowed a maximum speed of 32km/h and a 40km range.

对那个年代最有影响的技术进展是再生制动的发明，这一技术在 1897 年由法国人 M. A. 达奇拉在其小轿车上采用。再生制动技术在制动时回收车辆的动能，并向蓄电池组再充电，这样便大大增加了行驶里程。这是对电动汽车和混合动力电动汽车应用技术最有价值的贡献之一。正是再生制动技术对能量效率的贡献，使电动汽车在市区行车中优于其他任何车辆。

The most significant technological advance of that era was the invention of regenerative braking by Frenchman M. A. Darracq on his 1897 coupe. This method allows for recuperating the vehicle's kinetic energy while braking and recharging the batteries, which greatly enhances the driving range. It is one of the most significant contributions to electric and HEV technology as it contributes to energy efficiency more than anything else in urban driving.

当燃油汽车变得功率更大、更灵活，尤其是更易于操作时，电动汽车开始消失。电动汽车的高成本对于与燃油汽车的对抗毫无帮助,而其有限的续驶里程和性能确实削弱了它面对燃油汽车的竞争力。最后交付使用的、商业上有影响力的电动汽车发售于大约 1905 年。在近 60 年期间所销售的电动汽车仅是一般的高尔夫球车和运送货车。

As gasoline automobiles became more powerful, more flexible, and above all easier to handle, EVs started to disappear. Their high cost did not help, but it is their limited driving range and performance that really impaired them versus their gasoline counterparts. The last commercially significant EVs were released around 1905. For nearly 60 years, the only EVs sold were common golf carts and delivery vehicles.

1945 年,贝尔实验室的三位研究员发明了一种电器,即晶体管。这意味着全球电子学革命。晶体管迅速替代了电子仪器中的电子管,而且不久发明了晶闸管,它可以在高电压下切换大电流,从而在没有低能耗变阻箱情况下,也能调节输送给电动机的功率,并使交流电动机得以在可变频率下运转。1966 年,通用汽车公司制造了异步电动机驱动的电动汽车,该电机由晶闸管做成的逆变器供电。

In 1945, three researchers at Bell Laboratories invented a device that was meant to revolutionize the world of electronics and electricity: the transistor. It quickly replaced vacuum tubes for signal electronics and soon the thyristor was invented, which allowed switching high currents at high voltages. This made it possible to regulate the power transmitted to an electric motor without the very inefficient rheostats and allowed the running of AC motors at variable frequencies. In 1966, General Motors (GM) built the Electrovan, which was propelled by induction motors that were fed by inverters built with thyristors.

在 20 世纪 60—70 年代,对环境的忧虑触发了电动汽车的研究。然而,尽管蓄电池制造技术和电子应用技术有一定的进展,电动汽车的续驶里程和性能仍然是制约其发展的因素。

During the 1960s and 1970s, concerns about the environment triggered some research on EVs. However, despite advances in battery technology and power electronics, their range and performance were still obstacles.

现代电动汽车时代在 20 世纪 80 年代达到顶峰,并在 90 年代初期由厂商展示了几种实用的电动汽车,例如通用汽车公司的 EV1 以及标志(雪铁龙公司)的 106 电动车。虽然这些电动汽车展示了现实的成就,尤其与早期电动汽车相比时更是如此,但很明显,在 90 年代初期,电动汽车决然不可能与燃油汽车在续驶里程和性能方面相竞争。究其原因,在于就蓄电池组,其能量储存在金属电极内。对同等能量容量来说,电池重量远超过汽油。汽车制造工业放弃电动汽车而转向混合动力电动汽车的研究。

The modern EV era culminated during the 1980s and early 1990s with the release of a few realistic vehicles by firms such as GM with the EV1 and Peugeot Société Anonyme (PSA) with the 106 Electric. Although these vehicles represented a real achievement, especially when compared with early realizations, it became clear during the early 1990s that electric automobiles could never compete with gasoline automobiles for range and performance. The reason is that in batteries the energy is stored in the metal of the electrodes, which weigh far more than gasoline for the same energy content. The automotive industry abandoned the EV to research hybrid electric vehicles.

在电动汽车研发方面，关于蓄电池的应用技术显得非常薄弱，这阻碍了电动汽车进入市场。以改进蓄电池性能、满足电动汽车需求为目的，在蓄电池的研究方面也已付出巨大努力和投资。遗憾的是，进展非常有限。电动汽车的性能远落后于需求，尤其是单位重量和体积所对应的能量储存指标太低。受此限制，电动汽车仅适于某些特定的场合使用，例如机场、车站、邮件运送和高尔夫球场等。

In the context of the development of EVs, it is the battery technology that is the weakest, blocking the way of EVs to the market. Great effort and investment have been put into battery research, to improve performance to meet the EV requirement. Unfortunately, progress has been very limited. Performance is far behind the requirement, especially energy storage capacity per unit weight and volume. This poor energy storage capability of batteries limits EVs to only some specific applications, such as at airports, railroad stations, mail delivery routes, golf courses, and so on.

2.2.2 混合动力电动汽车发展历史
History of HEVs

令人意想不到的是，混合动力电动汽车的概念几乎与汽车的概念一样悠久。然而其原始目的并非是有效地降低燃油的消耗量，而是辅助内燃机汽车以保证其合适的性能水平。事实上早期内燃机工程技术的进步并不及电机工程技术。

Surprisingly, the concept of an HEV is almost as old as the automobile itself. The primary purpose, however, was not so much to lower fuel consumption but rather to assist the IC engine to provide an acceptable level of performance. Indeed, in the early days, IC engine engineering was less advanced than electric motor engineering.

有记录的最早的混合动力电动汽车出现在1899年巴黎美术展览会上。共有两辆电动汽车，第一辆电动汽车是由比利时的皮珀组织和法国的维多利亚电动汽车公司制造的。该电动车是一辆并联式的混合动力电动汽车，它装有一台由电动机和铅酸蓄电池组辅助的小型空冷汽油发动机。记录表明，当该混合动力电动汽车滑行或停车时，蓄电池组即由发动机予以充电；当所需驱动功率大于发动机额定值时，电动机即时提供辅助功率。该电动车是第一辆并联式混合动力电动汽车，无疑是混合动力电动汽车的开端。

The first hybrid vehicles reported were shown at the Paris Salon of 1899. These were built by the Pieper establishments, in Belgium, and by the Vendovelli Electric Carriage Company, in France. The vehicle was a parallel hybrid with a small air-cooled gasoline engine assisted by an electric motor and lead-acid batteries. It is reported that the batteries were charged by the engine when the vehicle coasted or was at a standstill. When the driving power required was greater than the engine rating, the electric motor provided additional power. For the first parallel hybrid vehicle, the vehicle was undoubtedly the first electric starter.

1899年巴黎美术展览会上展出的另一辆混合动力电动汽车，是由法国的维多利亚公司与普利斯利公司制造的，这是第一辆串联式混合动力电动汽车。它由商品化的纯电动汽车衍生而来，是一辆三轮车，在其两个后轮上分别装有独立的电动机。一个额外的3/4hp的汽油发动机与一个1.1kW的发电机一同被安装在拖车上，通过对蓄电池组的再充电扩展其续驶里程。

The other hybrid vehicle introduced at the Paris Salon of 1899 was the first series HEV and was derived from a pure EV commercially built by the French firm Vendovelli and Priestly. This vehicle was a tricycle, with two rear wheels powered by independent motors. An additional 3/4 hp gasoline engine coupled to a 1.1kW generator was mounted on a trailer and could be towed behind the vehicle to extend the range by recharging the batteries.

法国人卡米尔·热纳茨在1903年巴黎美术展览馆上展示了又一辆并联式混合动力电动汽车。该车将6hp的汽油发动机和14hp的电动机相组合，由汽油发动机给蓄电池组充电或由蓄电池组辅助驱动。1902年，另一位法国人H.克里格制造了第二辆串联式混合动力电动汽车。该车采用两个独立的直流电动机驱动前轮。电动机由44个铅酸蓄电池供电，而蓄电池则由一个4.5hp燃用乙醇的火花点燃式发动机驱动并励直流发电机给蓄电池充电。

Frenchman Camille Jenatzy presented a parallel hybrid vehicle at the Paris Salon of 1903. This vehicle combined a 6hp gasoline engine with a 14hp electric machine that could either charge the batteries from the engine or assist them later. Another Frenchman, H. Krieger, built the second reported series hybrid vehicle in 1902. His design used two independent DC motors driving the front wheels. They drew their energy from 44 lead-acid cells that were recharged by a 4.5hp alcohol spark-ignited engine coupled to a shunt DC generator.

早期混合动力电动汽车是为了辅助功率偏小的内燃机汽车，或是为了增加电动汽车的续驶里程。混合动力电动汽车利用了纯电动汽车应用技术且使之实用化。尽管在电动汽车设计中体现了很多的创造性，然而在第一次世界大战后，混合动力电动汽车技术发展缓慢，而内燃机技术已经很成熟。就功率密度而言，汽油发动机取得了惊人的进步，发动机变得更小、更高效，并且不再需要电动机予以辅助。使用电动机的附加成本高，以及使用酸性蓄电池组公害性大，使得第一次世界大战后混合动力电动汽车从市场中消失。

Early hybrid vehicles were built in order to assist the weak IC engines of that time or to improve the range of EVs. They made use of the basic electric technologies that were then available. In spite of the great creativity featured in their design, these early hybrid vehicles could no longer compete with the greatly improved gasoline engines that came into use after World War I. The gasoline engine made tremendous improvements in terms of power density, the engines became smaller and more efficient, and there was no longer a need to assist them with electric motors. The supplementary cost of having an electric motor and the hazards associated with lead-acid batteries were key factors in the disappearance of hybrid vehicles from the market after World War I.

然而，混合动力电动汽车设计必须解决的最大问题是电动机控制，这是个技术难点。在20世纪60年代中期以前，电子技术尚未达到适合应用的水平，且早期的电动机是利用机械开关和电阻器控制的，它们都受制于有限的运行范围，与汽车高效的运行要求不匹配。

However, the greatest problem that these early designs had to cope with was the difficulty of controlling the electric machine. Electronic technology did not become available until the mid-1960s and early electric motors were controlled by mechanical switches and resistors. They had a limited operating range incompatible with efficient operation.

虽然历经1973年和1977年两次石油危机，环境忧虑也在不断增加，但这些并没有促使混合动力电动汽车成功地进入市场。20 世纪 80 年代，研究者们的工作聚焦于电动汽车，制成许多电动汽车的原型。期间对混合动力电动汽车兴致不高，归因于电子控制技术、现代电动机和蓄电池应用技术的欠缺。反而是 20 世纪 80 年代见证了传统内燃机汽车体积减小、催化转化器引用以及燃料喷射普及化等技术的进展。

Despite the two oil crises of 1973 and 1977, and growing environmental concerns, no HEV made it to the market. The researchers' focus was drawn by the EV, of which many prototypes were built during the 1980s. The lack of interest in HEVs during this period may be attributed to the lack of practical power electronics, modern electric motors, and battery technologies. The 1980s witnessed a reduction in conventional IC engine-powered vehicle sizes, the introduction of catalytic converters, and the generalization of fuel injection.

20 世纪 90 年代，人们清楚地认识到纯电动汽车难以达到节能目标，对混合动力电动汽车又产生了很大的兴趣。福特汽车公司启动了福特混合动力电动汽车挑战计划，该计划得到众多大学援助，开发新款混合动力汽车。

The HEV concept drew great interest during the 1990s when it became clear that EVs would never achieve the objective of saving energy. The Ford Motor Corporation initiated the Ford Hybrid Electric Vehicle Challenge, which got help from universities to develop new hybrid versions of production automobiles.

此时，汽车公司生产的混合动力电动汽车原型取得了巨大的进步。它们在燃油经济性方面超过了内燃机汽车。在美国，道奇汽车公司制造了无畏混合动力电动汽车。该混合动力电动汽车是串联式结构，它装备一个小型涡轮增压的三缸柴油机和一个蓄电池组；在后轮上安置了两个 100hp 的电动机。

Automobile manufacturers around the world built prototypes that achieved tremendous improvements in fuel economy over their IC engine-powered counterparts. In the United States, Dodge built Intrepid. The Intrepid was a series hybrid vehicle, powered by a small turbocharged three-cylinder diesel engine and a battery pack. Two 100hp electric motors were located in the rear wheels.

欧洲方面的成果由法国的雷诺·耐克斯特展示。该车是一辆小型的并联式混合动力电动汽车，它采用了一个排量 750CC 的火花点燃型发动机和两个电动机。这一原型车的燃油经济性达到 29.4km/L，其最高车度和加速性能已可与传统内燃机汽车相媲美。大众汽车公司也制造了原型车奇科，它装备了镍氢蓄电池组和一台三相异步电动机，并安装有一台小型的双缸汽油发动机给蓄电池组再充电，并为高速巡航提供附加动力。

Efforts in Europe are represented by the French Renault Next, a small parallel hybrid vehicle using a 750CC spark-ignited engine and two electric motors. This prototype achieved 29.4km/L with maximum speed and acceleration performance comparable to conventional vehicles. Volkswagen also built a prototype, the Chico. The base was a small EV, with a nickel-metal hybrid battery pack and a three-phase induction motor. A small two-cylinder gasoline engine was used to recharge the batteries and provide additional power for high-speed cruising.

日本汽车公司对混合动力电动汽车的发展和商品化带来最大影响。1997 年，丰田公司在日本推出了普锐斯混合动力电动轿车，本田公司也推出了音赛特和思域混合动力电动轿车。这些混合动力电动汽车目前在全世界得到了广泛的应用，实现了燃油消耗量的最小化。普锐斯和音赛特等混合动力电动汽车是当时首批商品化的混合动力电动汽车，具有历史性意义，它们解决了私家车燃油消耗难题。

The most significant effort in the development and commercialization of HEVs was made by Japanese manufacturers. In 1997, Toyota released the Prius sedan in Japan. Honda also released its Insight and Civic Hybrid. These vehicles are now available throughout the world. They achieve excellent figures for fuel consumption. Toyota's Prius and Honda's Insight vehicles have historical value in that they are the first hybrid vehicles commercialized in the modern era to respond to the problem of personal vehicle fuel consumption.

丰田汽车公司将这一设计理论应用到小型车如凯美瑞，后来应用到豪华车雷克萨斯，并生产了一批豪华电动汽车。

Toyota began providing this design option on the main smaller cars such as Camry and later with the Lexus divisions, producing some hybrid luxury vehicles.

2020 年丰田生产并在全世界销售的混合动力电动汽车达到 200 万辆，在 50 多个国家销售。正是普锐斯主导了混合动力电动汽车的销售，截至 2020 年 8 月 31 日，其累积销售量达到 443 万辆。丰田总裁宣称：最终公司制作的每一辆车都是混合动力电动汽车。雷克萨斯也有其混合动力成员组，包括 LS600h 和 LS66hL（配备 6L 排量和 V8 发动机）。

Worldwide sales of hybrid vehicles produced by Toyota reached 2.0 million in 2020, sold in more than 50 countries. Toyota's hybrid sales are led by the Prius, with worldwide cumulative sales of 4.43 million by August 31, 2020. Toyota's CEO has committed to eventually making every car of the company a hybrid vehicle. Lexus also has their own hybrid lineup, consisting of the LS600h/LS600hL (With 6L displacement and V8 engine).

迄今，丰田汽车公司在电动汽车方面以完美的技术和销售保持第一。

By now, Toyota keeps number one in EVs with its consummate technologies and sales.

比亚迪是一家中国汽车制造公司，总部位于广东省深圳市，公司成立于 2003 年。2008 年 12 月，比亚迪汽车开始销售世界上第一批量产的插电式混合动力车，并计划在不久的将来大规模生产廉价的电动汽车。

BYD Auto is a Chinese automobile manufacturer based in Shenzhen, Guangdong Province, China. The firm was founded in 2003. In December 2008, BYD Auto began selling the world's first mass-produced plug-in hybrid vehicle and plans to mass-produce affordable electric vehicles in the near future.

比亚迪几乎生产了全部汽车配件，从空调零件到发动机。这与许多美国、日本、欧洲汽车厂商形成了对比，国外生产厂家通常外包汽车使用的零件，仅在自己的工厂里进行最终的组装。

BYD produces nearly all of the components used in its vehicles, from the air conditioning units to the engines. This is in contrast to many American, Japanese and European auto manufacturers, which normally outsource a great deal of the components used in their vehicles, only performing final assembly at their own factories.

2009年比亚迪已经将汽车出口到非洲、南美洲和中东地区。该公司计划进入欧洲和以色列市场，同时也希望在美国销售汽车。比亚迪生产基地包括西安汽车装配基地，北京配件生产厂，深圳研发中心和初期的汽车装配基地及上海研发中心。

In 2009, BYD exports its cars to Africa, South America and the Middle East. The company has plans to enter the European and Israeli markets and hopes to sell vehicles in the United States, too. Production bases include an automobile assembly base in Xi'an, a module manufacturing plant in Beijing, an R&D center and nascent automobile assembly base in Shenzhen and an R&D center in Shanghai.

2014年，在北美国际汽车展览会上，比亚迪公司展示了一款电动车E6。E6具有250km的续驶里程，得到了媒体和公众的广泛关注。公司能够生产自己的锂离子电池。该电池有10年的寿命，能在10分钟内充电总电容量的50%。

The BYD Company exhibited an electric car E6 in 2014 at the North American International Auto Show. It had a driving range of 250km and got lots of attention from the media and the general public. The company was able to produce its own lithium-ion battery. The battery was designed to have a lifetime of 10 years and can be charged to 50% of its capabilities within 10 min.

目前比亚迪SUV主流车型是比亚迪唐、宋、元。其中，比亚迪唐定位为中型SUV，比亚迪宋定位为紧凑型SUV，比亚迪元定位为小型SUV。2018年6月26日，比亚迪全新唐正式上市，新车基于比亚迪BLP大型豪华车打造，同时提供了三种类型选择。其中，内燃机车辆搭载205马力的2.0T涡轮增压发动机，共推出5款车型，指导售价区间为12.99万～16.99万元。唐DM是插电式混动车型，共推出了5款车型，售价为23.99万～32.99万元。唐DM搭载2.0T插电式混动系统，匹配6速湿式双离合变速箱，并且唐DM采用双电机四驱系统。其前轴电机的最大功率为149hp，峰值扭矩为250N•m，后轴电机的最大功率为245hp，峰值扭矩为380N•m，总的最大功率超过500hp，0～100km/h加速时间为4.3s。比亚迪唐EV是纯电动车型，拥有500km的续驶里程，0～100km/h加速时间小于4.5s，体现了比亚迪唐优越的技术性能。

At present, the major SUV vehicles in BYD were Tang, Song and Yuan. Among them, BYD Tang was a kind of mid-size SUV, BYD Song was compact and BYD Yuan was small size. On June 26, 2018, the new Tang generation based on BYD BLP, a large-scale and luxurious type was put into market with three type choices. Among them, an internal combustion engine vehicles with a 2.0T turbocharging engine of 205hp provided 5 models which sold in a guided price of 129.9–169.9 thousand Yuan RMB. Tang DM, a plug-in hybrid electric vehicle provided 5 models with a market price of 239.9–329.9 thousand Yuan RMB. Tang DM is equiped with a 2.0T plug-in hybrid system, 6 speeds transmission matching wet-type dual clutches. In addition, it is equipped with 4-wheel drive with two electric motors which got a maximum power of 149hp, peak torque of 250N·m on the front axle and a maximum power of 245hp, peak torque of 380N·m on the rear axle. The total maximum power reached more than 500hp which got acceleration from 0 to 100km/h in 4.3 seconds. BYD Tang EV was a pure electric vehicle which possessed a range of 500km, an acceleration from 0 to

100km/h in less than 4.5 seconds, behaving superior technology of the BYD Tang.

2.2.3 燃料电池车发展历史
History of fuel cell vehicles

早在 1839 年，威廉姆·格罗夫（常称其为燃料电池之父）已发现通过反向电解水即可产生电能。直到 1889 年才有两位研究员查尔斯·兰格和路德维希·蒙德，利用空气和煤气尝试设计制作了第一个实用的燃料电池。20 世纪初，进一步发展燃料电池以使煤或碳可转换为电能的研究本有望深入，但内燃机使用性能高，暂时压制了燃料电池技术开发。

As early as 1839, Sir William Grove (often referred to as the "Father of the Fuel Cell") discovered that it may be possible to generate electricity by reversing the electrolysis of water. It was not until 1889 that two researchers, Charles Langer and Ludwig Mond, made the name "fuel cell" as they were trying to engineer the first practical fuel cell using air and coal gas. Although further attempts were made in the early 1900s to develop fuel cells that could convert coal or carbon into electricity, the advent of the IC engine temporarily quashed any hopes of further development of the fledgling technology.

1932 年，弗朗西斯·培根成功研制了第一台燃料电池装置，该装置含有用碱性电解液和镍电极构成的氢氧燃料电池，其中有蒙德和兰格所使用的廉价催化剂。由于一些实质性的技术困难，直至 1959 年，培根和公司才首次对外公布其实用的 5kW 燃料电池系统。哈里·凯瑞·伊律格在同一年展示了当时名噪一时的牵引车，该车装备有 20hp 的燃料电池。

Francis Bacon developed what was perhaps the first successful fuel cell device in 1932, with a hydrogen-oxygen cell using alkaline electrolytes and nickel electrodes inexpensive alternatives to the catalysts used by Mond and Langer. Due to a substantial number of technical hurdles, it was not until 1959 that Bacon and company first demonstrated a practical 5kW fuel cell system. Harry Karl Ihrig presented his now-famous 20hp fuel-cell-powered tractor that same year.

在 20 世纪 50 年代后期，美国国家航空航天局（NASA）也开始制造应用于太空飞行任务的紧凑型发电机，并且不久即为涉及燃料电池应用技术的数百个研究项目提供资金，在成功完成数次太空飞行供电任务后，燃料电池在空间项目中作用已确认无疑。

National Aeronautics and Space Administration (NASA) also began building compact electric generators for use on space missions in the late 1950s. NASA soon came to fund hundreds of research contracts involving fuel cell technology. Fuel cells now have a proven role in the space program, after supplying electricity for several space missions.

在最近几十年，很多汽车制造厂加大投入进行燃料电池应用技术研发，用于燃料电池车和其他项目。目前，氢的生成、储存和分配也是面临的最大挑战。

In more recent decades, a number of manufacturers, including major automakers and various federal agencies have supported ongoing research into the development of fuel cell technology for use in fuel cell vehicles and other applications. Hydrogen production, storage, and distribution are the biggest challenges.

在日本，两款燃料电池车于 2014 年 1 月实现了量产并推向市场，这两款车型分别是途胜以及未来（Mirai）。未来欲复制丰田普锐斯的成功。"Mirai"在日语中意为"未来"。在混合动力汽车市场获得成功的丰田，意图借助"未来"车型开拓燃料电池汽车这片新领域。

In 2014, in Japan, two kinds of fuel cell vehicles named Tucson FCV and Toyota Mirai came to mass production and were put into market. Toyota Mirai desired to copy the success of Toyota Prius. "Mirai" means "future". Toyota, made some achievements developed in new field of fuel cell vehicles with the aid of Toyota Mirai.

2014年6月，量产的途胜正式登陆美国加州市场。该车型以出租车方式运营，收益不菲。丰田未来于2018年5月在英国上市，售价为53105英镑，减去15000英镑的政府补贴，用户只需用38105英镑（约合人民币28.1万元）即可买到一台丰田未来燃料电池车。

In June 2014, mass-produced Tucson FCV formally landed the California market in America. The model is running as a taxi and got a higher income. Toyota Mirai was launched into England in May 2018. The sale payment was £53105. Cutting off the government subsidy of £15000, customers paid only £38105 (about 281000 yuan RMB) for a Toyota Mirai.

相比途胜，未来在动力性能和续驶里程上都有一定的优势。未来的动力系统输出功率已达到甚至超越1.8L自然吸气汽油发动机的水平，加上400km的续航里程，使未来具备了较好的实用性。

Compared with Tucson FCV, Toyota Mirai was more superior in power performance and range. The output power of power system on Toyota Mirai had reached or surpassed the level of naturally inspired engine with displacement of 1.8L. In addition to the range of 400km, Toyota Mirai owned the nice practicability.

习　　题

一、选择题

1．1770年，（　　）发明了蒸汽机车。
　　A．潘哈德　　　　　　　　　B．勒瓦瑟
　　C．戈特利布·戴姆勒　　　　D．约瑟夫·屈尼奥

2．1870年，（　　）制造了第一台四冲程内燃机。
　　A．瓦特　　　　　　　　　　B．尼古拉斯·奥托
　　C．卡尔·本茨　　　　　　　D．丹尼尔

3．（　　）于1886年1月29日获得世界上第一个汽车专利。
　　A．卡尔·本茨　　　　　　　B．特利布·戴姆勒
　　C．福特　　　　　　　　　　D．宾利

4．1913年，（　　）首次推出的流水线产生了重大影响。
　　A．波许　　　B．道格拉斯　　C．亨利·福特　　D．迈巴赫

5．"甲壳虫"大众牌轿车由（　　）设计。
　　A．兰博基尼　　B．法拉利　　C．宾利　　D．费迪南德·保时捷

6．1881年，第一辆电动汽车由法国人（　　）制造。
　　A．莫里斯　　　　　　　　　　B．所罗门
　　C．古斯塔夫·特鲁韦　　　　　D．达奇拉
7．有记录的最早的混合动力电动汽车出现在（　　）巴黎美术展览会会上。
　　A．1889年　　　B．1899年　　　C．2009年　　　D．2019年
8．（　　）弗朗西斯·培根成功研制了第一台燃料电池装置。
　　A．1892年　　　B．1912年　　　C．1922年　　　D．1932年
9．1889年，两位研究员查尔斯·兰格和路德维希·蒙德命名"燃料电池"，并利用（　　）尝试设计制作第一个实用的燃料电池。
　　A．空气和汽油　　B．空气和煤油　　C．空气和煤气　　D．空气和氢气
10．在日本，两款燃料电池车于（　　）实现了量产并推向市场。
　　A．1984年1月　　B．1994年1月　　C．2004年1月　　D．2014年1月

二、简答题

1．轿车车身的演变经过哪些阶段？
2．简述1881年，第一辆电动汽车的相关情况。
3．简述第一辆商品化电动汽车的运行情况。
4．简述目前电动汽车的应用情况。
5．简述1899年巴黎美术展览会上展出的串联式混合动力电动汽车的相关情况。
6．简述日本汽车公司对混合动力电动汽车的发展和商品化带来的最大影响。
7．简述目前比亚迪SUV的主流车型。
8．简述日本两款燃料电池车途胜和未来的应用情况。

第 3 章　世界著名汽车公司

Famous companies over the world

3.1　大众汽车公司

Volkswagen Motor Company

1. 大众汽车集团

　　The Volkswagen Group

　　大众汽车集团，也称 VW，是德国沃尔夫斯堡的汽车制造公司。

　　The Volkswagen Group, also known as VW, is an automobile manufacturer based in Wolfsburg, Germany.

　　在德国，"大众汽车"并不是新概念。在 20 世纪 30 年代之前，曾有人努力创造大家都买得起的简洁汽车，但无一成功。在 1930 年以前，即使尽量作出足够简洁的款式，但还是要花费普通工人一年多的工资才能购买。

　　In Germany, the idea of a people's car wasn't exactly a new one. Before the 1930s, there had been many efforts to create simple cars that everyone could afford, but none met with profound success. Almost all cars before 1930, even if they were designed to be simple enough for the average person, they ended up costing more than the average worker's yearly wage.

　　1937 年大众汽车集团成立时，没有人能想到，它会成为欧洲最大的汽车制造公司。

　　When the company known as Volkswagen Group was founded, in 1937 no one could have guessed that it would one day be Europe's largest carmaker.

　　1938 年年初，在如今的沃尔夫斯堡市，开始建设大众汽车工厂，来生产由费迪南德·保时捷设计的新车型。

　　In early 1938, in what is today Wolfsburg, work begins on the construction of the Volkswagen plant which is to manufacture the new vehicle designed by Ferdinand Porsche.

　　大众甲壳虫被认为是本世纪最引人注目和设计最佳的车型之一，如图 3.1 所示。这款车起源于 20 世纪 30 年代，它的设计主要是在这十年之间，由费迪南德·保时捷博士完成。从他年轻时，就梦想为德国大众创作一款经济车型。

　　The Volkswagen Beetle is regarded as one of the most remarkable and best-engineered cars of the century (Fig.3.1). The car has its origins in the 1930s as it was designed mainly by Dr. Ferdinand Porsche during that decade. Porsche had dreams of creating an economical car for the masses in

Germany since he was a young man.

图 3.1 甲壳虫型轿车

Fig.3.1 Beetle type car

第二次世界大战期间，大众汽车集团改为生产军用装备。大约两万名被强迫的劳工、战俘，还有后来集中营里的囚犯，都在该工厂工作过。

During the Second World War, Volkswagen's production is switched to armaments. Some 20000 forced labourers, prisoners of war, and later also concentration camp prisoners, work at the plant.

1998 年 9 月，在承认历史事件的前提下，大众集团为第二次世界大战时被强迫征收的劳工建立了人道主义基金，目的是维护这些劳工的权益。到 2001 年为止，来自 26 个国家超过 2050 位第二次世界大战的劳工接受了来自此基金的人道主义援助。此外，为纪念那时在大众工厂工作的劳工，在沃尔夫斯堡市建立了一座纪念碑。

In September 1998, in recognition of the events of that time, VW established a humanitarian fund on behalf of the forced labourers compelled to work at Volkswagen during the Second World War. By the end of 2001 more than 2050 people in 26 countries had received humanitarian aid from the fund. Furthermore, a Memorial in remembrance of the forced labour employed at the Volkswagen plant is currently being established at Wolfsburg.

第二次世界大战结束之后，1945 年 6 月中旬，大众汽车公司由英国军政府掌控。在伊万•赫斯特少校的管理经营下，大众甲壳虫开始大批量生产。

After the end of the Second World War, in mid-June 1945, responsibility for Volkswagen is placed in the hands of the British Military Government. Under the management of Major Ivan Hirst, mass production of the Volkswagen Beetle started.

1956 年在汉诺威为大众 T 型车成立了另外一个生产基地，同时为今天的大众商用车品牌奠定了基础。

In 1956, a separate manufacturing base for the Transporter is established in Hanover, at the same time setting down the roots of today's Volkswagen Commercial Vehicles brand.

1972 年 2 月 17 日，大众汽车打破了世界汽车生产记录：因组装生产了共计超过 1500 万辆，甲壳虫产量超越了传奇的福特汽车公司 T 型车。

On February 17, 1972, VW broke the production record: with more than 15000000 units assembled, the Beetle surpasses the legendary mark achieved by the Ford Motor Company's Model T.

1973 年，帕萨特成为大众新生代第一款车型，该车采用前轮驱动，配备水冷式四汽缸 110hp 发动机。帕萨特的制造过程符合模块化发展战略，其一个标准化的组件可一定范围内用于不同型号的系列产品中，这使大规模生产更加容易。

In 1973 the Passat is the first model of the new generation of Volkswagen vehicles to go into production—with front wheel drive, a water-cooled four-cylinder engine and a range of engines up to 110hp. The Passat is built in line with the modular strategy, by which standardized components are usable in a range of different models vehicles. It made a mass production easier.

1974 年 1 月，第一台高尔夫车在沃尔夫斯堡的工厂下线。这种紧凑型轿车很快风靡一时，进而成为了一代传奇甲壳虫轿车的合理继任者。

In January 1974 the first Golf is built at the Wolfsburg plant. The compact saloon quickly becomes a hit and becomes the legitimate heir to the legendary Beetle.

1983 年 6 月，第二代高尔夫诞生。基于大规模自动化装配流水线，在特别建立的总装大厅，机器人被首次引入到汽车制造业中。

In June 1983 production of the second-generation Golf begins. The car is designed for a largely automated assembly process, and in the specially erected final assembly hall, robots are deployed for the first time in vehicle manufacture.

1999 年 7 月，第一辆百千米耗油仅 3L 的路波轿车下线，大众汽车再次创造了汽车历史。

With the production launch of the Lupo 3L Car, the first production car to offer fuel consumption of just three liters per 100 kilometers, in July 1999, Volkswagen once again makes automotive history.

2009 年 8 月 13 日，大众集团董事会与保时捷签署协议，在大众的领导下，建立一个联合汽车集团。

On August 13, 2009, the Board of Volkswagen signed the agreement of an integrated automotive group with Porsche under the leadership of Volkswagen.

2009 年 11 月，大众—保时捷联合汽车集团已经超越丰田，成为世界上最大的汽车制造公司。

In November 2009, Volkswagen-Porsche has overtaken Toyota to become the world's largest car manufacturer.

迄今为止，大众集团公司旗下包括九个汽车品牌：大众、奥迪、保时捷、斯柯达、西亚特、兰博基尼、宾利、布加迪和斯堪尼亚。

By now, the VW group contains the nine-car brands VW, Audi, Porsche, Skoda, SEAT, Lamborghini, Bentley, Bugatti and Scania.

2018 年 8 月 25 日，大众官方宣布，独立推出电动"汽车共享"服务，2019 年春季首次在德国柏林开展活动。2021 年《财富》世界 500 强车辆和零部件行业第一位。

On August 25, 2018, Volkswagen officially announced that it push forward electric the "We share" service carried out in Berlin, Germany in 2019. In 2021, Volkswagen was honored the top 1 on *Fortune* 500 in the vehicle and spare part industry.

2. 中国大众汽车集团

Volkswagen Group China (VGC)

中国大众汽车集团（VGC）是德国大众汽车集团在中华人民共和国境内的全资子公司。大众汽车集团占有中国市场约 16%（2017 年）的市场份额，是最大的外国汽车制造商。中国也是该集团的主要市场之一。大众汽车在中国的业务包括整车、零部件、发动机和变速器系统的生产、销售及服务。中国大众汽车集团在本地生产和进口多种品牌汽车，如在中国有大众、奥迪、斯柯达、宾利和兰博基尼等多个品牌。

Volkswagen Group China (VGC) is a fully-owned subsidiary of the German Volkswagen Group in the People's Republic of China. Volkswagen Group enjoys sales of about 16% (2017) of the Chinese market and is the largest foreign carmaker. The Chinese market is one of the main markets of the Group. Operations of Volkswagen in China include the production, sales and services of whole cars, parts and components, engines and transmission systems. The company's locally manufactured and imported vehicles are sold under various brand names such as Volkswagen, Audi, Skoda, Bentley, and Lamborghini in China.

大众汽车集团是中国汽车行业最大、最早和最成功的跨国合作公司。从 1978 年与中国合作，大众汽车集团已经在中国汽车市场处于领先地位 40 多年。大众汽车集团在中国的第一个合资企业是 1984 年 10 月成立的上海大众汽车有限公司。第二个合资企业是 1991 年 2 月在长春成立的一汽大众汽车有限公司。

Volkswagen Group is the largest, earliest and most successful international partner in China's Automotive Industry. It started its connection with China as early as 1978 and has been taking the leading position in the Chinese automotive market for more than 40 years. Its first joint venture in China, Shanghai Volkswagen Automotive Company Limited was established in October 1984. The second joint venture, FAW-Volkswagen Automotive Company Limited was established in Changchun in February 1991.

大众汽车集团在中国的目标是通过本地强大的制造网络迎接挑战，作为最成功的企业，巩固在中国市场的领先地位。

The goal of Volkswagen Group China is to continue its market leadership as the most successful car manufacturer by responding to the challenges with a strong local manufacturing network.

3.2 福特汽车公司

Ford Motor Company

福特汽车公司（简称为福特）是一家世界跨国汽车制造公司,总部设在美国密歇根州的迪尔伯恩（位于底特律的郊区）。

Ford Motor Company (also known as simply Ford) is an American multinational automaker headquartered in Dearborn, Michigan, a suburb of Detroit.

1901 年 11 月 3 日亨利·福特以他的名字命名亨利·福特公司。1902 年 8 月 22 日，福特离开该公司并带走了公司的名称，剩下的这个公司变成了凯迪拉克汽车公司。在 1903 年，福特汽车公司又在 12 个投资者 2.8 万美元的现金支持下，以一家改装厂重新经营。在这些投资者中，最有名的是约翰·道奇和贺拉斯·道奇兄弟（他们俩后来成立了自己的汽车公司）。早期的时候，在密歇根州底特律的麦克大道的福特工厂，一天只能生产几辆汽车。两三个人一组负责一辆车的装配，零配件大多来自和福特签订合同的供应商。不到十年的时间，福特就以扩大和改善装配线而领先世界；福特也很快在其工厂内部以垂直整合的方式生产大部分汽车零配件，这在当时是一个更可行的办法。

Henry Ford's first attempt at a car company under his own name was the Henry Ford Company on November 3, 1901, which became the Cadillac Motor Company on August 22, 1902, after Ford left with the company name. The Ford Motor Company was launched in a converted factory in 1903 with $28000 in cash from twelve investors, most notably John and Horace Dodge (who would later found their own car company). During its early years, the company produced just a few cars a day at its factory on Mack Avenue in Detroit, Michigan. Groups of two or three men worked on each car, assembling it from parts made mostly by supplier companies contracting for Ford. Within a decade the company would lead the world in the expansion and refinement of the assembly line. And Ford soon brought much of the part production in-house in a vertical integration that seemed a better path for the era.

亨利·福特 40 岁的时候成立了福特汽车公司，当时是世界上最大的且盈利最多的公司之一，同时也是美国大萧条时期生存下来的一家公司。作为世界上最大的家族控股公司之一，福特汽车公司在家族的掌控下已经运行了 100 多年。

Henry Ford was 40 years old when he founded the Ford Motor Company, which would go on to become one of the world's largest and most profitable companies, as well as being one to survive the Great Depression. As one of the largest family-controlled companies in the world, the Ford Motor Company has been in continuous family control for over 100 years.

1914 年，福特在 T 型车中引入了第一台可移动汽缸盖发动机，如图 3.2 所示。1930 年，福特在车窗上使用安全玻璃（钢化玻璃）。福特在 1932 年率先推出了第一辆低价格、大功率 V8 发动机汽车，如图 3.3 所示。

In 1914 Ford introduced the first engine with a removable cylinder head, in the Model T (Fig.3.2). In 1930, Ford introduced safety glass (toughened glass) in the windshield. Ford launched the first low-priced V8 engine-powered car in 1932 (Fig.3.3).

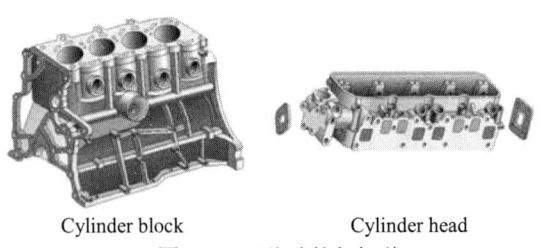

Cylinder block　　　　Cylinder head

图 3.2　可移动的气缸盖

Fig.3.2　Removable cylinder head

图 3.3　V8 发动机

Fig.3.3　V8 engine

20 世纪 80 年代，福特非常成功地在全球推出了几款车型。1990 年和 1994 年，福特分别购入了捷豹汽车和阿斯顿·马丁汽车。20 世纪 90 年代中后期，在美国股市飙升和油价低廉的经济繁荣背景下，福特汽车的销售也一路高涨。

In the 1980s, Ford introduced several highly successful vehicles around the world. In 1990 and 1994 respectively, Ford also acquired Jaguar Cars and Aston Martin. During the mid-to-late 1990s, Ford continued to sell large numbers of vehicles, in a booming American economy with a soaring stock market and low fuel prices.

随着新世纪的到来，医疗保健成本、不断上涨的油价和萎靡的经济导致了福特汽车市场份额下降、销量下降及利润减少。到 2005 年，福特和通用公司的股票双双成为垃圾股。

With the dawn of the new century, healthcare costs, higher fuel prices, and a faltering economy led to falling market shares, declining sales, and low profits. By 2005, both Ford's and GM's corporate bonds had been downgraded to junk status.

2005 年下半年，福特公司董事长比尔·福特要求新任福特美洲部总裁马克·菲尔兹制订一项计划，让公司重新盈利。菲尔兹于 2005 年 12 月 7 日在公司董事会提交了名为"未来之路"的计划，并于 2006 年 1 月 23 日公布于众。"未来之路"的计划包括调整公司的规模以与市场的实际情况相符合，停产一些不盈利和效益不高的车型，充实生产线，关闭 14 个工厂和裁减 3 万个工作岗位。

In the latter half of 2005, Chairman Bill Ford asked newly appointed Ford Americas Division President Mark Fields to develop a plan to return the company to profitability. Fields proposed the Plan, named The Way Forward, at the December 7, 2005 board meeting of the company and it was unveiled to the public on January 23, 2006. "The Way Forward" included resizing the company to match market realities, dropping some unprofitable and inefficient models, consolidating production lines, closing 14 factories and cutting 30000 jobs.

福特继续开发一系列新车型，包括"跨界 SUV"，该车实现车身和底盘一体化，即整体式车身。在为"福特翼虎混合动力 SUV"开发混合动力传动系统时，福特获得了丰田混合动力传动技术的支持。福特宣布利用家庭输电网络研究未来插电式混合动力汽车。在这个需要耗费数百万美元、数年时间的项目中，福特尝试把"福特翼虎混合动力汽车"转化成插电式混合动力汽车。

Ford moved to introduce a range of new vehicles, including "Crossover SUVs" built on unibody car platforms, rather than more body-on-frame chassis. In developing the hybrid electric powertrain technologies for the Ford Escape Hybrid SUV, Ford got support from Toyota hybrid technologies. Ford announced that it will examine the future of plug-in hybrids in terms of how home and vehicle energy systems will work with the electrical grid. Under the multi-million-dollar, multi-year project, Ford will convert a demonstration fleet of Ford Escape Hybrids into plug-in hybrids.

福特汽车公司报告显示，在 2006 年公司达到了 127 亿美元历史上最大的年度亏损，并且预计到 2009 年才能重新盈利。然而，福特汽车公司在 2007 年第二季度就公布了 7.5 亿美元的利润，令华尔街吃惊。尽管有第二季度的盈利，2007 年公司全年亏损 27 亿美元，亏损减少在很大程度上得益于公司的财务重组。

The automaker (manufacturer) reported the largest annual loss in company history in 2006 of $12.7 billion and estimated that it would not return to profitability until 2009. However, Ford surprised Wall Street in the second quarter of 2007 by posting a $750 million profit. Despite the gains, the company finished the year with a $2.7 billion loss, largely attributed to finance restructuring at the company.

2008 年 6 月 2 日，福特以 23 亿美元将捷豹和路虎的运营权卖给了塔塔（印度）汽车公司。

On June 2, 2008, Ford sold its Jaguar and Land Rover operations to Tata Motors for $2.3 billion. Tata Motors is an Indian company.

2008 年 11 月，由于 2008 年金融危机，福特与克莱斯勒和通用汽车公司一起，提交了汽车工业可持续发展的行动方案。该项举措让福特在 2009 年盈利 27 亿美元，这是公司 4 年来首次年度盈利。

During November 2008, by the 2008 financial crisis, Ford, together with Chrysler and General Motors presented action plans for the sustainability of the industry. The action yielded Ford a $2.7 billion profit in 2009, the company's first full-year profit in four years.

2012 年，Ford 公司债券重新由垃圾股升级为投资等级较高级别，证明了福特的价值可持续提升。

Finally, in 2012, Ford corporate bonds were upgraded from junk to investment grade again, citing sustainable, lasting improvements.

2021 年，福特汽车公司在世界汽车集团十强中排名第七。

In 2021, Ford Motor was honored No. 7 on Top 10 motor vehicle manufacturing companies.

3.3 通用汽车公司

General Motors Company

通用汽车公司，通常简称为 GM，是一家总部在美国密歇根州底特律市的跨国汽车公司，其标志如图 3.4 所示。

General Motors Company, commonly known as GM, is an American multinational automotive corporation headquartered in Detroit, Michigan. The logo of GM is as follows (Fig.3.4).

图 3.4　通用汽车标志

Fig.3.4　The logo of GM

1. 通用汽车发展简史

    Brief history of GM

通用汽车之父是威廉·杜兰特。当时这位精明的生意人看到：美国汽车制造公司的命运在很大程度上依赖于某一车型的成功或失败。他认为几个汽车生产商的联合能保证一个稳定的金融环境。因为汽车品牌的数量增加了，相应的产品分配周期会更加均匀。因此杜兰特在1903年买下了别克，在1909年买下了奥兹莫比，进而成立了通用汽车公司。

The father of GM was William C. Durant. This intelligent businessman saw the fate of many American car makers depended very much on the success or failure of individual models. He believed a consortium of several car makers would provide stable finance because the number of models would be multiplied and the product cycles would be more evenly distributed. Durant, therefore, bought Buick in 1903 and Oldsmobile in 1909 to form General Motors.

从20世纪20年代开始，通用采用了非常清晰的价格策略：每个部门和每个车型都有其价格范围和客户目标群，以避免通用内部的竞争。另一方面，通用发起了一个所谓的车身造型"革命"。它雇用了汽车工业的第一个造型师哈利·厄尔，对通用大量的各种车型进行多样化设计。这个策略也刺激了消费者经常换车的欲望，因此增加了汽车的销售。这种情况越来越走向极端。在20世纪50年代，通用受战斗机的启发，在汽车上采用了超长的后尾箱和尾翼。美国人在"美好的往日"里非常富有，因此他们能够负担得起这些高昂的费用。这也将通用的财富积累推向了顶峰。

Since the 1920s, GM adopted a clear pricing policy—each division and each model was assigned with a price range and target customers to avoid internal competition. On the other hand, GM started a so-called "revolution" in car styling. It employed the industry's first stylist, Harley Earl, to help diversifying the image of its wide range of models. This strategy stimulated customers' desire to change cars frequently, hence increasing sales. The situation went so extreme that the GM cars in the 1950s employed ultra long tails inspired by aircraft fighters. The American people were wealthy in those "good old days", so they could afford the excess. This pushed the fortune of General Motors to its peak.

从20世纪60年代开始，通用以庞蒂克GTO车型开始了"秀肌肉车"潮流。这将美国的汽车市场推向了另一个极端，每个人都追求大尺寸的V8发动机，其排量可高达7L，功率达到400hp。

From 1960s, GM started a trend of "muscle cars" with the Pontiac GTO. That pushed the American market to another extreme—everyone pursued big-block V8s with up to 7 liters capacity and 400 horsepower.

1967 年的第一次能源危机严厉地惩罚了通用（还有福特和克莱斯勒汽车公司）。由于能源危机很快过去，通用并未从中吸取教训。但是 1973 年的第二次和 1978 年的第三次石油危机就严重得多，执行更严格的汽车排放和安全规定更是雪上加霜。三大汽车公司发现，它们因为忽视小型经济轿车开发付出了代价，而同时日本进口车销量飙升。雪佛兰生产了第一辆所谓的"紧凑型车"科威尔，但以当时的标准来看并不紧凑。通用在 20 世纪 70 年代和 80 年代不时陷入亏损。1989 年，通用创造了世界工业亏损纪录，通用大量削减成本使它重新盈利，但是国内市场的份额再也没有回升。

The first energy crisis in 1967 punished GM (as well as Ford and Chrysler) heavily. But it did not learn from the lesson as the crisis passed away quickly. However, the second oil crisis in 1973 and then the third occasion in 1978 were not so kind, accompanied by stricter emission and safety regulations. The Big 3 found their ignorance about small economy cars paying the price. Sales of Japanese imports surged. Chevrolet made its first so-called "compact car", Corvair, but not too "compact" by our standards. GM ran into loss from time to time during the 1970s and 1980s. In 1989, it recorded the biggest loss ever experienced by the world's industry. Substantial cost-cutting measures afterward helped it to regain profitability, but its domestic market share never rose back.

在 20 世纪 90 年代和 21 世纪早期，通用实施了大规模并购。1990 年买入萨博（瑞典）、2003 年买入大宇（韩国）。通用持有斯巴鲁（日本）和铃木（日本）少量股票（后来为了筹措资金出售了这两个品牌的股票）。通用在 2000 年合并了菲亚特集团，但只持续了 5 年。其中，对大宇的收购和与中国上汽集团的合资非常成功，抵消了它在美国本土的部分损失。

In the 1990s and early 2000s, GM made some big-scale acquisitions. It bought Saab in 1990 and Daewoo in 2003. It took minority stakes in Subaru and Suzuki (both were sold off later to raise money). It merged with the FIAT group in 2000 but the marriage lasted for only 5 years. However, the Daewoo purchase and the joint venture with SAIC in China were very successful, offsetting part of the loss made in its home soil.

2021 年，通用汽车公司在世界汽车集团十强中排名第六。

In 2021, GM honored No. 6 on Top 10 motor vehicle manufacturing companies.

2. 通用汽车公司在中国

GM in China

通用汽车公司在中国市场的大部分车辆是由上海通用公司在上海本地制造的。这是一个与中国上汽集团合资的公司，于 1997 年 3 月 25 日创立。上海通用公司于 1998 年 12 月 15 日正式投产，恰逢在中国制造的首辆别克轿车下线。上汽通用五菱合资企业也以五菱品牌成功地销售微型面包车（通用拥有 34% 的股权）。最近通用销量增长主要发生在中国，它的汽车销售在 2021 年达到 176 万辆，创造了自己的历史纪录。

GM manufactures most of its China market vehicles locally through Shanghai GM, a joint venture with the Chinese company SAIC Motor, which was created on March 25, 1997. The Shanghai GM plant was officially opened on December 15, 1998, when the first Chinese-built Buick came off the assembly line. The SAIC-GM-Wuling Automobile joint venture is also successfully selling microvans under the Wuling marque (34 percent owned by GM). Much of General Motors' recent growth has been in China, where its selling reaches 1760000 vehicles and creates its historical record.

别克汽车在中国的发展势头很强劲，以别克凯越紧凑车型为主导。凯迪拉克品牌在2004年引入中国，开始向中国出口。2005年，通用开始在中国市场推广雪佛兰品牌，将原来的别克赛欧转至该品牌下。

The Buick is strong in China, led by the Buick Excelle subcompact. The Cadillac brand was introduced in China in 2004, starting with exports to China. GM pushed the marketing of the Chevrolet brand in China in 2005 as well, transferring Buick Sail to that marque.

3.4 宝马汽车公司

Bavarian Motor Works（BMW）

1. 宝马发展历史

BMW History

BMW 是巴伐利亚汽车制造厂的首字母缩写。无论怎么称呼它，这家德国公司都是世界上最受人尊崇的汽车制造公司之一，其负有盛名的精致豪华轿车和多功能运动型轿车，足以（为驾驶者）提供卓越的驾驶娱乐体验。

BMW is an acronym for Bavarian Motor Works. Whatever you call it, the German company is one of the world's most respected automakers, renowned for crafting luxury cars and SUVs that offer superior levels of driving enjoyment.

宝马总部位于德国慕尼黑，毗邻奥林匹克公园，被认为是慕尼黑最著名的现代建筑之一，由宝马塔楼和宝马博物馆组成。

The headquarters of BMW is located in Munich directly next to the Olympic Park. It is considered to be one of the most notable Munich modern buildings. It consists of BMW Tower and BMW Museum.

20世纪10年代，宝马公司由两个著名的德国飞机制造专家古斯塔夫·奥托和卡尔·拉普建立于慕尼黑，那时是一家飞机制造企业。宝马公司现在的标志，表达了白色螺旋桨迎着蓝天，反映的是企业自身的起源。这种蓝白色的设计方案也同巴伐利亚的蓝白方格旗相同，如图3.5所示。

Founded by two well-known airplane specialists Gustav Otto and Karl Rapp in Munich, the company began in the early 1910s as an aircraft manufacturer. BMWs current logo, designed to represent white propeller blades against a blue sky, reflects these origins; its blue-and-white color scheme also references Bavaria's blue-and-white checkered flag (Fig.3.5).

图 3.5 宝马标志

Fig.3.5 The logo of BMW

直到 1928 年公司才开始生产宝马牌汽车，首款车品牌是 Dixi（前置发动机，后轮驱动，747CC 直列四缸发动机）。这款车证明非常受欢迎，而且该款车成功推出帮助公司平安度过经济大萧条时期（20 世纪 30 年代的一次严重的经济衰退）。

It wasn't until 1928 that production began on the first BMW automobile, the Dixi (Front engine, rear-wheel drive, 4-cylinder inline engine with a displacement of 747CC). The car proved very popular, and its success helped the manufacturer weather the Depression (a severe economic depression in the 1930s).

第二次世界大战之前，宝马公司最知名的品牌是轻便灵活的双座 328 型跑车，它在 1936 年到 1940 年之间获得了超过 120 场汽车巡回赛的胜利。战后，宝马公司延续了这个传统，获得了多项汽车赛、拉力赛和山地赛的胜利。

BMW's best-known pre-World War vehicle was the Type 328 roadster, a supple two-seater that racked up over 120 victories on the motorsport circuit between 1936 and 1940. Postwar BMW cars maintained this tradition, winning several racing, rallying and hill climb victories.

20 世纪 50 年代早期，宝马 501 下线。这是一款宽敞、豪华型轿车，金光闪亮，给人以期望。很快宝马 502 型跟进，该车配备世界上第一台轻合金技术的 V8 发动机，显示出宝马公司开发新技术的积极性。

The early 1950s saw the launch of the BMW 501, a roomy, luxury sedan that was brilliant with all of the hopefulness of that era. It was soon followed by the 502 which was powered by the world's first light-alloy V8, foreshadowing BMW's ongoing commitment to developing new technology.

到 20 世纪 70 年代，宝马已成为一家成熟的汽车企业。它是开发众多先进技术的先锋，其中包括废气涡轮增压技术和高端汽车电子设备。70 年代，宝马 3 系、5 系、7 系和性能优越的 M 系轿车依次投产。

By the 1970s, BMW was establishing itself as a full-grown car company. It was a pioneer for many promising technologies, including turbocharging and advanced vehicle electronics. The 1970s also saw the birth of BMW's 3 Series, 5 Series and 7 Series cars and the M division in high performance.

近几年，宝马在电动车生产方面走在了前列。2022 年，宝马在中国市场推出 iX、i4、iX3 纯电动汽车和插电式混合动力电动汽车。

BMW went ahead in electric vehicle production in recent years. In 2022, BMW produces pure electric vehicles with iX、i4、iX3 models and plug-in hybrid electric vehicles in China market.

2. 宝马华晨汽车有限公司

BMW Brilliance Automotive Ltd.

2003 年 3 月，宝马集团与华晨中国汽车控股有限公司签订合资合同，于 7 月份正式成立宝马华晨汽车有限公司，总部设在沈阳。

The BMW Group and Brilliance China Automotive Holdings Limited signed a contract for a joint venture in March 2003, and in July, BMW Brilliance Automotive Ltd. was officially established with a production facility located in Shenyang.

2003 年 10 月，合资公司推出第一款国产宝马汽车。之后，宝马华晨汽车有限公司快速推出了宝马 318i、325i、520i、525i 和 530i 等型号轿车及各种配置的车型。

BMW Brilliance Automotive Ltd. has put into market models BMW 318i, 325i, 520i, 525i, and 530i of various equipment since the first locally produced BMW car was launched in October 2003.

2006 年 3 月，由宝马华晨沈阳工厂生产的宝马汽车在"中国汽车品牌顾客满意度调查"活动中，荣获最佳质量产品。

In March 2006, BMW cars produced at Shenyang Plant won Best Quality Product in the "Survey on the satisfaction degree with automobile brand in China".

3.5 丰田汽车公司

Toyota Motor Corporation

丰田汽车公司，一般称为丰田，是一家总部设在日本的跨国公司，也是世界上最大的汽车制造公司之一。它在美国汽车市场销售量处于龙头地位。

Toyota Motor Corporation, commonly known simply as Toyota, is a multinational corporation headquartered in Japan and one of the world's largest automakers. It is also the largest in US sales.

该公司于 1937 年由丰田喜一郎创办，总部设在东京。当时丰田汽车公司只是其父亲的丰田工业公司中一个汽车产业部门，拥有雷克萨斯和塞恩两个商标品牌。除了生产汽车，丰田公司还通过下属丰田金融机构提供金融服务，另外还从事机器人生产。丰田汽车公司（包括丰田金融机构）和丰田工业形成了丰田集团的主要部分，是世界上最大的企业集团之一。

The company was founded by Kiichiro Toyota in 1937 as a department in his father's company Toyota Industries to create automobiles. Toyota also owns and operates Lexus and Scion brands. Toyota is headquartered in Tokyo. In addition to manufacturing automobiles, Toyota provides financial services through its division Toyota Financial Services, and also builds robots. Toyota Motor Corporation (including Toyota Financial Services) and Toyota Industries form the bulk of the Toyota Group, one of the largest conglomerates in the world.

丰田卡罗拉是一款紧凑型轿车，如图 3.6 所示，自 1966 年首次投入市场以来，在世界各地大受欢迎。1997 年，卡罗拉成为世界上最畅销的品牌，到 2017 年为止销售量已超过 4000 万辆。在过去的 40 年里，平均每 40 秒，就会售出一辆卡罗拉车。

The Toyota Corolla is a compact car (Fig.3.6), which has become very popular throughout the world since the nameplate was first introduced in 1966. In 1997, the Corolla became the best-selling nameplate in the world, with over 40 million sold by the end of 2017. Over the past 40 years, a Corolla car has been sold on average every 40 seconds.

图 3.6 丰田卡罗拉
Fig.3.6 The Toyota Corlla

在 20 世纪 80 年代初期，丰田汽车公司获得了政府颁发的第一批日本质量控制奖，并在那时开始参加各种类型的赛车活动。由于 1973 年的石油危机，美国市场的消费者开始转向购买燃油经济性高的小型轿车，日本生产的轿车因而受益。而当时美国本土汽车公司认为小的经济型轿车只是一个"入门级"产品，不值得开发，并且，他们为了保持价格低廉，生产的小型车质量水平普遍偏低。

The Toyota Motor Company received its first Japanese Quality Control Award at the start of the 1980s and began participating in a wide variety of motorsports. Due to the 1973 oil crisis, consumers in the U.S. market began turning to small cars with better fuel economy. American car manufacturers had considered small economy cars to be an "entry-level" product, and their small vehicles employed a low level of quality in order to keep the price low.

20 世纪 80 年代末，丰田开始推出新品牌。1989 年，雷克萨斯豪华系列投入市场。

Toyota then started to establish new brands at the end of the 1980s, with the launch of their luxury division Lexus in 1989.

在 20 世纪 90 年代，丰田开始由生产紧凑型汽车转型，开发了许多更大、更豪华的车型，其中包括大尺寸皮卡 T100、多款凯美瑞 SUV，知名的有运动版凯美瑞速乐娜和塞恩品牌，这些车价格适中，同时又是运动款，目标客户定位在年轻群体。1997 年，丰田公司开始生产世界上最畅销的混合动力电动汽车——普锐斯。

In the 1990s, Toyota began to branch out from producing mostly compact cars by adding many larger and more luxurious vehicles, including a full-sized pickup, the T100; several lines of SUVs; a sport version of the Camry, known as the Camry Solara and the Scion brand, a group of several affordable, yet sporty, automobiles targeted specifically to young adults. Toyota also began production of the world's best-selling hybrid car, the Prius, in 1997.

在福布斯公布的 2005 年度世界顶级企业 2000 强名单中，丰田公司排名第八位。该公司在 2008 年第一季度中，全球汽车销量位居榜首。

Forbes 2000 list of the world's automobile companies, Toyota ranked eighth among the leading companies for the year of 2005. The company was number one in global automobile sales for the first quarter of 2008.

在 2009 年 5 月 8 日，丰田汽车公布年净亏损 44 亿美元，受 2007—2010 年金融危机影响严重的。它不得不向日本政府贷款。

On May 8, 2009, Toyota reported a record annual net loss of US $4.4 billion, making it the latest automobile maker to be severely affected by the 2007−2010 financial crisis. It had to ask the Japanese government for loans.

丰田是推动混合动力汽车发展最大力的公司，同时是第一家大规模商业化生产和销售混合动力汽车的公司，一个典型例子就是丰田普瑞斯的生产和销售。丰田最终在其主要的小型车上也采用这种技术，比如凯美瑞，后来扩展到雷克萨斯系列，开始生产混合动力豪华型汽车。

Toyota is one of the largest companies to push hybrid vehicles in the market and the first to commercially mass-produce and sell such vehicles, an example being the Toyota Prius. The company eventually began providing this option on the main smaller cars such as Camry and later with the Lexus divisions, producing some hybrid luxury vehicles.

到 2021 年 8 月，以普瑞斯为首的丰田混合动力车的全球累计销售已达 443 万辆。丰田汽车公司的首席执行官承诺：最终公司所生产的每一辆汽车均是混合动力汽车。

Toyota's hybrid sales are led by Prius, with worldwide cumulative sales of 4.43 million by August 2021. Toyota's CEO has committed to eventually making every car of the company a hybrid vehicle.

2021 年，丰田汽车公司在世界汽车集团十强中排名第 3。

In 2021, Toyota was honored No.3 on Top 10 motor vehicle manufacturing companies.

3.6 兰 博 基 尼

Lamborghini

兰博基尼是意大利系汽车品牌，1963 年由制造业巨头费卢西奥·兰博基尼创建，其标志如图 3.7 所示。兰博基尼品牌几易其主，直到 1998 年成为德国车企奥迪公司的子公司（奥迪公司本身是大众集团的子公司）。兰博基尼因其时尚、独特的设计赢得了世界范围内的认可，该品牌成为了性能和财富的标志。

Lamborghini is an Italian automaker that was founded in 1963 by manufacturing magnate Ferruccio Lamborghini (Fig.3.7). It has changed ownership numerous times, since most recently becoming a subsidiary of German car manufacturer AUDI (a subsidiary of the Volkswagen Group) in 1998. Lamborghini has achieved widespread recognition for its fashionable, exotic designs, and its cars have become symbols of performance and wealth.

1966 年兰博基尼发布了中置发动机缪拉跑车取得成功，1968 年发布埃斯帕达高级跑车，埃斯帕达在十年间卖出了 1200 多辆。十年的快速发展之后，虽然在 1974 年发布了康塔什等经典车型，但受到了 1973 年石油危机的影响，在 20 世纪 70 年代后期公司开始萎缩。

图 3.7　兰博基尼标志

Fig.3.7　The logo of Lamborghini

Lamborghini met with success in 1966 with the release of the mid-engined Miura sports coupe, and in 1968 with the Espada GT, with the 1200 units during ten years of production. After almost a decade of rapid growth, and the release of classic models like the Countach in 1974, hard times occurred for the company in the late 1970s, as sales plunged in the wake of the 1973 oil crisis.

1978 年，兰博基尼破产，转手瑞士企业，最后终于受到克莱斯勒工业巨头庇护。然而这家美国公司却并没有能够让这个意大利品牌盈利，1994 年，该公司被卖给了印尼企业。兰博基尼在 20 世纪 90 年代后期，依然保持公司产品的开发，并不断更新。1990 年推出迪亚波罗。90 年代的亚洲金融危机使得兰博基尼动荡飘摇，终于在 1998 年兰博基尼持有人把这个问题企业卖给了奥迪集团。奥迪集团是德国大众集团旗下生产豪华车的子公司。德国人拥有兰博基尼的所有权，兰博基尼从此开始一个稳定的生产增长期，在接下来的十年，销售增长了近十倍。

In 1978, Bankruptcy crippled the automaker, and after passing through the hands of a number of Swiss companies, Lamborghini came under the corporate umbrella of industry giant Chrysler. The American company failed to make the Italian manufacturer profitable, and in 1994, the company was sold to an Indonesian company. Lamborghini remained on life support throughout the rest of the 1990s, continuously updating the Diablo of 1990. Limping from the Asian financial crisis of the previous year, in 1998 Lamborghini's owners sold the troubled automaker to AUDI, the luxury car subsidiary of Volkswagen Group. German ownership marked the beginning of a period of stability and increased productivity for Lamborghini, with sales increasing nearly tenfold over the course of the next decade.

所有权归属德国后，兰博基尼出现了前所未有的稳定。2003 年，兰博基尼推出了搭载更小的 V10 发动机的盖拉多，盖拉多品牌更容易被接受，也更实用。

Under German ownership, Lamborghini found stability that it had not seen in many years. In 2003, Lamborghini equipped the V10 engine on Gallardo, intended to be a more accessible and more livable model.

2008 年兰博基尼推出蝙蝠，该品牌从隐形战斗机上获得灵感，是极其珍贵的限量版超级跑车，同时也是兰博基尼销售过的性能最强、价格最高的车型。随后公司发布 2014 款蝙蝠 LP670-4 SV 车型，超越兰博基尼所有品牌。

Murcielago was released in 2008, an extremely limited-edition supercar that carried the distinction of being the most powerful and expensive Lamborghini ever sold. The most recent models released are the 2014 Murcielago LP670-4 SV, overtaking all its previous products.

2021年，兰博基尼推出爱马仕（Concept S）概念跑车，是在盖拉多基础上进行设计和制造的跑车，乘客座位与驾驶员座位分开，如图3-8所示。爱马仕概念车目前仅有一辆，存放在兰博基尼博物馆，预估售价3.7亿元人民币。

In 2021, Lamborghini launched the sport car Concept S, based on Gallardo's design and development. The passenger seat was separated from driver's (Fig3.8). Concept S presents only one by now which is stored in the Lamborghini museum. The price estimated is about 370 million Yuan RMB.

图 3.8　爱马仕概念跑车

Fig.3.8　Concept S sport car

习　　题

一、选择题

1. 大众汽车集团，也称VWG，是德国（　　）的汽车制造公司。
   A．汉堡　　　　　　B．柏林　　　　　　C．沃尔夫斯堡　　　D．底特律
2. （　　），帕萨特成为大众新生代第一款车型，该车采用前轮驱动，配备水冷式四汽缸110马力发动机。
   A．1963年　　　　　B．1973年　　　　　C．1983年　　　　　D．1993年
3. （　　），第一台高尔夫车在沃尔夫斯堡的工厂下线。
   A．1954年1月　　　B．1964年1月　　　C．1974年1月　　　D．1984年1月
4. 2021年《财富》评选大众集团为世界500强车辆和零部件行业（　　）。
   A．第一位　　　　　B．第二位　　　　　C．第三位　　　　　D．第四位
5. 宝马公司现在的标志，表达了白色螺旋桨迎着蓝天，反映的是（　　）。
   A．企业自身的起源　　　　　　　　　B．企业自身的目标
   C．企业自身的文化　　　　　　　　　D．企业自身的性质

6．2008年6月2日，福特将捷豹和路虎的运营权卖给了塔塔（　　）汽车公司。

    A．菲律宾　　　　　B．印度尼西亚　　C．新西兰　　　　D．印度

7．通用汽车之父是（　　）。

    A．奥兹莫比　　　　B．凯迪拉克　　　C．别克　　　　　D．威廉·杜兰特

8．2021年，通用汽车公司在世界汽车集团十强中排名（　　）。

    A．第三　　　　　　B．第四　　　　　C．第五　　　　　D．第六

9．卡罗拉是（　　）公司一款紧凑型轿车。

    A．本田　　　　　　B．丰田　　　　　C．日产　　　　　D．铃木

10．兰博基尼是（　　）一个汽车品牌。

    A．意大利　　　　　B．法国　　　　　C．英国　　　　　D．德国

二、简答题

1．简述20世纪30年代大众甲壳虫的相关情况。

2．简述福特汽车公司的基本情况。

3．简述宝马汽车公司的基本情况。

4．简述通用汽车公司在中国市场的运营情况。

5．简述在丰田公司在混合动力汽车的发展情况。

第 4 章 汽车技术先锋

Pioneers of automotive technology

许多人为汽车的发展做出了贡献,在此列举了部分对汽车发展做出重要贡献的先驱们。

Owing to the large number of people who contributed to the development of the automobile, this list makes a part of completeness.

1866 年,尼古拉斯·奥古斯特·奥托(图 4.1)获得汽化器专利。

1866, Nikolaus August Otto (Fig.4.1) acquires the patent for the atmospheric gas machine.

图 4.1 尼古拉斯·奥古斯特·奥托

Fig.4.1 Nikolaus August Otto

尼古拉斯·奥古斯特·奥托(1832—1891),出生于德国霍兹豪森镇,他在很小的时候就对技术产生了兴趣。作为食品公司推销员,他还被燃气发动机吸引。从 1862 年起,他完全致力于发动机制造与开发。设法改进了由法国工程师艾蒂安·勒努瓦发明的燃气机,并于 1867 年在巴黎世界博览会上被授予金奖。基于他在 1861 年制定的四冲程原理,他与戴姆勒、迈巴赫一起开发出内燃机。由此产生的发动机被称为"奥托发动机",至今仍在沿用。1884 年,奥托发明了磁电机点火装置,打开了发动机由汽油驱动的先河。这项创新为罗伯特·博世一生的主要工作奠定了基础。奥托的独特贡献在于他是第一个制造四冲程内燃机的人,并展示出了其优于所有前辈的卓越能力。

Nikolaus August Otto (1832–1891), born in Holzhausen (Germany), developed an interest in technical matters at an early age. Besides his employment as a traveling salesman for food wholesalers, he was attracted by the functioning of gas-powered engines. From 1862 onward he dedicated himself totally to engine construction. He managed to make improvements to the gas engine invented by the French engineer, Étienne Lenoir. For this work, Otto was awarded the gold medal at the 1867 Paris World Fair. Together with Daimler and Maybach, he developed an internal-combustion engine based on the four-stroke principle he had formulated in 1861. The resulting engine is known as the "Otto engine" to this day. In 1884 Otto invented magneto ignition, which allowed engines to be powered by gasoline. This innovation would form the basis for the main part of Robert Bosch's life's work. Otto's singular contribution was his ability to be the first to build the four-stroke internal-combustion engine and demonstrate its superiority over all its predecessors.

戈特利布·戴姆勒（1834—1900），来自德国的绍恩多夫，如图 4.2 所示。他在斯图加特的卡尔斯鲁厄工程学院学习机械工程。1865 年，他遇到了才华横溢的工程师威廉·迈巴赫。从那一刻起，这两个男人将加入一个持久的相互合作的关系。除了发明第一辆摩托车，戴姆勒主要致力于开发适用于公路车辆的汽油发动机。1889 年，戴姆勒和迈巴赫在巴黎推出了第一辆使用双缸 V 型发动机的"钢轮汽车"。不到一年，戴姆勒就在全球范围内销售其快速运转的戴姆勒发动机。例如，在 1891 年，阿尔芒·标致成功地驾驶自己设计的汽车参加了巴黎马拉松赛。证明了其设计的价值和戴姆勒发动机的可靠性。

Gottlieb Daimler (1834−1900) (Fig.4.2) was from Schorndorf (Germany). He studied mechanical engineering at the Polytechnikum engineering college in Stuttgart. In 1865 he met the highly talented engineer Wilhelm Maybach. From that moment on, the two men would be joined in a lasting relationship of mutual cooperation. Besides inventing the first motorcycle, Daimler mainly worked on developing a gasoline engine suitable for use in road vehicles. In 1889 Daimler and Maybach introduced the first "steel-wheeled vehicle" in Paris featuring a two-cylinder V-engine. One year later, Daimler marketed his fast-running Daimler engine on an international scale scarcely. In 1891, for example, Armand Peugeot successfully entered a vehicle he had engineered himself in the ParisBrest-Paris long-distance trial. It proved both the worth of his design and the dependability of the Daimler engine he was using.

图 4.2　戈特利布·戴姆勒

Fig.4.2　Gottlieb Daimler

戴姆勒的成就在于汽油发动机的系统开发和戴姆勒发动机的全球销售。

Daimler's achievements lie in the systematic development of the gasoline engine and the international distribution of his engines.

威廉·迈巴赫（图 4.3）出生于德国的海尔布隆市，作为一名技术绘图员完成了他的学徒生涯。不久后，他成为了一名设计工程师。他的雇主之一是 Gasmotoren Deutz AG 公司（由奥托创立）。在他有生之年，获得"工程师之王"的称号。迈巴赫改进了汽油发动机并投入生产。他还发明了水冷、化油器和双点火系统。1900 年，迈巴赫制造了一辆带来革命性变化的合金赛车。这款车是应一位名叫耶利内克的奥地利商人的要求而开发。他订购了 36 辆这样的车，条件是这款车必须以他女儿的名字梅赛德斯命名。迈巴赫作为设计工程师的精湛技艺为当代汽车工业的未来指明了方向。他的去世标志着汽车先驱们辉煌时代的结束。

Wilhelm Maybach (Fig.4.3), a native of Heilbronn (Germany), completed his apprenticeship as a technical draftsman. Soon after, he worked as a design engineer. Among his employers was the firm of Gasmotoren Deutz AG (founded by Otto). He already earned the nickname of "king of engineers" during his own lifetime. Maybach revised the gasoline engine and brought it to production. He also developed water cooling, the carburetor, and the dual ignition system. In 1900 Maybach built a revolutionary, alloy-based racing car. This vehicle was developed in response to a suggestion by an Austrian businessman named Jellinek. His order for 36 of these cars was given on the condition that the model was to be named after his daughter Mercedes. Maybach's virtuosity as a design engineer pointed the way to the future of the contemporary automobile industry. His death signaled the end of the grand age of the automotive pioneers.

图 4.3　威廉·迈巴赫

Fig.4.3　Wilhelm Maybach

1886 年，作为第一辆装有内燃机的汽车发明者，本茨载入了世界历史史册。

In 1886, As the inventor of the first automobile fitted with an internal-combustion engine, Benz enters the annals of world history.

卡尔·弗里德里希·本茨（1844—1929）（图 4.4），出生于德国卡尔斯鲁厄，在家乡的工程学院学习机械工程。1871 年，他在曼海姆创立了自己的第一家公司（即奔驰公司），一家生产铸铁产品和工业零部件的工厂。不同于戴姆勒和迈巴赫，他还寻求在汽车上安装发动机的方法。当奥托的四冲程发动机专利被宣布无效时，除了他自己的四冲程发动机，本茨还开发了表面化油器、电子点火系统、离合器、水冷却系统和变速系统。1886 年，他申请了专利，并公开展示了他的汽车。直到 1990 年，奔驰公司能够提供 600 多种在售车型。1894 年至 1901 年期间，奔驰公司生产出维乐，总产量约为 1200 辆，可称为第一辆大规模生产的汽车。1926 年，奔驰与戴姆勒合并，成立了戴姆勒—奔驰股份公司。卡尔·本茨发明了第一辆汽车，并为汽车工业化生产奠定了基础。

Carl Friedrich Benz (1844–1929) (Fig.4.4), born in Karlsruhe (Germany), studied mechanical engineering at the Polytechnikum engineering college in his hometown. In 1871 he founded his first company, a factory for iron-foundry products and industrial components in Mannheim. Independently of Daimler and Maybach, he also pursued the means of fitting an engine in a vehicle. When the essential claims stemming from Otto's four-stroke engine patent had been declared null and void, Benz also developed a surface carburetor, electrical ignition, the clutch, water cooling, and a gearshift system, besides his own four stroke engine. In 1886 he applied for his patent and presented his motor carriage to the public. In the period until the year 1900, Benz was able to offer more than 600 models for sale. In the period between 1894 and 1901, the factory of Benz & Co. produced the "Velo", which, with a total output of about 1200 units, may be called the first mass-produced automobile. In 1926 Benz merged with Daimler to form "Daimler-Benz AG". Carl Benz introduced the first automobile and established the preconditions for the industrial manufacture of production vehicles.

图 4.4　卡尔·弗里德里希·本茨

Fig.4.4　Carl Friedrich Benz

亨利·福特（1863—1947）（图 4.5），来自美国密歇根州迪尔伯恩。尽管福特在 1891 年已经在爱迪生照明公司找到了一份稳定的工程师工作，他的个人兴趣还是致力于汽油发动机的发展。

Henry Ford (1863–1947) (Fig.4.5) was from Dearborn, Michigan (USA). Although Ford had found secure employment as an engineer with the Edison Illuminating Company in 1891, his personal interests were dedicated to the advancement of the gasoline engine.

图 4.5　亨利·福特

Fig.4.5　Henry Ford

　　1908 年，福特推出了传说中的"T 型车"，从 1913 年开始在装配线上大量生产。从 1921 年开始，福特凭借其在美国工业生产中 55%的份额，统治了美国国内的汽车市场。亨利·福特是美国汽车化的同义词，正是他的想法使汽车能为广大民众所接受。

　　In 1908 Ford introduced the legendary "Model T", which was mass-produced on assembly lines from 1913 onward. Beginning in 1921, with a 55-percent share in the country's industrial production, Ford dominated the domestic automobile market in the USA. The name Henry Ford is synonymous with the motorization of the United States. It was his ideas that made the automobile accessible to a broad segment of the population.

　　鲁道夫·克里斯蒂安·卡尔·迪赛尔（1858—1913）（图 4.6），出生于法国，14 岁时决定成为一名工程师。他以该学院成立以来的最好成绩毕业于慕尼黑工业大学。1892 年，迪塞尔获得了后来以他的名字命名的"柴油机"专利。该发动机很快被用作固定式动力装置和船用发动机。1908 年，第一辆商用卡车由柴油发动机驱动。但是要进入乘用车领域还需要几十年的时间。直到 1936 年，柴油发动机才成为奔驰 260D 系列的动力装置。现代柴油发动机的发展已达到了和汽油发动机一样的水平，应用和汽油发动机一样普遍。凭借他的发明，柴油机为内燃机的更经济利用做出了重大贡献。尽管迪塞尔通过颁发生产许可证活跃于国际舞台，但他生前的所做成就并没有得到应有的认可。

　　Rudolf Christian Karl Diesel (1858−1913) (Fig.4.6), born in Paris (France), decided to become an engineer at the age of 14. He graduated from the Techincal university of in Munich with the best marks the institution had given in its entire existence. In 1892 Diesel was issued the patent for the "Diesel engine" that was later to bear his name. The engine was quickly adopted as a stationary power plant and marine engine. In 1908 the first commercial truck was powered by a diesel engine. However, its entrance into the world of passenger cars would take several decades. The diesel engine became the power plant for the serial-produced Mercedes 260D as late as 1936. Today's diesel engine has reached a level of development such that it is now as common as the gasoline engine. With his invention, Diesel has made a major contribution to a more economical utilization of the internal-combustion engine. Although Diesel became active internationally by granting production licenses, he failed to earn due recognition for his achievements during his lifetime.

图 4.6　鲁道夫·克里斯蒂安·卡尔·迪赛尔

Fig.4.6　Rudolf Christian Karl Diesel

罗伯特·博世（图 4.7）："对我来说，无法忍受的是，有人检查我的任何一个产品，发现它在任何方面都是劣质的。出于这个原因，我一直努力制造经得起最严格审查的产品——证明在各方面都很优秀的产品。"

"It has always been an unbearable thought to me that someone could inspect one of my products and find it inferior in any way. For that reason, I have constantly endeavored to make products that withstand the closest scrutiny—products that prove themselves superior in every respect."

—Robert Bosch (Fig.4.7)

图 4.7　罗伯特·博世

Fig.4.7　Robert Bosch

罗伯特·博世（1861—1942）于 1861 年 9 月 23 日出生在德国乌尔姆附近的阿尔贝克，来自于一个富裕的农民家庭。在完成了作为精密钳工的学徒生涯后，他开始做起了临时工以继续磨炼自己的工程技能，扩大自己的销售能力和经验。在斯图加特理工大学学习电气工程六个月后，他前往美国为"爱迪生照明公司"工作。后来受雇于英国的"西门子兄弟"。1886 年，他决定在斯图加特西区一所住宅的后面开设一个"精密机械和电气工程工作室"，并雇佣了一名机械师和一名学徒。起初，他的工作领域是安装和修理电话、电报、避雷针和其他光工程工作。他致力于为新问题寻找快速的解决方案，这也帮助他在后来的活动中获得了竞争优势。

Robert Bosch, born on September 23, 1861, in Albeck near Ulm (Germany), was the scion of a wealthy farmer's family. After completing his apprenticeship as a precision fitter, he worked temporarily for a number of enterprises, where he continued to hone his technical skills and expand his merchandising abilities and experience. After six months as an auditor studying electrical engineering at Stuttgart technical university, he traveled to the United States to work for "Edison Illuminating". He was later employed by "Siemens Brothers" in England. In 1886 he decided to open a "Workshop for Precision Mechanics and Electrical Engineering" in the back of a dwelling in Stuttgart's west end. He employed another mechanic and an apprentice. In the beginning, his field of work lay in installing and repairing telephones, telegraphs, lightning conductors, and other light-engineering jobs. His dedication to finding rapid solutions to new problems also helped him gain a competitive lead in his later activities.

1897 年，对汽车行业而言，由博世开发的低压磁电机点火装置实现了一项真正的突破，这一点与其不可靠的前辈大不相同。这一产品是罗伯特·博世业务迅速扩张的跳板。他总是设法使技术和经济与人类的需求相协调。博世在社会关怀的许多方面都是先驱者。罗伯特·博世在开发和推动下列产品成熟发展方面进行了开创性的工作：用于高速发动机的低/高压磁电机点火装置（由他的同事戈特罗布·霍诺德设计）、火花塞点火分电器、蓄电池（客车和摩托车用）、起动机、发电机（交流发电机）、第一个前大灯照明系统、柴油喷油泵、车载收音机（由"Ideal-Werke"制造，1938 年更名为"Blaupunkt"）、第一个自行车照明系统、博世喇叭、蓄电池点火系统、博世信号转向灯（最初被嘲笑为典型的德国组织意识——现在是不可或缺的方向指示灯），在这一方面，在社会参与领域的许多其他成就也都值得大书特书。他们都是博世走在时代前列的见证。他的前瞻性思维极大地推动了汽车的发展。越来越多的自驾游行动促进了维修设备需求的增长。20 世纪 20 年代，罗伯特·博世发起了一场旨在创建综合性服务机构的运动。

To the automobile industry, the low-voltage magneto ignition developed by Bosch in 1897 represented—much unlike its unreliable predecessors—a true breakthrough. This product was the launching board for the rapid expansion of Robert Bosch's business. He always managed to bring the purposefulness of the world of technology and economics into harmony with the needs of humanity. Bosch was a trailblazer in many aspects of social care. Robert Bosch performed technological pioneering work in developing and bringing the following products to maturity: low-voltage magneto ignition, high-voltage magneto ignition for higher engine speeds (engineered by his colleague Gottlob Honold), spark plug ignition distributor, battery (passenger vehicles and motor cycles) electrical starter, generator (alternator), lighting system with first electric headlamp, diesel injection pumps, car radio (manufactured by "Ideal-Werke", renamed "Blaupunkt" in 1938), first lighting system for bicycles, bosch horn, battery ignition, Bosch semaphore turn signal (initially ridiculed as being typical of the German sense of organization—now the indispensable direction indicator). At this point, many other achievements, also in the area of social engagement, would be worthy of note. They are clear indicators that Bosch was truly ahead of his time. His forward-thinking mind has given great impetus to advances in automobile development. The rising number of self-driving motorists fostered a corresponding increase in the need for repair facilities. In the 1920s Robert Bosch launched a campaign aimed at creating a comprehensive service organization.

1926年，在德国国内，这些服务维修中心被统一命名为"博世—迪恩斯特"（博世服务），并被注册为商标。博世公司在实现社会关怀方面同样雄心勃勃。1906年，在引入8小时工作制后，他给工人们提供了丰厚的工资作为补偿。1910年，博世捐赠了100万德国马克用来支持技术教育。博世以生产第50万台永磁电机为契机，推出周六下午免工作制。在博世提出的其他改进措施中，也包括养老金、重度残疾人工作间和休假计划。1913年，博世的信条"学徒的职业和实践是比理论更有知识的教育者"推动成立了一个学徒车间，该车间为104名学徒提供了充足的工作空间。1914年中期，博世的名字已经在全世界范围内成为一种象征。1914年以前，88%由斯图加特生产的产品计划出口。博世能够在大量军事特遣队的帮助下继续扩张。然而，鉴于战争年代的暴行，他不认同由此产生的利润。故捐赠了1300万德国马克用于社会福利事业。第一次世界大战结束后，博世已很难在国外市场重新站稳脚跟。例如，博世公司的工厂、销售办事处以及公司标志和符号被没收，并出售给一家美国公司。其中一个结果便是以"博世"品牌出现的产品并非真正由博世制造。

In 1926, within Germany, these service repair centers were uniformly named "Bosch-Dienst" (Bosch Service) and the name was registered as a trademark. Bosch had similarly high ambitions with regard to the implementation of social-care objectives. Having introduced the 8-hour day in 1906, he compensated his workers with ample wages. In 1910 he donated one million reichsmarks to support technical education. Bosch took the production of the 500000th magneto as an occasion to introduce the work-free Saturday afternoon. Among other Bosch-induced improvements were old-age pensions, workplaces for the severely handicapped, and the vacation scheme. In 1913 the Bosch credo, "Occupation and the practice of apprenticeship are more knowledgeable educators than mere theory" resulted in the inauguration of an apprentice workshop that provided ample space for 104 apprentices. In mid-1914 the name of Bosch was already represented around the world. Prior to 1914, 88% of the products made in Stuttgart were slated for export. Bosch was able to continue expansion with the aid of large contingents destined for the military. However, in light of the atrocities of the war years, he disapproved of the resulting profits. As a result, he donated 13 million German marks for social-care purposes. After the end of WWI, it was difficult to regain a foothold in foreign markets. In the United States, for example, Bosch factories, sales offices, and the corporate logo and symbol had been confiscated and sold to an American company. One of the consequences was that products appeared under the "Bosch" brand name that was not truly Bosch-made.

直到 20 世纪 20 年代末，博世才收回了他以前的所有权利，并能够在美国重新立足。创始人克服一切障碍的坚定决心让公司重返世界市场，同时，也让博世员工意识到博世作为一家企业的国际意义。1936 年，他捐资修建了一所医院，并于 1940 年正式开放。在他的就职演说中，罗伯特·博世强调了他在社会参与方面的个人奉献："每一份工作都很重要，即使是最底层的工作。不要让任何人欺骗自己去认为自己的工作比同事的工作更重要。"1942 年，罗伯特·博世逝世，全世界都在哀悼这位企业家，他不仅是技术和电气工程领域的先驱，也是社会参与领域的先驱。直到今天，罗伯特·博世仍然是进步的时代精神、不懈的奋斗、推动社会进步、企业家精神的典范，也是教育事业的坚定拥护者。他对进步的愿景以这样一句话达到顶点："知识、能力和意志都很重要，但成功只能来自它们之间的和谐互动。"1964 年，罗伯特·博世基金会成立。其活动包括促进和支持卫生保健、福利、教育，以及赞助艺术和文化、人文和社会科学。该基金会至今仍致力于培养创始人的理念。

It was not until the end of the 1920s before Bosch had reclaimed all of his former rights and was able to reestablish himself in the United States. The Founder's unyielding determination to overcome any and all obstacles returned the company to the markets of the world and, at the same time, imbued the minds of Bosch employees with the international significance of Bosch as an enterprise. In 1936 he donated funds to construct a hospital that was officially opened in 1940. In his inaugural speech, Robert Bosch emphasized his personal dedication in terms of social engagement: "Every job is important, even the lowliest. Let no man delude himself that his work is more important than that of a colleague." With the passing of Robert Bosch in 1942, the world mourned an entrepreneur who was a pioneer not only in the arena of technology and electrical engineering, but also in the realm of social engagement. Until this day, Robert Bosch stands as an example of progressive zeitgeist, untiring diligence, social improvements, of entrepreneurial spirit, and as a dedicated champion of education. His vision of progress culminated in the words, "Knowledge, ability, and will are important, but success only comes from their harmonious interaction." In 1964 the Robert Bosch Foundation was inaugurated. Its activities include the promotion and support of health care, welfare, and education, as well as sponsoring the arts and culture, humanities, and social sciences. The Foundation continues to nurture the founder's ideals to this day.

习　　题

一、单选题

1. （　　）改进了由法国工程师艾蒂安·勒努瓦发明的燃气机，发明了"奥托发动机"。
   A．迈巴赫　　　　　B．奥托　　　　　C．卡尔·本茨　　D．戴姆勒
2. （　　）的成就在于汽油发动机的系统开发和戴姆勒发动机的全球销售。
   A．迈巴赫　　　　　B．奥托　　　　　C．卡尔·本茨　　D．戴姆勒

3．（　　）曾获得"工程师之王"的称号。
　　A．迈巴赫　　　　B．奥托　　　　C．卡尔·本茨　D．戴姆勒
4．（　　）发明了第一辆汽车，并为汽车工业化生产奠定了基础。
　　A．迈巴赫　　　　B．奥托　　　　C．卡尔·本茨　D．戴姆勒
5．第一个开始在装配线上大量生产的车是（　　）。
　　A．福特　　　　　B．奔驰　　　　C．丰田　　　　D．红旗
6．下面获得"柴油机"专利的是（　　）。
　　A．福特　　　　　B．狄赛尔　　　C．罗伯特·博世　D．迈巴赫
7．创建博世公司的是（　　）。
　　A．福特　　　　　B．狄赛尔　　　C．罗伯特·博世　D．迈巴赫
8．下面属于国产自主品牌的汽车是（　　）。
　　A．福特　　　　　B．奔驰　　　　C．丰田　　　　D．红旗

二、简答题

1．简述罗斯·奥古斯特·奥托的主要贡献。
2．叙述卡尔·弗里德里希·本茨的主要成就。
3．分析福特汽车能迅速占据美国国内汽车市场的原因。
4．查阅资料，总结与分析红旗轿车的发展历程以及关键人物。
5．查阅资料，阐述博世公司的生产经营范围。

第 5 章 汽车标志和超豪华轿车

Car logo and ultra luxurious car

5.1 汽车标志简述

Introduction to automobile logo

汽车标志是代表汽车类型和身份的符号或文字。作为汽车公司独特的文化视觉符号，汽车标志有助于汽车公司在世界范围内获得产品认同。

A car logo is a symbol or letter that represents the identity of a particular type of car. Car logos will help you to distinguish one brand from another. Logos serve as unique visual marks of the identity of a company. They help companies gain product recognition in the world market.

（1）奥迪标志。奥迪公司是德国历史最悠久的汽车制造商标志之一，如图 5.1 所示。标志有"四个圈"，象征着 1932 年四个独立的汽车制造商合并成一家公司：奥迪、DKW、霍希和流浪者。1969 年，NSU 品牌加入，这些公司一起成为今天奥迪股份公司的根基。奥迪公司新车标于 2009 年 9 月发布，改变了字体，同时也对四个圈的三维描绘做了修改。

Audi logo. The Audi badge the "Four Rings" is the emblem of one of the oldest car manufacturers in Germany (Fig.5.1). It symbolizes the 1932 merger of the four independent motor-vehicle manufacturers: Audi, DKW, Horch, and Wanderer. Together with the NSU brand, which joined in 1969, these companies are the roots of the present-day AUDI AG. The new logo, released in September 2009 changes the font and also improves on the 3-dimensional aspect of the rings.

图 5.1 奥迪标志

Fig.5.1 Audi logo

（2）宝马标志。20 世纪 10 年代，宝马公司由两个著名的德国飞机制造专家古斯塔夫·奥托和卡尔·拉普建立于慕尼黑，那时是一家飞机制造商。宝马公司现在的标志，被设计成白色的螺旋桨迎着蓝天，反映的就是自身的起源；这种蓝白色的设计方案也与巴伐利亚的蓝白方格旗色调一致，如图 5.2 所示。

BMW Logo. Founded by two well-known airplane specialists Gustav Otto and Karl Rapp in

Munich, the company began in the early 1910s as an aircraft manufacturer. BMWs current logo, designed to represent white propeller blades against a blue sky (Fig.5.2), reflects these origins: its blue-and-white color scheme also references Bavaria's blue-and-white checkered flag.

图 5.2　宝马标志

Fig.5.2　BMW logo

（3）梅赛德斯—奔驰标志。梅赛德斯—奔驰车标是世界上最著名的车标之一。奔驰的车标是一个简洁的三叉星，它代表着奔驰车在陆地、海洋和天空中的统治地位，如图 5.3 所示。奔驰著名的三叉星由戈特利布·戴姆勒设计，表明他的汽车能够在陆地、天空和海洋中使用。奔驰的车标在 1909 年的一辆戴姆勒汽车上首先使用，在 1926 年加上了奔驰的花环以表示戴姆勒和奔驰两家公司的联合。

Mercedes-Benz logo. The Mercedes-Benz logo is one of the most famous brands in the world. The Benz logo is a simplistic three-pointed star that represents its domination of the land, the sea, and the air (Fig.5.3). The famous three-pointed star was designed by Gottlieb Daimler to show the ability of his motors for land, air, and seausage. It was first seen on a Daimler in 1909 and was combined with the Benz laurel wreath in 1926 to signify the union of the two firms.

图 5.3　梅赛德斯—奔驰标志

Fig.5.3　Mercedes-Benz logo

（4）大众汽车标志。大众汽车公司的车标的含义很明显。这个车标包含了蓝色背景下的字母 V 和 W，字母的外面被一个圆包围，如图 5.4 所示。"Volks" 的意思是 "大众" 而 "Wagen" 表示 "汽车"。所以 "Volkswagen" 在德语中就是 "大众汽车"。现在大众汽车公司的车标是第四代，和第三代非常相似，只做了一些小的改动。主要的变化是颜色，主题颜色由原来的黑白色变成了蓝色和灰色。现在的大众车标非常有影响力，且引人注意。

Volkswagen logo. The Volkswagen logo story is simplistic (Fig.5.4). The logo contains the letters V and W on a blue background surrounded by a circle. "Volks" means people and "Wagen" car. So the name "Volkswagen" means "People's car" in German. The current logo is the fourth version and basically is very similar to the previous one with minute modifications. The major change is its color. The color theme has changed altogether from black and white to blue and grey. The current logo is exceptionally impactful and eye-catching.

图 5.4　大众汽车标志

Fig.5.4　Volkswagen logo

（5）别克标志。别克标志有三个盾牌，来源于别克汽车的创始人大卫•邓巴•别克的先祖盾徽。这个车标经历了几次大变动。在 20 世纪 80 年代后，别克三盾车标重新出现，图案有所简化，只是保留了与美国国旗相同的红白蓝颜色，如图 5.5 所示。

Buick logo. The Buick Tri-shield is rooted in the ancestral coat of arms of the automaker's founder, David Dunbar Buick. The logo underwent several major overhauls. The trishield reemerged in the 1980s, simplified, but with its same patriotic colors (Fig.5.5).

图 5.5　别克标志

Fig.5.5　Buick logo

（6）雪佛兰标志。雪佛兰采用了蝴蝶结图案，如图 5.6 所示。普遍的说法是：公司的创立人之一的威廉•杜兰特，在巴黎一家旅馆墙上看到了一张壁纸的主题很好，就顺手撕下那片壁纸，经过改进作为雪佛兰汽车的标志。

Chevrolet logo. The long-accepted version of how Chevrolet got its Bowtie logo (Fig.5.6) is that the company co-founder William. C. Durant saw the motif on the wallpaper of a Parisian hotel, tore off a piece of the wallpaper, and adapted the pattern for his cars' nameplate.

图 5.6　雪佛兰标志

Fig.5.6　Chevrolet logo

（7）雪铁龙标志。雪铁龙的标志看来像两个呈倒 V 字的美国工兵，如图 5.7 所示。安德烈•雪铁龙在进入汽车行业前生产齿轮，而双人字形则表示齿轮轮齿形状，是向这位老工程师早期的修理工作表示纪念。

Citroën logo. The Citroën logo looks like something you might see on an American cartoon soldier-two inverted Vs. Andre Citroën started in the motor trade by building gear wheels before branching out into the motorcar (Fig.5.7), and the twin chevrons are meant to represent gear teeth in honor of the old engineer's early fettlings.

图 5.7 雪铁龙标志

Fig.5.7 Citroën logo

（8）法拉利标志。全球闻名的法拉利，标志是一匹跃起的黑马映衬在黄色背景下，有两个字母 S 和 F，代表斯库德里亚·法拉利，如图 5.8 所示。这匹跃起的黑马原来是弗朗西斯科·巴拉卡伯爵的标志，他是第一次世界大战期间意大利空军的传奇飞行员，他把一匹马涂在他飞机的侧面。巴拉卡在 34 次空中决斗和多次团队作战中取得胜利，在 1918 年 6 月 19 日一次战斗中所驾驶的飞机被击落后牺牲，当时非常年轻。

Ferrari logo. The famous symbol of Ferrari is a black prancing horse on yellow background, usually with the letters S F for Scuderia Ferrari (Fig.5.8). The horse was originally the symbol of Count Francesco Baracca, a legendary "asso" (ace) of the Italian air force during World War I, who painted it on the side of his planes. Baracca died very young on June 19, 1918, shot down after 34 victorious duels and many team victories.

图 5.8 法拉利标志

Fig.5.8 Ferrari logo

（9）福特标志。椭圆形的福特车标是世界上最为人们所熟知的车标之一，该车标已经使用了 50 多年。这个标志的脚本可以追溯到福特工程公司创立的时候，亨利·福特设计出一种奇特风格的、程式化的"福特汽车公司"字样。这个蓝色椭圆形车标是福特汽车公司在 2003 年为了纪念福特汽车公司成立 100 周年而发布的。它被称为"世纪蓝色椭圆"，如图 5.9 所示。

Ford logo. The oval of the Ford brand is one of the best-known symbols in the world and has been used for more than 50 years. The script trademark dates back to the beginning of the engineering firm of Henry Ford developed a wizard version of the stylized words "Ford Motor Company".

This logo is the blue oval that Ford released in 2003 in honor of 100 years of the Ford Motor Company was about. It is named the "Centennial Blue Oval" (Fig.5.9).

图 5.9　福特标志

Fig.5.9　Ford logo

（10）捷豹标志。捷豹的标志是一只美洲虎正从公司的名字上跃起。跃起的美洲虎代表捷豹汽车的速度、力量和敏捷，如图 5.10 所示。

Jaguar logo. The Jaguar logo is a Jaguar leaping across the company name (Fig.5.10). The leaping Jaguar is possibly built to represent the speed, power, and quickness of the car.

图 5.10　捷豹标志

Fig.5.10　Jaguar logo

（11）兰博基尼标志。兰博基尼的车标是一头充满力量、向对方攻击的斗牛，如图 5.11 所示。它代表了其创始人费鲁基欧·兰博基尼，他的星座是金牛座。兰博基尼公司大部分的汽车都是以有名的斗牛来命名。

Lamborghini logo. The Lamborghini Charging Bull Logo stands for the founder, Ferruccio Lamborghini, zodiacal sign (Taurus) (Fig.5.11). Most of the company's cars have been named after famous fighting bulls.

图 5.11　兰博基尼标志

Fig.5.11　Lamborghini logo

（12）马自达标志。马自达车标时尚的大写"M"让人联想到飞翔的翅膀，寓意着马自达飞向未来，如图 5.12 所示。"M"之间的"V"向外展开就像一个运转的风扇，代表着马自达的创造力、活力、灵动和热情。车标整体感觉就是马自达旗下产品追寻锐意进取、坚实可靠。富有动感的圆象征着马自达在进入 21 世纪时，随时准备展翅高飞。

Mazda logo. Mazda, the stylized "M" evokes an image of wings in flight and symbolizes the Mazda's flight toward the future (Fig.5.12). The "V" in the center of the "M" spreads out like an opening fan, representing the creativity, vitality, flexibility, and passion that in Mazda. The symbol as a whole expresses the sharp, solid feeling that Mazda will be seeking in all of its products. The dynamic circle symbolizes Mazda's readiness to spread its wings as it enters the 21st century.

图 5.12　马自达标志

Fig.5.12　Mazda logo

（13）劳斯莱斯标志。劳斯莱斯的车标包含了两个 R，表示罗尔斯和罗伊斯两人，如图 5.13 所示，他们是劳斯莱斯汽车公司的创始人。这个车标没有什么特别之处，但由于劳斯莱斯的品牌非常有名，这使得它的车标看起来也与众不同。1884 年，弗雷德里克·亨利·罗伊斯开始了他的机械电力生意。1904 年，他在自己的曼彻斯特工厂里制造出他的第一辆汽车——"罗伊斯"。同年 5 月 4 日，经人介绍他见到了住在曼彻斯特旅馆的查尔斯·斯图尔特·罗尔斯，双方达成了交易：由罗伊斯制造汽车，罗尔斯专门负责销售。在合同中加了一项条款，规定汽车的名字就叫"劳斯莱斯"。

Rolls Royce logo. Two R in the Rolls Royce logo stands for the Rolls and Royce, the two founders of this car manufacturing company. There is nothing special about the design of the logo, but the brand name is so strong that make the logo looks special (Fig.5.13). In 1884 Frederick Henry Royce started an electrical and mechanical business. He made his first car, a "Royce", in his Manchester factory in 1904. He was introduced to Charles Stewart Rolls in a Manchester hotel on

May 4 of that year, and the pair agreed with a deal where manufacture cars, to be sold exclusively by Rolls. A clause was added to the contract, stipulating the cars would be called "Rolls Royce".

图 5.13　劳斯莱斯标志

Fig.5.13　Rolls Royce logo

（14）丰田标志。丰田的车标由三个椭圆组成，代表了顾客的心意、生产者的心意和丰田汽车未来不断发展的技术和机遇。另外一种解释是这三个椭圆代表了公司文化的三个密不可分的方面：自由、团队精神和进步，如图 5.14 所示。同样，在日语中，"Toyo"意思是丰收、富裕，而"ta"是"大米、水稻"的意思（尽管丰田的名字取自创建者的姓氏而不是其字面意思）。在一些亚洲国家的文化中，有很多大米的人被认为享有大量的财富。

Toyota logo. The Toyota logo is comprised of three ellipses, representing the heart of the customer, the heart of the producer, and the ever-expanding technological advancements and opportunities that lie ahead. Another interpretation is that it represents the three interlocking aspects of the culture of the company—freedom, team spirit, and progress (Fig.5.14). Also, in Japanese "Toyo" means an abundance of, and "ta" is rice (though the name Toyota was chosen as it was the founder's name, not for its literal meaning). In some Asian cultures, those blessed with an abundance of rice are believed to be blessed with great wealth.

图 5.14　丰田标志

Fig.5.14　Toyota logo

（15）沃尔沃标志。沃尔沃的名字来自于拉丁词"volvere"，意思是滚动。这个名字最初来源于公司原始时期为汽车工业生产轴承。沃尔沃的车标是表示钢铁的古老标志，这就是一个带有箭头指向对角线右上方的圆，如图 5.15 所示。这个符号也代表着"马尔斯，战争之神"，同样也代表"男人"。沃尔沃汽车历来以其很高的安全性而闻名于世。钢铁符号也用来反映瑞典钢铁工业优秀的传统，比如安全、高质量和耐用。

Volvo logo. The name Volvo is derived from the Latin word "volvere" which means "roll", the name originated from the original company that manufactured bearings for the car industry

(Fig.5.15). The logo for Volvo is the ancient symbol of Iron, which is a circle with an arrow pointed diagonally upwards to the right. This symbol also represented "Mars, the God of War" and also the symbol for "Man" as well. Volvo cars are also traditionally known for their safety features. The iron symbol was used to also reflect the strong tradition of the Swedish Iron Industry along with its properties such as safety, quality, and durability.

图 5.15　沃尔沃标志

Fig.5.15　Volvo logo

（16）特斯拉标志。特斯拉是美国一家电动汽车和能源公司，由马丁•艾伯哈德和马克•塔彭宁于 2003 年共同创立。特斯拉首次在电动汽车上使用锂基电池，主要产品有 Model S, Model X 和 Model 3，其标志如图 5.16 所示。

Tesla logo. Tesla is an American electric vehicle and energy company co-found by Martin Eberhard and Mark Tarpenning in 2003. Tesla first used lithium-based batteries inits electric vehicles, with its main product being the Model S, Model X and Model 3, whose logo is shown in Fig.5.16.

图 5.16　特斯拉标志

Fig.5.16　Tesla logo

（17）克莱斯勒标志。克莱斯勒是美国一家历史悠久的汽车公司，在美国汽车公司中位居前三。老标志是五角星，新标志于 2010 年开始使用，是两个飞翔的翅膀，如图 5.17 所示，给人以流线型的感觉。

Chrysler logo. Chrysler is founded in America. It is one of the 3 top automobile companies in America. The old logo is a five-angle star and the new logo used from 2010 is double fly wings meaning the streamlined sense (Fig.5.17).

（18）吉利标志。吉利标志中的椭圆象征地球，表示面向世界，走向国际。椭圆在动态中最稳定，喻示吉利事业稳定发展。椭圆内的尖角寓意男人的六块腹肌，代表年轻、力量和健康，如图 5.18 所示。

Geely logo. The oval of the Geely logo symbolizes the Earth and represents facing the world international. The oval is stable in dynamic situations indicating the stable development of Geely undertaking (Fig.5.18). Sharp angle means the 6 abdomen muscles of man which stands for youth, power, and health.

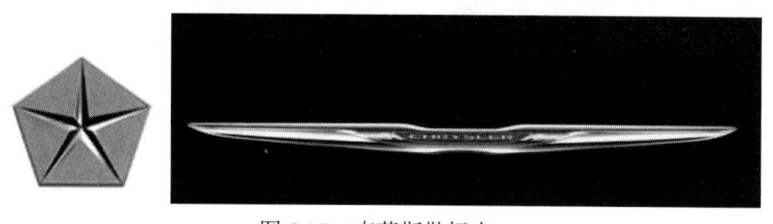

图 5.17　克莱斯勒标志

Fig.5.17　Chrysler logo

图 5.18　吉利标志

Fig.5.18　Geely logo

（19）比亚迪标志。比亚迪标志在 2007 年已由蓝天白云的老标志转换成只有三个字母和一个椭圆组成的标志了，如图 5.19 所示。BYD 的意思是成就梦想。

BYD logo. BYD logo has converted to the symbol which is composed of three letters and one oval from the old one with a blue sky and white cloud in 2007. The meaning of BYD is "build your dreams" (Fig.5.19).

图 5.19　比亚迪标志

Fig.5.19　BYD logo

5.2　不同国家汽车品牌

Automobile brands from different countries

（1）中国制造品牌如表 5.1 所示。

Brands made in China (Table 5.1).

表 5.1 中国制造品牌

Table 5.1 Brands made in China

比亚迪 BYD	中国一汽 China FAW	奇瑞 Chery	长城 Great Wall
吉利 Geely	东风 Dong Feng	红旗 Hong Qi	广汽 Guang Qi

（2）德国制造品牌如表 5.2 所示。

Brands made in Germany (Table 5.2).

表 5.2 德国制造品牌

Table 5.2 Brands made in Germany

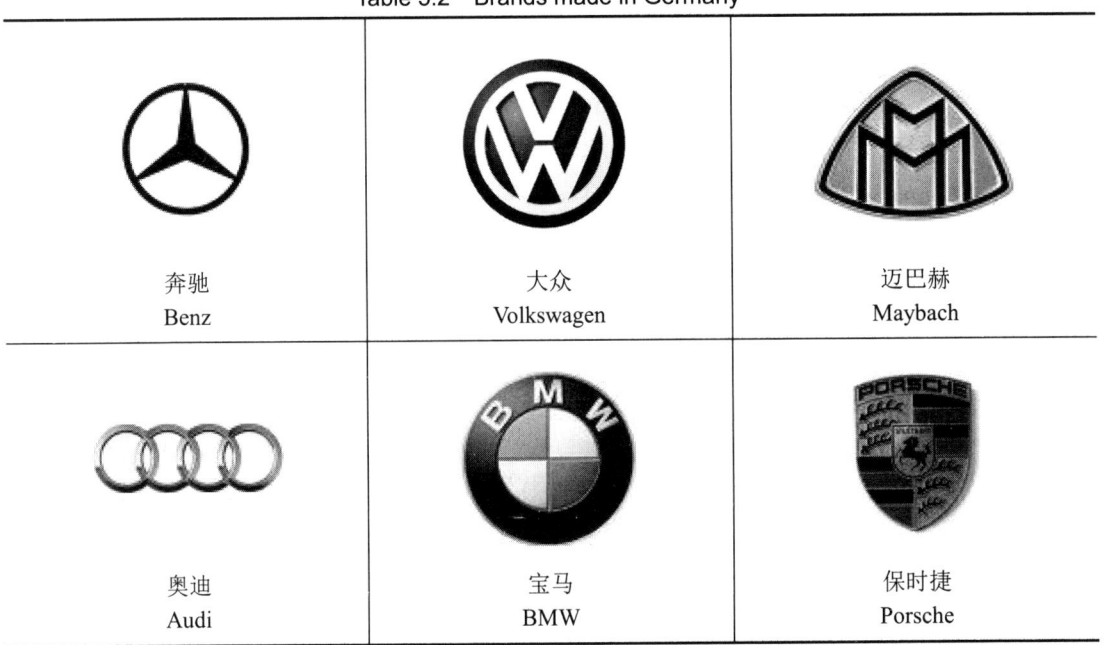

奔驰 Benz	大众 Volkswagen	迈巴赫 Maybach
奥迪 Audi	宝马 BMW	保时捷 Porsche

（3）日本制造品牌如表 5.3 所示。

Brands made in Japan (Table 5.3).

表 5.3　日本制造品牌

Table 5.3　Brands made in Japan

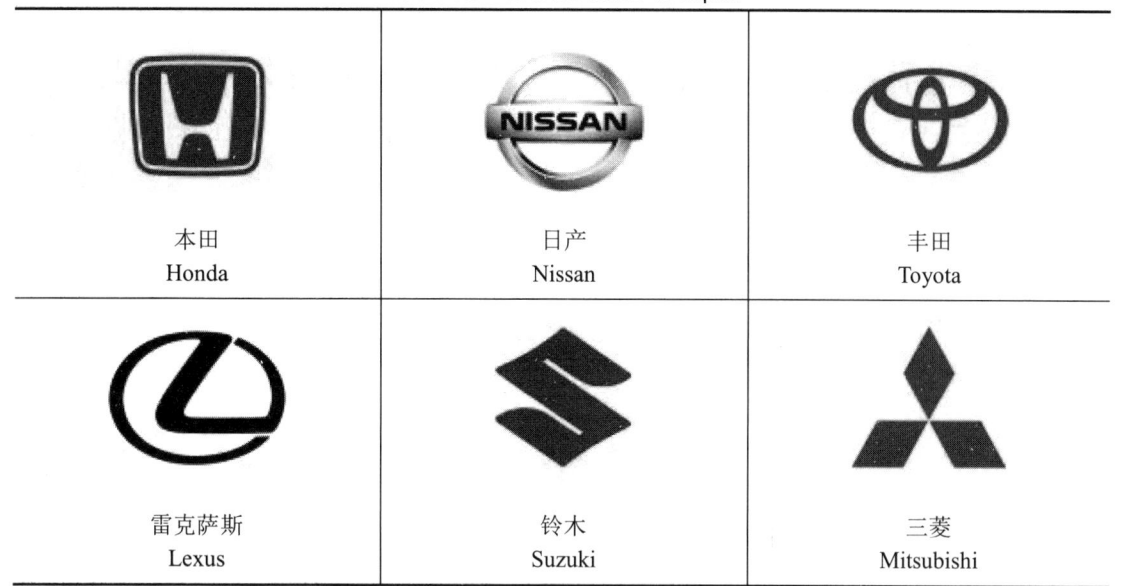

本田 Honda	日产 Nissan	丰田 Toyota
雷克萨斯 Lexus	铃木 Suzuki	三菱 Mitsubishi

（4）美国制造品牌如表 5.4 所示。

Brands made in America (Table 5.4).

表 5.4　美国制造品牌

Table 5.4　Brands made in America

林肯 Lincoln	吉普 Jeep	道奇 Dauge
别克 Buick	悍马 Hummer	通用 GM

（5）意大利和法国制造品牌如表 5.5 所示。

Brands made in Italy and France (Table 5.5).

表 5.5 意大利和法国制造品牌
Table 5.5 Brands made in Italy and France

玛莎拉蒂 Maserati	帕加尼 Pagani	依维柯 Iveco
菲亚特 Fiat	雷诺 Renault	标志 Peugeot

5.3 超豪华轿车

Ultra luxurious car

世界三大顶级豪华车品牌是哪三个？答案是劳斯莱斯、宾利和迈巴赫。宝马、大众和奔驰是这些超级品牌的幕后东家。

Who are the top 3 luxury car brands in the world? They are Rolls-Royce, Bentley, and Maybach. BMW, Volkswagen, and Mercedes-Benz, are the puppet masters behind the three ultra-luxury brands.

1. 劳斯莱斯

    Rolls-Royce

劳斯莱斯汽车公司是一家位于英国古德伍德的豪华汽车制造商。该公司是当前劳斯莱斯品牌汽车的生产商，其历史可以追溯到1904年。该公司是宝马集团的全资子公司（宝马汽车公司在德国）。

Rolls-Royce Motor Cars is a British manufacturer of luxury automobiles based in Goodwood, England. It is the current producer of Rolls-Royce branded automobiles, whose historical production dates back to 1904. The factory is a wholly owned subsidiary of the BMW Group (Bavarian Motor Works is based in German).

2003年1月，劳斯莱斯公司在底特律举办的北美国际汽车展上推出劳斯莱斯幻影。这款车安装了6.75L V12宝马发动机，但大多数其他零部件是专门为该车制作的，这些零部件来源于欧洲。幻影在尺寸和外形绝无仅有的感受，真正诠释出劳斯莱斯的时尚气息。2∶1 车轮与车高的比例是基于对开门设计的。柔和的下弯曲线形车顶和向上轻掠的曲线形车身底部构造，使得该车即使在静止状态，也似乎正在前行。仅是来自于直喷 V12 发动机提供的动力就令人印象深刻。在以 70 英里每小时的速度行驶时，仍有超过 90%的后备功率可用，可以轻松加速。结合电子控制六速自动变速器，无论是在起步或是在行驶过程中，踩下加速踏板时会使驾驶者享受到平顺、无限加速的感觉。

In January 2003, Rolls-Royce Phantom was launched at Detroit North American International Auto Show. The car has a 6.75L V12 engine sourced from BMW, but most other components are unique to the car. Parts are sourced from Europe. The car Phantom has a rare sense of scale and shape that makes it a truly modern interpretation of a Rolls-Royce. The 2:1 wheel-to-height ratio is fundamental to this as are the coach doors. The gentle downward curve of the roofline and upward sweep of the lower body line suggest movement even when the car is stationary. Just as Phantom's delivery of power from the direct-injection V12 engine is much more impressive. At 70mph over 90% of the power is available in reserve, making for easy acceleration. Combined with the electronically controlled six-speed transmission, pressing the accelerator gives the driver a feeling of smooth, endless acceleration from standing or at speed.

幻影独特、先进的铝合金车身框架是由 500 多个零部件手工焊接而成，焊缝长度超过 100m。难以置信的轻便而结实，既坚硬又有韧性。结合最先进的悬挂技术，该款车创造出了独特的似气垫般的魔力坐垫。车身双层底板隐藏了许多技术，但表面丝毫不露痕迹。通过隔离路面噪声为乘客营造了安静的车内氛围，平铺地板为乘客营造了足够舒展的空间。

Phantom's unique, advanced aluminum spaceframe is hand-welded from over 500 separate parts, with over 100 meters of the weld. Incredibly light but strong, it is both stiff and dynamic. When combined with the most advanced suspension technologies, it creates the air-cushioned magic carpet that is unique to Rolls-Royce. The double-skinned flat floor of the spaceframe conceals much of the technology, making it conspicuous by its apparent absence. This adds to the calm, quiet ambiance inside by isolating passengers from road noise and the flat floor leaves plenty of space to stretch out.

顶级劳斯莱斯幻影 6.7T 于 2018 年推出，如图 5.20 所示，其售价高达 1200 多万元人民币。

The top-of-the-line Rolls-Royce Phantom 6.7T was launched in 2018, as shown in the Fig.5.20, and its price reaches more than 12 million Yuan RMB.

2. 宾利

Bentley

宾利汽车有限公司是一家英国汽车制造商，由沃尔特·欧文·宾利（简称 W.O.宾利或 W.O.）创立于 1919 年 1 月 18 日。宾利先前以在第一次世界大战中从事航空发动机制造业而广为人知，最有名的发动机当属宾利 BR1。宾利标志有两个机翼，如图 5.21 所示，1998 年以后，公司归属德国大众汽车集团。

Bentley Motors Limited is a British manufacturer of automobiles founded on 18 January 1919 by Walter Owen Bentley (known as W. O. Bentley or just "W.O."). Bentley had been previously known for his participating aero-engines in World War I, the most famous being the Bentley BR1. The logo shows two flying wings (Fig.5.21). Since 1998, the company has been owned by the Volkswagen Group of Germany.

图 5.20　顶级劳斯莱斯幻影

Fig.5.20　Top configuration of Rolls-Royce Phantom

图 5.21　宾利标志

Fig.5.21　Bentley logo

2002 年，宾利献给英国女王伊丽莎白二世限量版御驾专车，以庆祝她登基 50 周年。2003 年，宾利的双门敞篷车 Azure 停止生产。该公司推出了第二条生产线，宾利欧陆 GT，一款大型豪华轿车。这款车安装了在克鲁生产的 W12 发动机。

In 2002, Bentley presented Queen Elizabeth II with an official State Limousine to celebrate the Golden Jubilee. In 2003, Bentley's 2-door convertible, the Bentley Azure, ceased production, and the company introduced a second line, Bentley Continental GT, a large luxury coupe powered by a W12 engine built in Crewe.

该车需求如此之大，尽管位于克鲁郡的工厂年产约 9500 台车仍不能满足订单，以至于当收到订单一年之后，才能将产品交付至购买者手中。因此，部分新款如飞驰，欧陆 GT 四门款的生产，交由透明工厂（德国）来完成，大众辉腾豪华车也在这里组装。这项安排在 2006 年底生产约 1000 辆汽车后停止，此后所有生产回到克鲁工厂进行。

Demand had been so great, that the factory at Crewe was unable to meet orders despite an installed capacity of approximately 9500 vehicles per year; There was a waiting list of over a year for new cars to be delivered. Consequently, part of the production of the new Flying Spur, a four-door version of the Continental GT, was assigned to the Transparent Factory (Germany), where the Volkswagen Phaeton luxury car is also assembled. This arrangement ceased at the end of 2006 after around 1000 cars, with all car production reverting to the Crewe plant.

2005 年 4 月，宾利确定生产 4 座敞篷 Azure 的计划，该款车源自雅致软顶敞篷车，2006 年在克鲁开始生产。到 2005 年秋，欧陆 GT 敞篷款成功推出，欧陆 GTC 也同时亮相。这两款车在 2006 年年底成功上市。由 GT 改良的限量版 Zagato 叫做 "GTZ"，也于 2008 年 3 月宣布上市。2009 年日内瓦车展宾利推出了欧陆新版：欧陆 Supersports。该款车是一辆超级跑车，配有超强动力和 FlexFuel 环保技术。该车发动机是在当时宾利 W12 发动机基础上重新设计的。欧陆 Supersports 是宾利有史以来最快、最强劲的一款车。

In April 2005, Bentley confirmed plans to produce a 4-seat convertible model—the Azure. By the autumn of 2005, the convertible version of the successful Continental GT, the Continental GTC, was also presented. These two models were successfully launched in late 2006. A limited run of a Zagato-modified GT was also announced in March 2008, dubbed "GTZ". A new Bentley version of the Bentley Continental was introduced at the 2009 Geneva Auto Show: the Continental Supersports. This new Bentley is a supercar combining extreme power with environmentally FlexFuel technology. The engine derived from Bentley's current W12 power unit was re-engineered. The Continental Supersports is the fastest, most powerful production of Bentley ever.

宾利的销量不断攀升，2021 年全球销量 11206 辆，创下品牌历史新高（另一高峰年是 2017 年，11089 辆）。在众多市场中，美洲地区为宾利汽车全球第一大市场，达到 3035 辆；其次是中国市场，2880 辆。2022 年推出的宾利飞驰限量版如图 5.22 所示。

Bentley sales continued to increase. In 2021, 11206 were sold worldwide with a new historical record (another annual record was 11089 in 2017). Among so many markets, The Americas became the biggest market in the world with a selling of 3035 and the second market in China with a selling of 2880. A limited brand of a Bentley Flying Spur in 2022 is shown as Fig.5.22.

图 5.22　宾利飞驰限量版轿车

Fig.5.22　A limited brand of a Bentley Flying Spur

3. 迈巴赫

Maybach

迈巴赫是一家德国的豪华汽车制造商。1909 年由威廉·迈巴赫创建，由其子卡尔·迈巴赫主管。该公司原是 Luftschiffbau Zeppelin GmbH 公司的子公司，自身以"Luftfahrzeug-Motoreinbau"（航空发动机装备公司）而闻名，直至 1918 年。如今，该品牌归属梅赛德斯·奔驰所有，本部在斯图加特。迈巴赫标志如图 5.23 所示，两个大写的"M"表示"迈巴赫制造"（Maybach manufaktur）。

Maybach is a German luxury car manufacturer. It was founded in 1909 by Wilhelm Maybach with his son Karl Maybach as director. The company was originally a subsidiary of Luftschiffbau Zeppelin GmbH and was itself known as "Luftfahrzeug-Motoreinbau GmbH" (literally "Aircraft Engine Installation Company") until 1918. Today, the brand is owned by Mercedes-Benz and based in Stuttgart. The logo contains two capital letters "M" representing "Maybach manufaktur" (Fig.5.23).

图 5.23　迈巴赫标志

Fig.5.23　Maybach logo

1997 年，梅赛德斯·奔驰在东京车展推出豪华概念车：梅赛德斯·奔驰迈巴赫（V12 发动机，5987 毫升排量，550 马力）。梅赛德斯·奔驰公司原本打算发展该车，但最终决定以独立品牌迈巴赫上市该款车。因此，随着新款车的生产，迈巴赫品牌在 21 世纪初得以复兴，该款车有两种不同尺寸的型号——迈巴赫 57 和迈巴赫 62。2005 年，增加了 57S，该型号配备 V12 涡轮增压发动机，具备 604hp（450kW）功率和 999N·m 的扭矩。公司为顾客提供个性化选择，并提供多种装配组合。

In 1997, Mercedes-Benz presented at the Tokyo Motorshow a luxury concept car under the name Mercedes-Benz Maybach (V12, 5987CC, 550 horsepower). Mercedes-Benz decided to develop it; However, Benz made the decision to market the car under the sole brand name of Maybach. Maybach was therefore revived as a brand in the early 2000s, with the production of the new model in two sizes—the Maybach 57 and the Maybach 62. In 2005, the new 57S was added, with a V12 turbo engine, producing 604hp (450kW) of power and 999N·m of torque. The company offers various options for customers to personalize their vehicles, and provides various equipment combinations.

迈巴赫 2021 年全球总销量为 15730 辆，在中国销量为 6600 辆。最新款顶配迈巴赫 GSL680 在中国售价高达 500 多万元人民币。迈巴赫轿车同时有奔驰车标和"MAYBACH"标注，如图 5.24 所示。

In 2021, Maybach sales reached 15730, with 6600 in China. The selling price of a new model

Maybach GSL680 with a top configuration reaches more than 5000000 Yuan RMB. The Maybach sedan has both the Mercedes-Benz badge and the "MAYBACH" label as shown in Fig.5.24.

图 5.24　迈巴赫车标志和标注

Fig.5.24　The logo and remark of Maybach

习　　题

一、选择题

1. 奥迪标志的"四个圈"象征着（　　）。
   A．四个企业管理人　　　　　　B．四个车轮
   C．四个主要公司品牌　　　　　D．四个汽车制造商合并成一家公司
2. 奔驰的车标是一个简洁的三叉星，它代表着（　　）。
   A．奔驰车在陆地、海洋和天空中的统治地位
   B．方向盘
   C．三家企业合并
   D．天、地和人共处
3. 福特汽车公司蓝色椭圆形车标是在（　　）发布的。
   A．2001 年　　　B．2002 年　　　C．2003 年　　　D．2004 年
4. 雪佛兰采用了（　　）车标。
   A．十字星　　　B．蝴蝶结　　　C．交叉路口　　　D．国际红十字协会
5. 雪铁龙的标志两个倒 V 字，代表了（　　）。
   A．两颗牙齿　　　　　　　　　B．齿轮轮齿
   C．两个潜水运动员　　　　　　D．两座山
6. 劳斯莱斯汽车公司最早是一家在（　　）的豪华汽车制造商。
   A．英国　　　　B．德国　　　　C．法国　　　　D．美国
7. 2022 年推出的宾利（　　）限量版。
   A．宾利　　　　B．欧陆　　　　C．飞驰　　　　D．飞翔

8．迈巴赫标志两个大写的"M"表示（　　）。

　　A．迈巴赫设计　　　　B．迈巴赫制造　　C．迈巴赫文化　　D．迈巴赫技术

二、简答题

1．简述梅赛德斯—奔驰汽车标志的含义。
2．简述宝马汽车标志的含义。
3．简述法拉利汽车标志的含义。
4．简述兰博基尼汽车标志的含义。
5．简述丰田汽车标志的含义。
6．简述克莱斯勒汽车标志的含义。
7．简述劳斯莱斯汽车标志的含义。
8．简述吉利汽车标志的含义。
9．简述劳斯莱斯幻影轿车的特点。

第 6 章　发动机的构造与原理

Construction and operating principle of engine

发动机是汽车的动力装置，传统的发动机车辆装备有内燃机（IC）（新能源汽车装备有电动机，可以装备内燃机，也可以没有）。它通过燃烧液体燃料获得动力，如汽油和柴油。燃料中的化学能通过燃料燃烧转化为热能，燃烧室内释放的热能提高了燃烧气体的温度，气体温度的升高推动气体压力上升。上升的气体压力作用在活塞头部，然后转化为有用的机械能，为变速器输入轴提供动力。

The engine acts as the power unit. A traditional engine vehicle equips internal combustion (IC) engine (EV equips electric motor with or without IC engine). It obtains its power by burning liquid fuel, such as gasoline (or petrol) and diesel fuel. The chemical energy in fuel is converted to heat by the burning of the fuel at a controlled rate. The heat energy released in the combustion chamber raises the temperature of the combustion gases with the chamber. The increase in gas temperature causes the pressure of the gases to increase. The pressure developed within the combustion chamber is applied to the head of a piston to produce a usable mechanical force, which is then converted into useful mechanical power, and supply power to rotate a shaft connected to the transmission.

6.1　发动机的分类

Engine classification

汽车发动机可以有以下几种分类：

（1）按发动机布置和驱动形式划分。为了满足不同的应用要求，车辆的整体结构和布局可以不同。根据发动机和这些部件的相对位置，现代汽车的布局通常有以下三种类型（表 6.1）：

The automobile engines can be classified by engine arrangement and driving type. To meet the different requirements of application, the overall structure and layout of vehicle can be different. According to the relative position of the engine and those components, four types of modern cars' layouts are usually as follows (Table 6.1):

发动机前置，前轮驱动（FF）——在汽车上日益流行，结构布局紧凑，减轻了汽车的重量，提高了车辆稳定性。

Front engine, front-wheel drive (FF)—is increasingly popular in the car on the layout pattern with a compact structure, reducing the car's weight, and improving stability.

表 6.1　发动机布置和驱动形式

Table 6.1　Engine arrangement and driving type

Engine arrangement and driving type	diagram
Front engine, front-wheel drive	
Front engine, rear-wheel drive	
Rear engine, rear-wheel drive	
All-wheel drive	

发动机前置，后轮驱动（FR）——在良好的路面上启动、加速或爬坡时，驱动轮的负荷增大（即驱动轮的附着压力增大），其牵引性能比前置前驱型式优越；轴荷分配比较均匀，因而具有良好的操纵稳定性和行驶平顺性，并有利于延长轮胎的使用寿命。

Front engine, rear-wheel drive (FR)—When starting, accelerating or climbing on a good road, the load of the driving wheel increases (the adhesion pressure of the driving wheel increases), and its traction performance is superior to the front drive; The axle load distribution is uniform, so it has good handling stability and ride comfort, and is beneficial to prolong tire life.

发动机后置，后轮驱动（RR）——是中型客车流行的布局模式。这种模式有利于降低车内噪声，也有利于车身内部布局。

Rear engine, rear-wheel drive (RR)—is a popular layout pattern for the large and medium-sized passenger cars. Such a kind of pattern is good for lowering interior noise, as well as the interior layout of the body.

全轮驱动（AWD）——这种布置更安全，驱动力分配给所有车轮。加速过程中车轮之间负载的分担降低了车轮空转的风险。

All-wheel drive (AWD)—This arrangement is safer because it distributes the drive to all four wheels. The sharing of the load between the wheels during acceleration reduces the risks of wheel spin.

（2）按气缸数划分。可分为单缸发动机和多缸发动机。

Classified by the number of cylinders. The automobile can be classified single-cylinder engine and multi-cylinder engine.

（3）按气缸布置形式划分。发动机布置形式指发动机气缸的布置方法，有直列式、对置式、V 型发动机（图 6.1），在这三种基本的布置形式中，也存在一些形式变化。

Classified by the arrangement of cylinders. The term of engine configuration refers to the way that the cylinders of an engine arrangement. The cylinders can be in-line, opposed, or at an angle (V-type) (Fig.6.1). Within three basic arrangements, there are a number of variations.

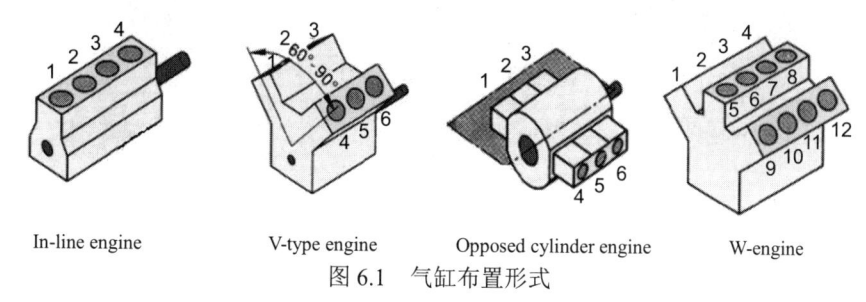

图 6.1　气缸布置形式

Fig.6.1　The arrangement of cylinders

（4）按气门布置形式划分。发动机可以分为三缸发动机、四缸发动机、五缸发动机等等。

Classified by the arrangement of valves. The engine can be classified into three-cylinder engine, four-cylinder engine, five-cylinder engine and so on.

（5）按循环次数划分。发动机可以分为四冲程和二冲程循环发动机（图6.2）。

Classified by the number of cycles. The engine can be classified into four-stroke cycle and two-stroke cycle (Fig.6.2)

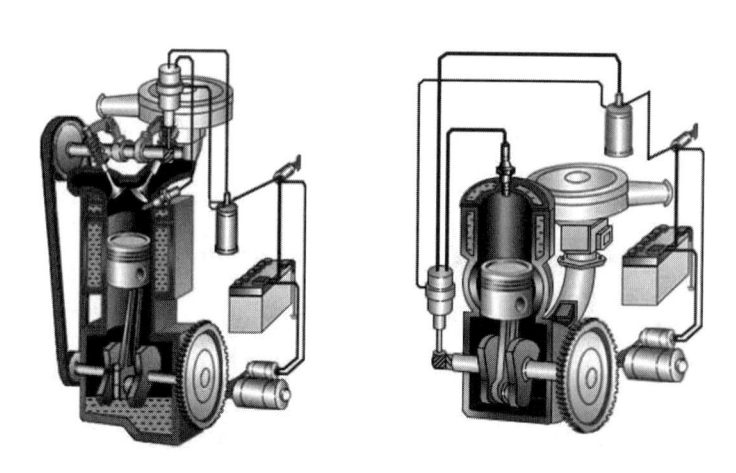

图 6.2　四冲程和二冲程发动机

Fig.6.2　Four-stroke cycle and two-stroke cycle engine

（6）按冷却方式划分。发动机可分为水冷式和风冷式两种（图6.3）。

Classified by the type of cooling. The engine can be classified into water-cooled or air-cooled (Fig.6.3).

（7）按燃烧燃料类型划分。发动机可分为汽油发动机和柴油发动机。

Classified by the type of fuel burned. The engine can be classified into gasoline engine and diesel engine.

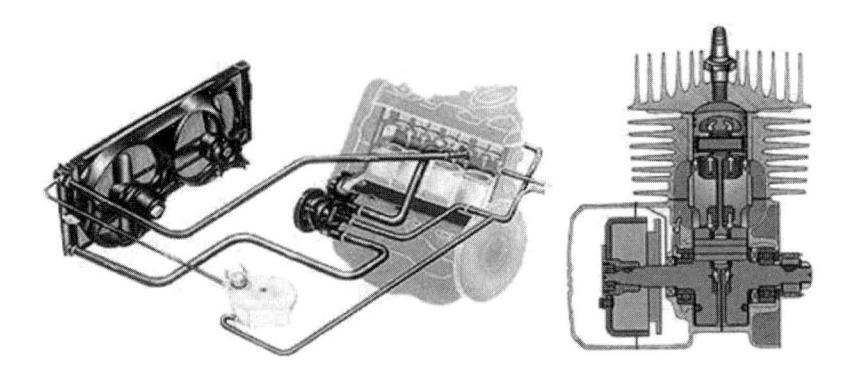

图 6.3　水冷式和风冷式发动机

Fig.6.3　Water-cooled and air-cooled engine

6.2　发动机基本术语

Engine terms

上止点：活塞顶离曲轴回转中心最远处。

下止点：活塞顶离曲轴回转中心最近处（图 6.4）。

TDC (Top Dead Center): the position of the crank and piston when the piston is farther away from the crankshaft.

BDC (Bottom Dead Center): the position of the crank and piston when the piston is nearest to the crankshaft (Fig.6.4).

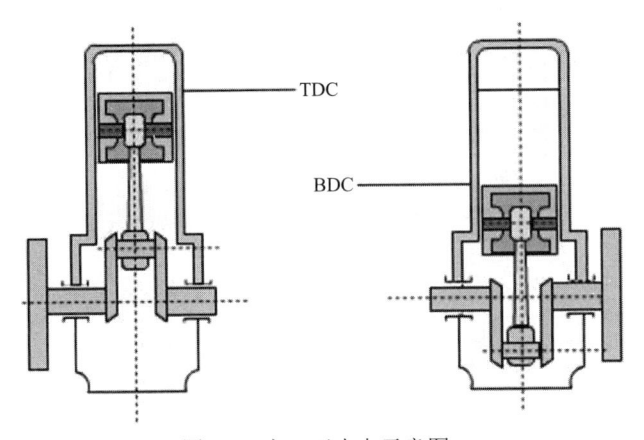

图 6.4　上、下止点示意图

Fig.6.4　Diagram of TDC and BDC

活塞行程：上、下止点间的距离称为活塞行程。

Stroke: the distance between BDC and TDC stroke is controlled by the crankshaft.

气缸工作容积：上、下止点间所包容的气缸容积称为气缸工作容积（图 6.5），表示为：

Swept volume: the volume between TDC and BDC (Fig.6.5), as follows:

$$V_h = \frac{\pi d^2 s}{4000} \text{cm}^3 \tag{6.1}$$

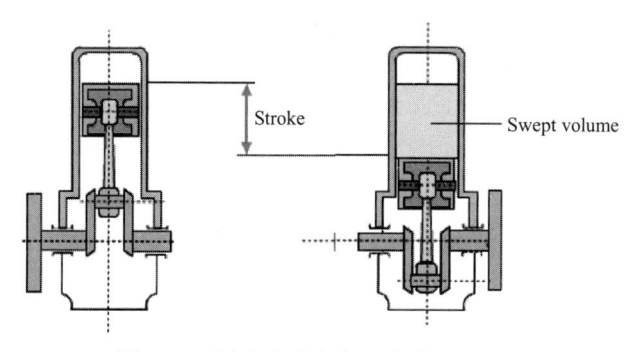

图 6.5 活塞行程和气缸工作容积示意图

Fig.6.5 Schematic diagram of stroke and swept volume

发动机排量：所有气缸的工作容积总和，表示为：

Engine capacity: this is the swept volume of all the cylinder, as follows:

$$V_H = V_h z \tag{6.2}$$

z 为气缸数量。

z is the number of cylinders.

燃烧室容积：当活塞位于上止点时，活塞上方空间的容积 V_c（图 6.6）。

Clearance volume: the volume of the space above the piston when it is at TDC V_c (Fig.6.6).

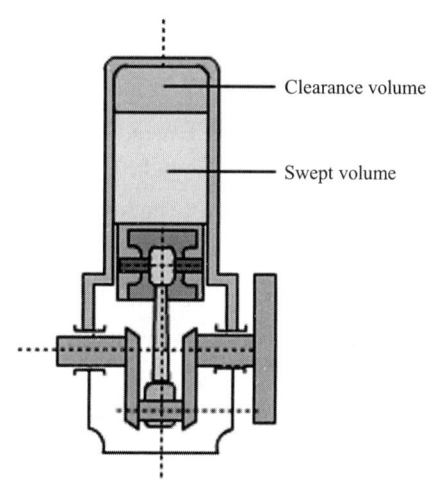

图 6.6 燃烧室容积简图

Fig.6.6 Schematic diagram of clearance volume

压缩比：气缸总容积与燃烧室容积之比称为压缩比，表示为：

Compression ratio = (swept vol + clearance vol)/(clearance vol), as follows:

$$\varepsilon = \frac{V_h + V_c}{V_c} \qquad (6.3)$$

发动机转矩：是指发动机转动驱动桥的能力。

Engine torque: It means the ability of turning the live axle.

燃油消耗量：车辆行驶一定距离所消耗的燃油量。

Specific fuel consumption: The fuel consumption in the given distance.

发动机功率：发动机在额定时间内输出的功率，单位 kW。

Engine Power: The output of the engine in the given time. The unit of measurement is kW.

二行程：曲柄每转一圈做一次功。

Two-stroke: The crank does work once per revolution.

四行程：曲柄每转两圈做一次功。

Four-stroke: The crank does work once per two revolutions.

6.3　四冲程汽油机工作原理

Operating principles of four-stroke petrol engine

正如自然界中事件的各种重复循环一样，汽油发动机也需要以一种不断重复的循环方式运行，这种循环被称为四冲程工作原理。大众普遍知道的是1876年，第一台四冲程内燃机的成功运转。这位自学成才的德国工程师成为了在他那个时代最杰出的研究人员之一，并且其所在公司多年来一直是世界上最大的内燃机制造商。

As with the various repeating cycles of events in nature, so does the motor vehicle petrol engine need to operate on a constantly repeating cycle known as the four-stroke principle. It would seem to be generally accepted that the first internal combustion engine to operate successfully on the four-stroke cycle was constructed in 1876. This self-taught German engineer was to become one of the most brilliant researchers of his time and for many years was the largest manufacturer of internal combustion engines in the world.

在这种发动机中，以下冲程在其运行的整个时间内不断重复（图6.7）：

In this type of engine the following sequence of events is continuously repeated all the time when it is running (Fig.6.7):

（1）进气行程，在此行程中，由于活塞向下运动产生的部分真空或低压，可燃空气和燃料被吸入燃烧室和气缸。在进气行程中，进气门打开，排气门关闭。

The intake stroke, during which combustible air and fuel are drown into the combustion chamber and cylinder due to the partial vacuum or low pressure created by the downward movement of the piston. During the intake stroke, the intake valves open and the exhaust valves close.

（2）压缩行程，活塞的上移将可燃混合气压缩到较小的燃烧室容积中，气门关闭紧密。该行程用于提高可燃混合气的压力和温度。

The compression stroke, which serves to raise both the pressure and temperature of the combustible charge as it is compressed into the lesser volume of the combustion chamber by the advancing piston.

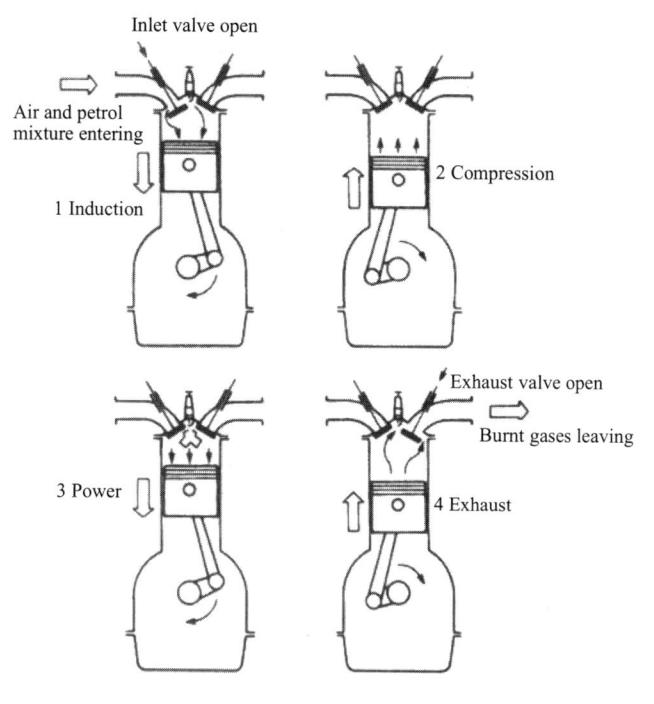

图 6.7 四冲程汽油机发动机循环

Fig.6.7 The four-stroke petrol engine cycle

（3）做功行程，在此之前可燃混合气被火花塞点燃，在此行程中气体膨胀并对向下运动的活塞做有用功，推动曲轴旋转。

The power stroke, immediately preceding which the combustible charge is ignited by the sparking plug, the valves are closed tightly. The gas expand and perform useful work on the retreating piston and turns the crankshaft with great force.

（4）排气行程，在做功行程即将结束时，排气门打开。曲轴推动活塞向上运动，通过打开的排气门将热的、燃烧过的气体推出。然后，在活塞到达最高点之前，排气门关闭，进气门打开。当活塞到达气缸的最高点，也就是上止点时，又开始下降。因此，一个循环结束，另一个循环立即开始。

Just before the bottom of the power stroke, the exhaust valve opens. This allows the piston, as it moves upward, to push the hot, burned gases out through the open exhaust valve.

Then, just before the piston reaches its highest point, the exhaust valve closes and the inlet valve opens. As the piston reaches the highest point in the cylinder, known as TDC, it starts back down again. Thus, one cycle ends and another begins immediately.

因此，一个完整的工作循环占据了曲轴的两个旋转周期。因为在点火发生之前，活塞的进气和压缩行程必然需要能量，故起动机用于给发动机提供初始力矩。一旦发动机运转，随后进气、压缩和排气行程所需的能量就源于其从曲轴和飞轮系统获得的旋转动能。动能是一个物理量，用来表示物体因其质量和运动而具备的能量。因此，发动机飞轮便成了动能的储能元件，以便在加速时吸收能量，在减速时释放能量。

It thus follows that one complete cycle of operations occupies two complete revolutions of the engine crankshaft. Since energy is necessarily required to perform the initial induction and compression strokes of the engine piston before firing occurs, an electrical starter motor is used for preliminary cranking of the engine. Once the engine is running, the energy required for performing subsequent induction, compression and exhaust strokes is derived from the crankshaft and flywheel system, by virtue of its kinetic energy of rotation. Kinetic energy is a term used to express the energy possessed by a body due to its mass and motion. The principle of an engine flywheel is therefore to act as a storage reservoir for rotational kinetic energy, so that it absorbs energy upon being speeded up, and delivers it when slowed down.

6.4 发动机总体结构

Engine overall structure

发动机由大量零件组成（图 6.8）。发动机的主要部件有气缸体、活塞、连杆、曲轴和气门。

The engine consists of a large number of parts (Fig.6.8).The main components of engine are cylinder block, pistons, connecting rods, crankshaft and valves.

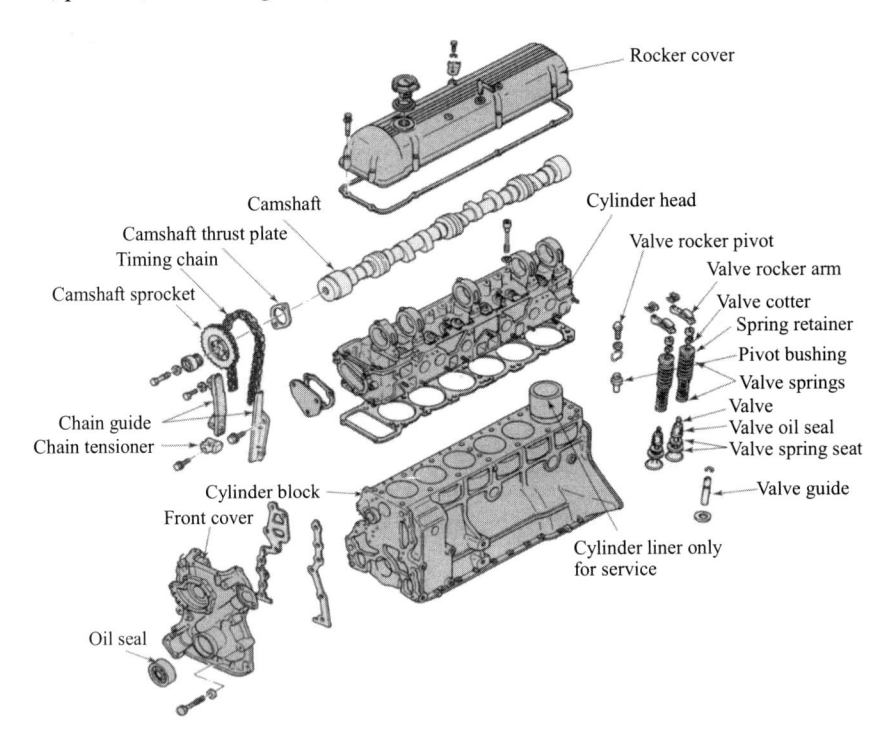

图 6.8 发动机总体结构简图

Fig.6.8 General structure diagram of engine

气缸是一端封闭的简单圆管,活塞紧紧地嵌在气缸里。理想情况下,它应该是完全密封的,但在气缸内活塞可以完全自由地上下移动。连杆将活塞连接到曲轴上。在连杆的活塞端有一个可转动的销,称为"活塞销"。活塞销安装在活塞和连杆的孔中,将它们连接在一起。曲轴是发动机的主轴,装在曲轴箱的轴承上。连杆安装在曲柄销上,曲柄销偏离轴的主要部分可以自由转动,形成曲柄连杆机构,配气机构用来控制气门的开启和关闭。两个机构与其他部分连接在一起形成系统。这些系统是燃油供给系统、冷却系统、润滑系统、点火系统和启动系统。每一部分都有其明确的功能。

The cylinder with the simplest form, is circular tube, which is closed at one end. The piston fits closely inside the cylinder. Ideally it would be perfectly gas-tight yet perfectly free to move up and down inside the cylinder. The connecting rod connects the piston to the crankshaft. At the piston end of connecting rod is a swivel pin called the "gudgeon pin". The gudgeon pin is fitted into holes in the piston and the connecting rod, thus coupling them together. The crankshaft is the main shaft of the engine and is carried in bearings in the crankcase. Offset from the main part of the shaft is the crankpin to which the connecting rod is fitted and is free to turn, a crank-connecting rod mechanism is formed, and the valve train is used to control the opening and closing of the valve. The two mechanisms are connected with other parts to form a system. These systems are the fuel system, valve system, ignition system, cooling system, lubrication system. Each of them has a definite function.

6.4.1 曲柄连杆机构
Crank-connecting rods and valve mechanism

内燃机中曲柄与连杆构成曲柄连杆机构完成工作循环,并将燃料的热能转化为转动曲轴的动能。其功能是实现能量转换以传递动力,并将活塞的往复运动转变为曲轴的旋转运动。该机构的工作环境相当恶劣,要承受高温、高压、高速和化学腐蚀。曲柄连杆机构主要由三部分组成,分别是机体组、活塞连杆组和曲轴飞轮组。

The combination of crank and connecting rod in an internal combustion engine forms a kind of mechanism that can fulfill working cycle and convert the potential energy of the fuel into the kinetic energy which rotates the crankshaft. Its function is to achieve energy conversion to transmit force and change the reciprocating motion of the piston into the rotary motion of the crankshaft. The working condition in this mechanism is rather severe due to withstanding high temperature, high pressure, high-speed and chemical corrosion. The crank and connecting rod mechanism can be divided into three groups, such as the engine body, piston-connecting rod and crankshaft-flywheel group.

(1)机体组。机体组是构成发动机的骨架,是发动机各机构和各系统的安装基体。由于承受各种载荷,车身必须具有足够的强度和刚度。机体组主要由气缸体、曲轴箱、气缸盖、气缸垫等零件组成(图6.9和图6.10)。

Cylinder group. The body constitutes the backbone of the engine, which is regarded as the base on the internal and external installation of all the major parts and accessories in an engine. The body must have sufficient strength and stiffness because it is subjected to various loads. It is mainly composed of the cylinder block, crankcase, cylinder head, cylinder gasket and other parts (Figs.6.9-6.10).

气缸体：发动机的基础零件之一，是许多其他零件的安装机体，如曲轴、活塞连杆机构。

Cylinder block: one of the base parts of an engine. Many other parts are mounted on it, such as crankshaft, and pistin-connecting rod mechanism.

气缸盖：位于气缸体之上，气缸盖是发动机的第二个基本部件。配气机构、进气管和排气管都安装在上面。

Cylinder head: it is above cylinder block, the second base part of an engine. The valve train, intake manifold and exhaust pipe are mounted on it.

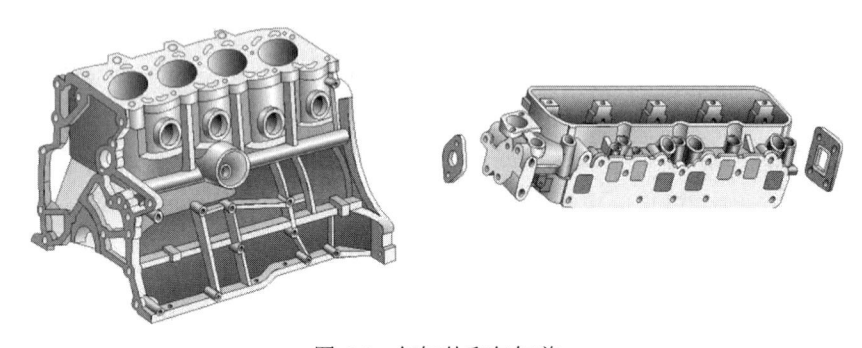

图 6.9 气缸体和气缸盖

Fig.6.9 Cylinder block and cylinder head

气缸垫：在气缸体和气缸盖之间的一个衬垫。其作用是密封燃烧室，并减少气缸体和气缸盖之间因振动而产生的摩擦。

Gasket: Between cylinder block and cylinder head, there is a gasket. The function is sealing the combustion chamber, and reduce the friction between cylinder block and cylinder head due to vibration.

油底壳：在气缸体的底部，用来储存机油。机油是润滑系统的润滑剂。通常油底壳内有一个油尺，用来检查油量和机油质量。

Oil pan: it is on the bottom of cylinder block. It reserves engine oil. Engine oil is the lubricant for lubrication system. Usually there is an oil ruler in oil pan used to check oil quantity and quality.

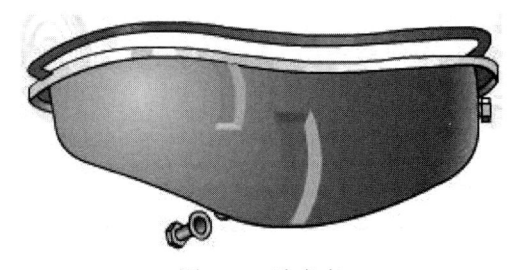

图 6.10 油底壳

Fig.6.10 Oil pan

（2）活塞连杆组。活塞组由活塞、活塞销、活塞环、连杆和曲柄销轴承组成（图6.11）。活塞在气缸中上下移动。连杆安装在曲轴的曲柄销上，其大端随曲轴转动，而小头通过活塞销随活塞运动。

Piston and connecting rod mechanism. Piston group consists of piston, piston pin, piston rings, connecting rod and crankpin bearings (Fig.6.11). Piston moves up and down in cylinder bore. By crankpin bearing, connecting rod is mounted on crankpin of crankshaft and its big end rotates with crankshaft while small eng move with piston by piston pin.

图 6.11　活塞连杆组

Fig.6.11　Piston and connecting rod mechanism

通常活塞上有三个活塞环。两个气环用于气体密封，一个油环用于防止机油进入燃烧室（图6.12）。

Usually there are three piston rings on piston. Two rings are for gas sealing and one ring is for preventing oil into combustion chamber (Fig.6.12).

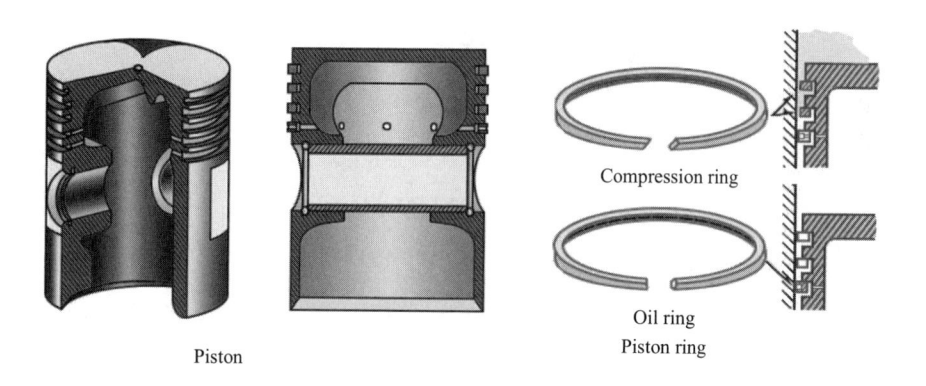

图 6.12　活塞环

Fig.6.12　Piston ring

（3）曲轴飞轮组。曲轴飞轮组主要由曲轴、飞轮和其他附件组成（图6.13）。

Crankshaft and connecting rod mechanism. The group of crankshaft-flywheel is mainly composed of crankshaft, flywheel and other accessories (Fig.6.13).

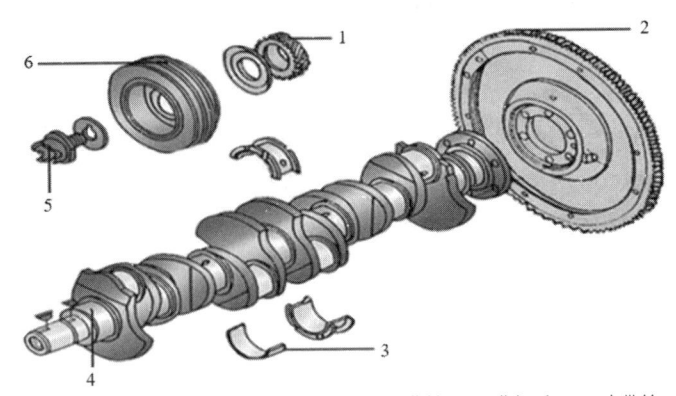

1—正时齿轮；2—飞轮；3—主轴承半壳；4—曲轴；5—曲柄爪；6—皮带轮
1-Timing gear; 2-Flywheel; 3-Main bearing half shell; 4-Crankshaft; 5-Cranking claw; 6-Pulley

图 6.13　曲轴飞轮组分解图

Fig.6.13　Crankshaft-flywheel exploded view

曲轴是发动机上重要的旋转部件。图 6.14 为 4 缸直列式发动机的曲轴。有 4 个曲柄销，适合 4 缸布局，5 个曲轴轴颈用于固定曲轴。

Crankshaft is an important rotary part on engine. Fig.6.14 shows a crankshaft on 4-cylinder inline type engine. There are 4 crankpins to suit 4-cylinder layout and 5 crankshaft journals to fasten crankshaft.

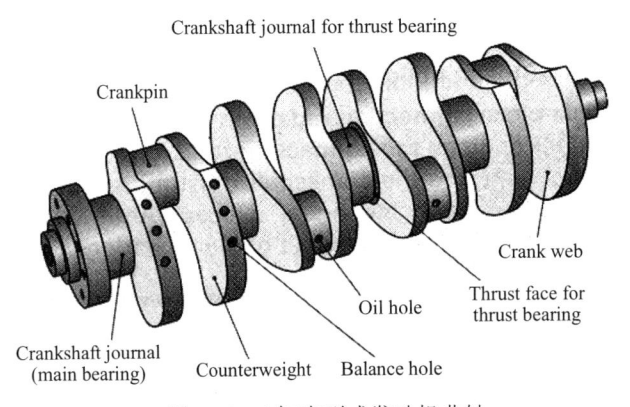

图 6.14　4 缸直列式发动机曲轴

Fig.6.14　A crankshaft on 4-cylinder inline type engine

曲轴通过主轴承、主轴承盖和螺栓安装在气缸体上。每个轴承都由上下两部分组成，使装配变得简单可行。

Crankshaft is mounted on cylinder block by main bearings, main bearings caps and bolts. Every bearing consists of upper and lower parts to make assembly simple and possible.

曲轴上可布置多个零件。飞轮用于储存动能和启动发动机，凸轮轴用来驱动气门机构，油泵齿轮用于驱动油泵，曲轴皮带轮用于驱动水泵、发电机、空调压缩机等发动机附件。

There are some parts on crankshaft. Flywheel is used to reserve kinetic energy and start engine.

Camshaft sprocket is used to drive valve train. Oil pump gear is used to drive oil pump. Crankshaft pulley is used to drive engine accessories such as water pump, generator and air conditioner compressor.

6.4.2 配气机构
The valve operating mechanism

配气机构用于控制进气门和排气门，使新鲜空气及时进入气缸并排出废气。同时，气门根据气缸的点火顺序和要求打开和关闭气缸盖上的进、排气门，气缸通过进、排气门与进气和排气歧管连通。气门传动广泛应用于四冲程发动机中。

The valve operating mechanism is used to control the intake and exhaust ports, which provides timely admission of the fresh charge into the cylinders and emission of exhaust gases. Simultaneously, the valves punctually open and close those ports in the cylinder head through which the cylinders communicate with the intake and exhaust manifold according to the ignition order of the cylinder and the process requirements. The valve gear is widely applied in the four-stroke engines.

配气机构由两部分组成，包括气门组和气门传动组（图6.15）。每组包含一些部件或零件，如气门、气门座、气门导管、气门弹簧、锁片、凸轮轴、挺柱、推杆、摇臂等。根据气门和凸轮轴位置的不同，布局会有所不同。例如，气门位于气缸的顶部或侧面。凸轮轴设置在下方、中间或上方（图6.16）。这些装置分别用于不同的发动机。由于侧气门发动机效率低，这种布置形式已被淘汰。

The valve gear is composed of two parts, including the valve group and the valve drive group (Fig.6.15). Each group contains some components or parts, such as valve, valve boss, valve guide, valve spring, locking plate, retainer, camshaft, tappet, push rod, rocker arm etc. According to the different location of valves and camshafts, the layout will be different. For example, valves are located on the top or the side of the cylinder. Camshafts are set on the beneath, the mid or the overhead (Fig.6.16).These arrangements are respectively used in different engines. Due to the inefficiency of side-valve engines, vehicle manufactures no longer use this layout.

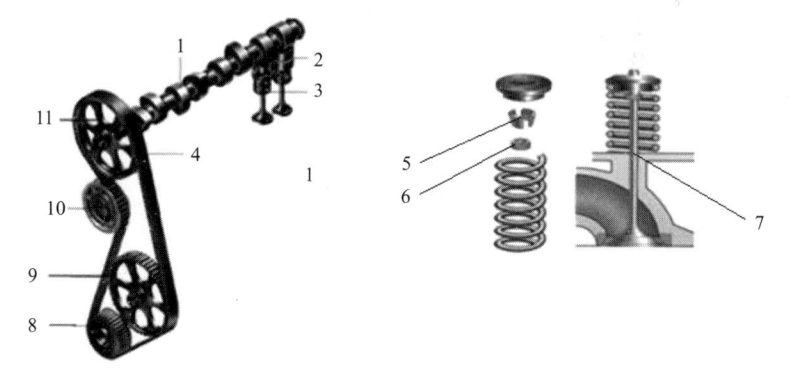

1—凸轮轴；2—挺柱；3—气门弹簧；4—正时皮带；5—气门弹簧上环；6—气门导管；7—阀杆；
8—曲轴正时皮带轮；9—中轴皮带轮；10—张紧器；11—凸轮轴正时皮带轮
1-Camshaft; 2-Tappet; 3-Valve spring; 4-Timing belt; 5-Upper valve spring collar; 6-Valve guide; 7-Valve stem;
8-Crankshaft timing pulley; 9-Mid-shaft pulley; 10-Tensioner; 11-Camshaft timing pulley

图 6.15 配气机构
Fig.6.15 Valve operating mechanism

Beneath-camshaft　　　Mid-camshaft　　　Overhead-camshaft

图 6.16　凸轮轴三种布置形式

Fig.6.16　Three ways of the camshaft arrangement

凸轮轴传动有带传动、链传动和齿轮传动三种方式（图 6.17）。一般来说，下置式凸轮轴和中置式凸轮轴的机构大多采用圆柱正时齿轮传动。从曲轴到凸轮轴通常只需要一对正时齿轮。如果齿轮直径太大，可以加一个中间齿轮。链传动适用于顶置式凸轮轴，但其可靠性和耐用性不如齿轮传动。近年来，低噪声、低成本的齿形带逐渐取代传动链被广泛应用于高速发动机。

As for the camshaft drive, there are three ways such as belt drive, chain drive and gear drive (Fig.6.17). Generally speaking, the mechanism with both the beneath-camshaft and the mid-camshaft is mostly adopted the cylindrical timing gear drive. It usually needs just a pair of timing gears from crankshaft to camshaft. If the gear diameter is too large, an intermediate gear may be added. The chain drive is suitable for the overhead camshaft, but the reliability and the durability of the drive is not as good as that of the gear drive. In recent years, the toothed belt with low noise and low cost is widely used in high-speed car engine instead of the drive chain.

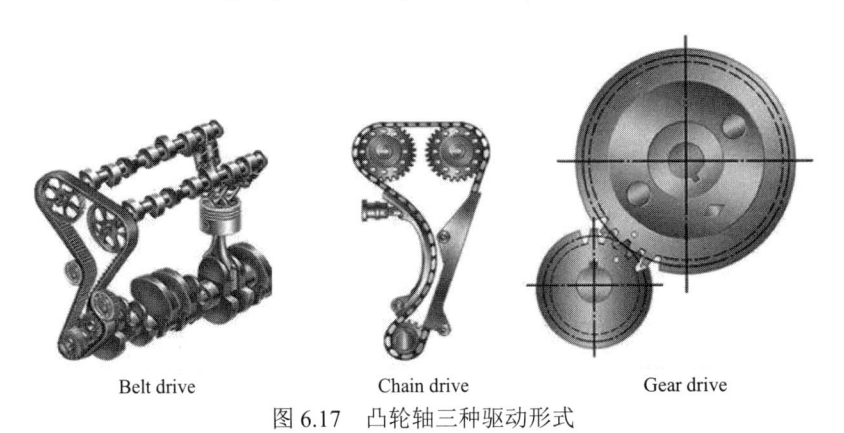

Belt drive　　　Chain drive　　　Gear drive

图 6.17　凸轮轴三种驱动形式

Fig.6.17　Three ways of the camshaft drive

大多数发动机的正时齿轮都装在一个特殊的壳体内，壳体安装在发动机的前端。这些是从曲轴向凸轮轴、喷油泵轴、油泵和其他机构传递转矩所必需的。齿轮由钢制成，使用螺旋齿来降低噪声。本田发动机上使用的一种系统叫做 VTEC。VTEC（可变气门正时和升程电子控制系统）是本田发动机中控制气门正时和升程的电子、机械系统，允许发动机具有多个凸轮轴。VTEC 发动机有一个额外的进气凸轮，具有跟随相应的凸轮的摇臂。此凸轮上的轮廓使进气门打开的时间比另一个凸轮轮廓长。

The timing gears in most engines are housed in a special case fitted at the front end of the engine. These are necessary to transmit rotation from the crankshaft to the camshaft, fuel injection pump shaft, and to oil pumpand other mechanisms. The gears are made of steel and use helical teeth to reduce noise. One system used on some Honda engines is called VTEC.VTEC (Variable Valve Timing and Lift Electronic Control) is an electronic and mechanical system in some Honda engines that allows the engine to have multiple camshafts.VTEC engines have an extra intake cam with its ownrocker, which follows this cam.The profile on this cam keeps the intake valve open longer than the other camprofile.

6.4.3 电子燃油喷射系统
Electronic fuel injection system

在老式汽车上，化油器将混合好的空气与燃油混合物输送到发动机。化油器是一种混合汽油和空气的装置。为了适应发动机的工作条件，混合气必须不断地改变浓度。因此，在现代汽车发动机中，电子燃油喷射系统已经取代了化油器。

On old cars, it is a carburetor that sends the correct air-fuel mixture to the engine. The carburetor is a mixing device that mixes liquid gasoline with air. The mixture must vary degree of richness continually to suit engine operation conditions. Therefore, the electric fuel injection system has replaced the function of the carburetor in modern car engines.

电子燃油喷射系统提供更精确的空燃比控制（图 6.18）。因此，发动机可具有更好的经济性和排放控制。传感器读取发动机信号。计算机处理信号，并向发动机的燃料控制器发出适当的指令。然后，喷油器向发动机喷射一定量的燃油。

Fuel injection system provides more exact air-fuel ratio control (Fig.6.18). Thus, engine develops better economy and emission control. Sensors read changes on the engine. A computer interprets the information and sends appropriate instruction to the engine's fuel controller. Then the injector sprays a measured amount of fuel down to the engine.

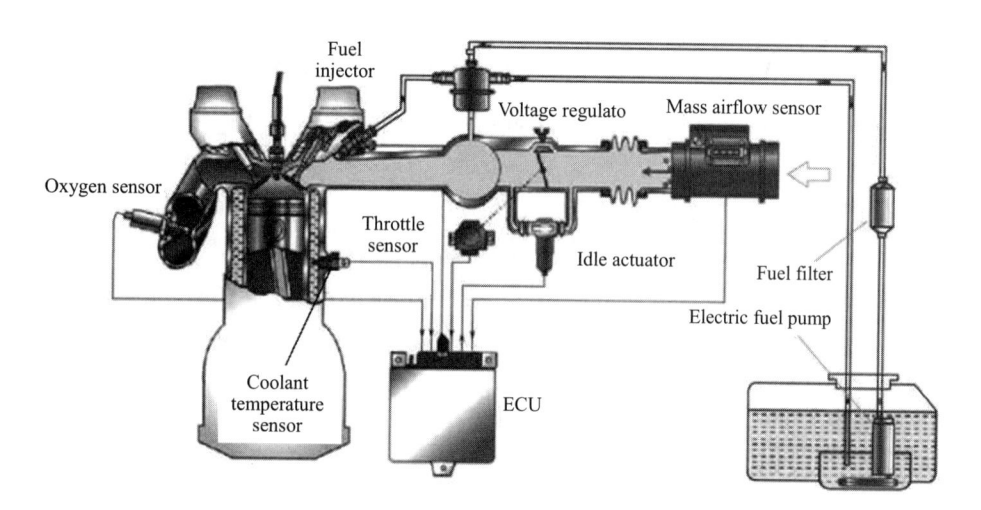

图 6.18　汽油电子燃油喷射系统

Fig.6.18　Electronic petrol fuel system

现代燃油供给系统是电子控制的,这种控制方式可以精确地设定燃油量,以适应发动机的工作条件。严格的排放控制法规要求对燃料进行精确计量,尽管汽油喷射系统比化油器燃料系统昂贵,但现在它们被用来控制所有发动机的燃料供给。大多数汽油喷射系统与点火系统集成在一个发动机管理系统中,包括三个系统(燃油供给、空气供给和电子控制系统)。

Modern systems are controlled electronically because this form of control enables the fuel quantity to be accurately set to suit the engine operating conditions. Strict emission control regulations have demanded precise metering of the fuel, and although petrol injection systems are more expensive than carburetor fuel systems, they are now used to control the fuelling on all engines. Most petrol injection systems are integrated with the ignition system into an engine management system, including three systems (fuel delivery, air induction, electronic control).

输送适量高度雾化燃料的汽油喷射系统具有以下优点:
(1)较低的废气污染。
(2)油耗更低。
(3)更高的功率输出。
(4)由于每个气缸的功率输出均匀,发动机运转更加平稳。
(5)自动调节空燃比,以适应所有运行条件。

A petrol injection system that delivers the correct quantity of highly atomized fuel gives the following advantages:

(1) Lower exhaust pollution.

(2) Lower fuel consumption.

(3) Higher power output.

(4) Smoother engine operation due to an even power output from each cylinder.

(5) Automatic adjustment of the air/fuel ratio to suit all operating conditions.

1. 燃油供给系统

    Fuel delivery system

燃油供给系统(图6.19)通过电动燃油泵为喷油器提供燃油。

The fuel delivery system (Fig.6.19) is to supply the injectors with the fuel. Pressure is provided by an electric fuel pump.

燃油系统由油箱、燃油泵、燃油滤清器、分配管、喷油器和燃油压力调节器组成。分配管中的燃油压力较低(约0.3kPa)。燃料被喷入歧管。

For gasoline engine, fuel system consists of fuel tank, fuel pump, fuel filter, distributor pipe, fuel injector and fuel pressure regulator. The fuel pressure in distributor pipe is lower (about 0.3kPa). Fuel is sprayed into manifold.

2. 空气供给系统

    Air supply system

空气供应系统(图6.20)用于引导新鲜空气在气缸中形成混合气,包括空气滤清器总成、节气门体和进气歧管。节气门体部分包含节气门,由驾驶员打开和关闭,以控制进入进气歧管的空气量。在节气门体燃油喷射系统中,节气门体也包含燃油喷射部件。进气歧管在节气门体和气缸盖之间形成了一个封闭的通道。

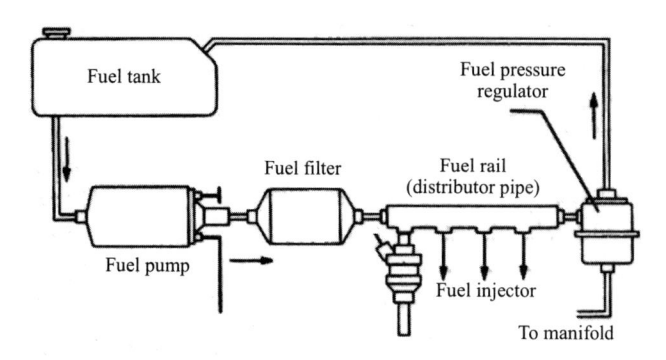

图 6.19　燃油供给系统

Fig.6.19　Fuel delivery system

The air supply system (Fig.6.20) is to induce the fresh air to form the mixture in the cylinder, consisting of an air cleaner assembly, throttle body, and intake manifold. The throttle body section contains the throttle valve, which is opened and closed by the driver to control the amount of air entering the intake manifold. On throttle body fuel injection systems, the throttle body also contains the fuel injection components. The intake manifold forms a closed passage between the throttle body and the cylinder head.

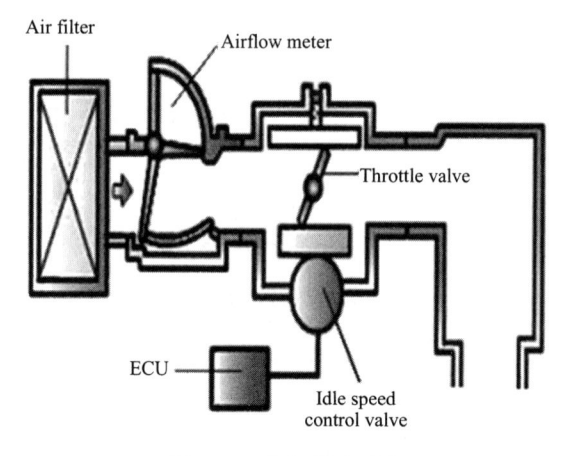

图 6.20　空气供给系统

Fig.6.20　The air induction system

3. 电子控制系统

Electronic control system

发动机的电子控制系统主要由 ECU、传感器和执行器组成（图 6.21）。发动机控制部分由许多不同的电子电路和元件构成。除了喷油器之外，现代计算机还控制许多其他的发动机系统。计算机通常位于远离发动机振动和热量的保护区域，并通过密封的线束插头连接到喷射系统的其余部分。每当发动机运转时，计算机就接收来自许多传感器的信号。根据这些输入，计算机评估发动机的燃油需求，并相应地调整喷油器脉冲宽度。

The electronic control system of an engine is mainly composed of ECU, sensors and actuators (Fig.6.21). Engine control computers are constructed by using many different electronic circuits and components. Modern computers control many other engine systems in addition to the fuel injectors. The computer is usually located in a protected area away from engine vibration and heat, and is connected to the rest of the injection system by means of a sealed wiring harness plug. The computer receives signals from a number of sensors whenever the engine is running. From this input, the computer evaluates engine fuel needs and adjusts injector pulse width accordingly.

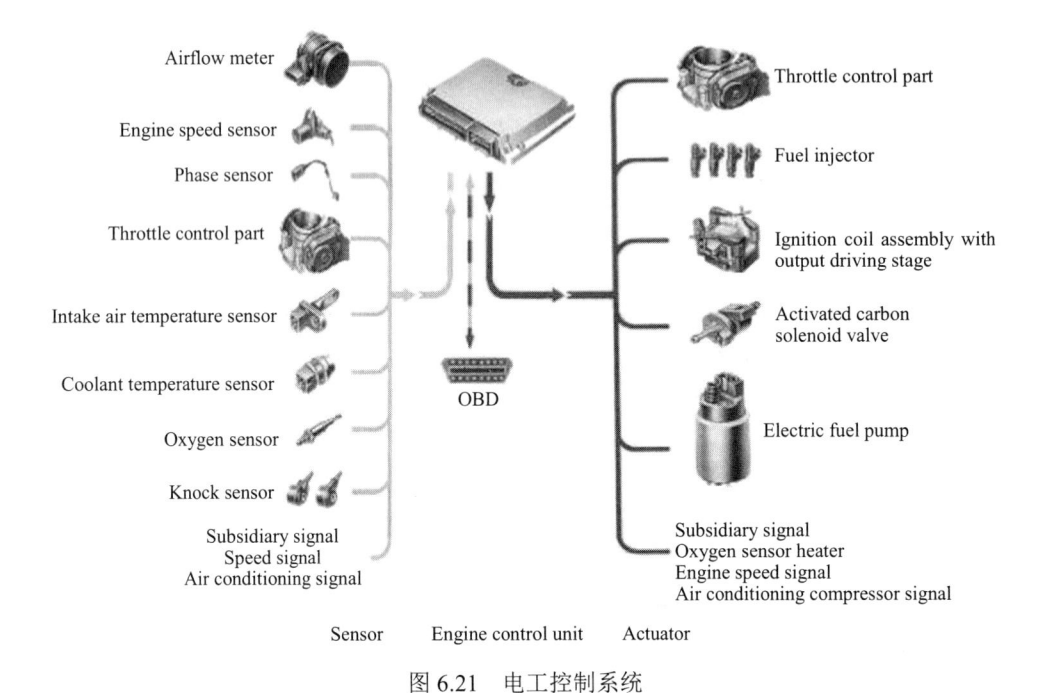

图 6.21 电工控制系统

Fig.6.21 The electronic control system

为了在各种工况下提供正确的燃油量，发动机控制单元（ECU）必须通过大量的传感器监控各机构的运行状态。

In order to provide the correct amount of fuel for every operating condition, the engine control unit (ECU) has to monitor a huge number of input sensors.

（1）空气流量传感器——测量进入发动机的空气质量。

（2）氧传感器——监控废气中的含氧量，以便电子控制单元能够确定燃料混合物的浓度，并做出相应的调整。

（3）节气门位置传感器——监控节气门位置（决定进入发动机的空气量），以便ECU能够快速响应变化，根据需要增加或减少燃油率。

（4）冷却液温度传感器——确定发动机何时达到其正常工作温度。

（5）电压传感器——监控汽车中的系统电压，因此如果电压下降（这表明电气负载较高），ECU可以提高怠速。

（6）进气歧管绝对压力传感器——监控进气歧管中的空气压力。吸入发动机的空气量可以很好地表明发动机产生了多少功率；进入发动机的空气越多，歧管压力越低，用来测量产生了多少功率。

（7）发动机转速传感器——监控发动机转速，用于计算脉冲宽度的指标之一。

(1) Mass airflow sensor—Tells the ECU the mass of air entering the engine.

(2) Oxygen sensor(s)—Monitors the amount of oxygen in the exhaust so the ECU can determine how rich or lean the fuel mixture is and make adjustments accordingly.

(3) Throttle position sensor—Monitors the throttle valve position (which determines how much air goes into the engine) so the ECU can respond quickly to change, increasing or decreasing the fuel rate as necessary.

(4) Coolant temperature sensor—Allows the ECU to determine when the engine has reached its proper operating temperature.

(5) Voltage sensor—Monitors the system voltage in the car so the ECU can raise the idle speed if voltage is dropping (which would indicate a high electrical load).

(6) Manifold absolute pressure sensor—Monitors the pressure of the air in the intake manifold. The amount of air being drawn into the engine is a good indication of how much power it is producing; and the more air that goes into the engine, the lower the manifold pressure.

(7) Engine speed sensor—Monitors engine speed, which is one of the factors used to calculate the pulse width.

6.4.4 润滑系统
The lubrication system

要求润滑系统不断地润滑发动机的运动部件是非常重要的。它用于收集、清洁、冷却和再循环发动机中的机油。润滑系统的主要功能是将润滑油循环输送到所有运动部件的表面，以减少它们之间的摩擦。具体来说，润滑剂在发动机运动部件中循环，执行重要的工作：

It is very important for the lubrication system to be required to lubricate the moving parts of an engine constantly. It is used for collecting, cleaning, cooling and re-circulating oil in the engine.The main function of the lubrication system is to circulate and deliver oil to the surfaces of all the moving parts in order to reduce friction between them. In detail, the lubricant circulates through the engine moving parts and performs important jobs:

润滑运动部件以减少磨损；
润滑运动部件以减少摩擦造成的能量损失；
通过充当冷却剂来吸收发动机零件的热量；
吸收轴承和其他发动机部件之间的震动，从而降低噪声，延长发动机寿命；
在活塞环和气缸壁之间形成良好的密封；
作为一种清洁剂，清洗工作表面的化学沉积物，灰尘和污垢，以保护他们免受腐蚀。

To lubricate moving parts to minimize wear;

To lubricate moving parts to minimize power loss from friction;

To remove heat from engine parts by acting as a cooling agent;

To absorb shocks between bearings and other engine parts, thus reducing the noise and extending the engine life;

To form a good seal between piston rings and cylinder walls;

To act as a cleaning agent, washing the working surfaces free of chemical deposits, dust and dirt to protect them from corrosion.

为了使汽车保持良好的运行状态，车主必须每行驶5000km更换一次润滑油。如果润滑系统发生故障，不仅发动机会停止运转，而且一些零件也可能被损坏，无法修复。因此，当出现润滑故障时，发动机很少能在不大修的情况下再次运行。

To keep a car in good running conditions, a car owner must change the lubricant once every 5000km. If the lubricating system should fail, not only will the engine stop, but also some parts are likely to be damaged beyond repair. Therefore, when lubrication failure occurs, the engine can seldom be run again without a major overhaul.

该系统的主要部件有油泵、机油滤清器、主油道、油底壳、机油压力调节器、安全阀、机油冷却器等。图6.22显示了润滑系统布局。常见的润滑方式有三种：飞溅润滑、压力润滑和常规润滑。

The main components of the system are oil pump, oil filters, main oil galleries, oil pan, oil pressure regulators, relief valve, and oil coolers and so on. Fig.6.22 shows the lubrication system layout. The lubrication way comprises three types: splash lubrication, pressure lubrication and regular lubrication.

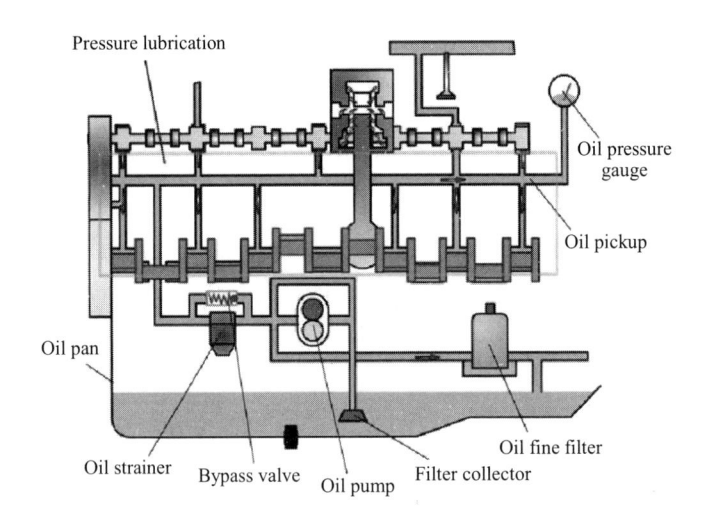

图6.22　润滑系统

Fig.6.22　The lubrication system

飞溅润滑是利用发动机工作时运动部件溅起的油滴或油雾来润滑摩擦表面的一种简单方法。压力润滑或强制润滑是由油泵以一定的压力向发动机的大部分零件，特别是主轴承和连杆轴承连续供油来实现的。常规润滑是通过定期定量添加某种润滑油来实现的。

The splash lubrication is a simple method to lubricate the friction surfaces via using those oil droplets or oil mist splashed up by the moving parts when the engine works. Pressure or forced lubrication is carried out by the oil pump supplying the oil continuously with a certain pressure to the majority of engine parts, especially to main bearings and connecting rod bearings. The regular lubrication is fulfilled by adding some a kind of lubricating grease regularly and quantificationally.

6.4.5 冷却系统
The cooling system

毫无疑问，可燃混合气在发动机气缸内燃烧时会产生大量的热量。如果热量不能及时传递出去，发动机将会因温度过高而无法正常工作。有些部分会因膨胀过度，粘在一起或破裂。冷却系统的功能是通过冷却水将热量传递给空气，使发动机保持在最有效的工作温度。

Without doubt, the burning of the fuel air mixture inside the cylinders of an engine will produce a great deal of heat. If the heat is not transferred timely outside, the engine will not work normally due to too high temperature. Some parts will be subjected to expand too much and stick together or crack. The function of the cooling system is to keep the engine at its most efficient operating temperature by transferring the heat to the air.

燃料中大约三分之一的热能被转化为动力。另外三分之一未经使用就从排气管中排出，剩下的三分之一必须由冷却系统处理。这三分之一经常被低估，有时被认为会更少。一辆普通汽车的冷却系统带走的热量足以让一个有六个房间的房子在零度的天气里保持温暖。

It is said that about one-third of the heat energy in the fuel is converted into power. Another one-third goes out the exhaust pipe unused, and the remaining one-third must be handled by the cooling system. This one-third is often underestimated and even less understood. The heat removed by the cooling system of an average automobile at normal speed is enough to keep a six-room house warm in zero weather.

冷却发动机最常用的方法是让冷却液在发动机缸体和气缸盖的通道中循环。然后冷空气吹过液体，将热量传递给空气。在液冷发动机中，冷却系统包括水泵、水套、散热器、膨胀水箱、压力盖、节温器、冷却风扇和软管等部件，如图 6.23 所示。

The most common way to cool an engine is to circulate a liquid coolant through passages in the engine block and cylinder head.Then cold air is blown over the liquid to transfer the heat to the air. In a liquid cooled engine the cooling system contains such parts as the water pump, the water jacket, the radiator, the expansion tank, pressure cap, the thermostat, the cooling fan and the hoses (Fig.6.23).

气缸由水套包围，水套的水道铸入发动机气缸体，水泵通过水套抽水。冷却系统的心脏是水泵，它的作用是将冷却液输送至冷却管道。通常，水泵由曲轴通过皮带轮和 V 形皮带驱动。水泵的设计大多数是离心式的，利用离心作用将流体输送到外部，使流体不断地从中心抽出，如图 6.24 所示，主要由旋转风扇或叶轮组成。来自水套的热水通过顶部软管流入散热器，在散热器中被外部空气冷却，然后通过底部软管再次泵入水套。

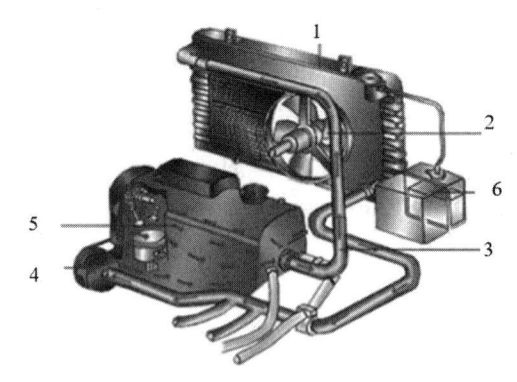

1—散热器；2—风扇；3—水管；4—泵；5—冷却水；6—储备箱
1-Radiator; 2-Fan; 3-Water hose; 4-Pump; 5-Cooling water; 6-Reserve tank

图 6.23 冷却系统

Fig.6.23 The cooling system

The cylinders are surrounded by a water jacket with water passages cast into the engine block, through water is pumped by a water pump. The heart of the cooling system is the water pump, which job is to move the coolant through the cooling system. Typically, the water pump is driven by the crankshaft through pulleys and drive V-belt. The water pumps are of many designs, but most are the centrifugal type, which uses centrifugal force to send fluid to the outside while it spins, causing fluid to be drawn from the center continuously (Fig.6.24), they consist of rotating fan or impeller. The hot water from the water jackets flows through the top hose into a radiator where it is cooled by the air outside before it is pumped back through the bottom hose into water jacket again.

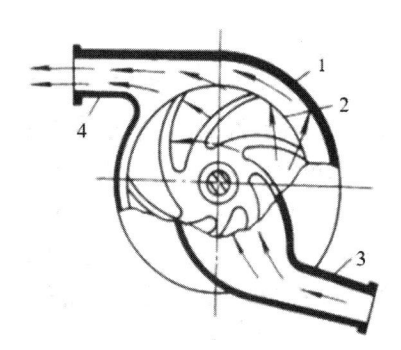

1—泵壳；2—叶轮；3—进水管；4—出水管
1-Pump shell; 2-Impeller; 3-Inlet tube; 4-Outlet tube

图 6.24 离心式水泵简图

Fig.6.24 Centrifugal water pump diagram

散热器是一种热交换器，如图 6.25 所示。它被设计成将流经它的冷却剂的热量传递给由风扇吹过它的空气。包括一个上水箱（在顶部）和一个下水箱，由一个包含许多细管的核心分隔开，热水通过这些细管流动。大多数现代汽车使用铝制散热器，这些散热器是通过将薄铝片钎焊到扁平铝管上制成。冷却液通过许多平行排列的管道从入口流向出口。散热片从管中传导热量，并将热量传递给流经散热器的空气。散热器通常在两侧各有一个水箱，水箱内有一个变速器冷却器。压力盖位于散热器上。它旨在增加冷却系统的压力，保护散热器软管并减少喘振。

A radiator is a type of heat exchanger (Fig.6.25). It is designed to transfer heat from the hot coolant that flows through it to the air blown through it by the fan. It comprises a header tank (at the top) and a bottom tank separated by a core containing a lot of narrow tubes through which the hot waterfalls. Most modern cars use aluminum radiators. These radiators are made by brazing thin aluminum fins to flattened aluminum tubes. The coolant flows from the inlet to the outlet through many tubes mounted in a parallel arrangement. The fins conduct the heat from the tubes and transfer it to the air flowing through the radiator. Radiators usually have a tank on each side, and inside the tank is a transmission cooler. Pressure cap is placed on the radiator. It is designed to increase the pressure on the cooling system, protect the radiator hoses and reduce surging.

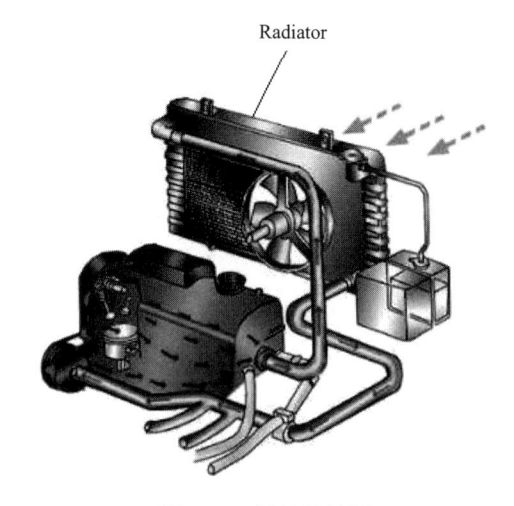

图 6.25　散热器简图

Fig.6.25　Radiator diagram

习　　题

一、单选题

1. 发动机一个完整的工作循环，曲轴旋转（　　）周。
   A．1　　　　　　　B．2　　　　　　　C．3　　　　　　　D．4
2. 在（　　）行程，气体膨胀并对向下运动的活塞做有用功，推动曲轴旋转。
   A．进气　　　　　　B．压缩　　　　　　C．做功　　　　　　D．排气
3. （　　）是构成发动机的骨架，是发动机各机构和各系统的安装基体。
   A．机体组　　　　　B．气缸体　　　　　C．气缸盖　　　　　D．油底壳
4. （　　）气体密封，（　　）用于防止机油进入燃烧室。
   A．气环，油环　　　　　　　　　　　　B．油环，气环
   C．气环，气环　　　　　　　　　　　　D．油环，油环

5．通常，上置式凸轮轴多数是通过（　　）驱动。

　　A．齿轮传动　　　　B．链传动　　　　C．带传动　　　　D．轴传动

6．（　　）测量进入发动机的空气质量。

　　A．氧传感器　　　　　　　　　　B．节气门位置传感器

　　C．爆震传感器　　　　　　　　　D．空气流量计

7．（　　）将油循环输送到所有运动部件的表面，以减少它们之间的摩擦。

　　A．机油泵　　　　B．润滑剂　　　　C．润滑系统　　　　D．机油泵

8．冷却系统的心脏是（　　），它的作用是将冷却液输送至冷却管道。

　　A．水泵　　　　　B．散热器　　　　C．冷却风扇　　　　D．节温器

9．（　　）的布置形式在汽车上日益流行，结构布局紧凑，减轻了汽车的重量，提高了车辆稳定性。

　　A．FF　　　　　　B．RR　　　　　　C．MR　　　　　　D．AWD

10．活塞扫过的体积称为气缸的（　　）。

　　A．总容积　　　　　　　　　　　B．燃烧室容积

　　C．压缩比　　　　　　　　　　　D．工作容积

二、简答题

1．什么叫上止点和下止点？
2．曲柄连杆机构的功能是什么？
3．曲柄连杆机构主要是由哪几部分组成？
4．电控燃油喷射系统中各传感器的功能是什么？
5．润滑系统和冷却系统的功能是什么？

第 7 章 底盘的结构与原理

Structure and principle of chassis

底盘集成了汽车中主要的运动部件。底盘通常包括传动系统、车身悬架系统、转向系统和制动系统。

The chassis is an assembly of those systems that are the major operating part of a vehicle. The chassis commonly includes power train, frame and suspension system, steering system, and brake system.

传动系统向车轮传递驱动力。主要组成机构为离合器、变速器、万向传动装置、主减速器和差速器,如图 7.1 所示。

Power train conveys the drive to the wheels. The main components of power train are clutch, gearbox, driveshaft, final drive, and differential (Fig.7.1).

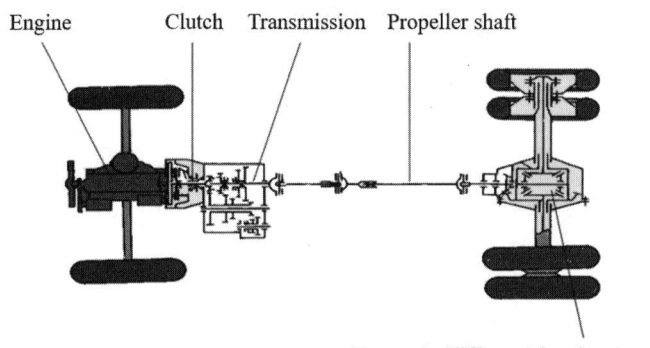

图 7.1 汽车传动系统

Fig.7.1 Power train of an automobile

车身悬架系统用于吸收路面震动。商用车底盘包含有明显的车架,而乘用车底盘大多是承载式车身,如图 7.2 所示。

Frame and suspension absorb the road vibrations. Commercial vehicle chassis contain a distinct frame, while passenger vehicle chassis are mostly load-baring beodies (Fig.7.2).

转向系统控制汽车转向。制动系统使汽车减速,如图 7.3 所示。

Steering system controls the direction of the movement. Brake system slows down the vehicle. (Fig.7.3).

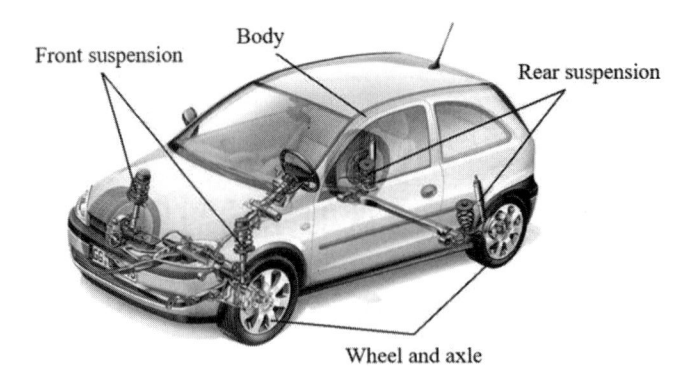

图 7.2 行驶系统

Fig.7.2 Frame and suspension

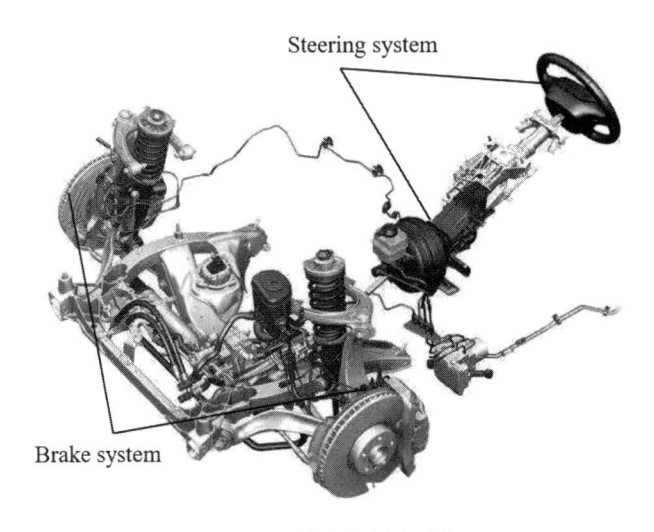

图 7.3 转向与制动系统

Fig.7.3 Steering and brake system

7.1 传 动 系 统

Power train

  传动系统将发动机的转矩和转速传递到驱动轮。其主要组成为离合器、变速器、传动轴、后桥（主要包括主减速器和差速器）。

  Power train systems conveys the torque and rotation speed from engine to the driving wheels. The main components of power train are clutch, gearbox (transmission), drive shaft, rear axle (includes main reducer and differential).

  （1）离合器。离合器是位于发动机和变速器之间的一个旋转装置，包括飞轮、从动盘、压盘、压紧弹簧、离合器盖以及操作离合器所需的连接杆件（操纵系统）等。离合器通过螺栓安装在飞轮的后表面（图7.4）。挂挡之前可以通过离合器切断动力传递并且离合器可以防止传动系统过载。

Clutch. The clutch which includes the flywheel, driven plate, pressure plate, springs, pressure plate cover and the linkage necessary to operate the clutch is a rotating mechanism between the engine and the transmission. The clutch is mounted on back surface of flywheel by bolts (Fig.7.4). Clutch can break power transmitting before handling transmission and protect power train when overloading.

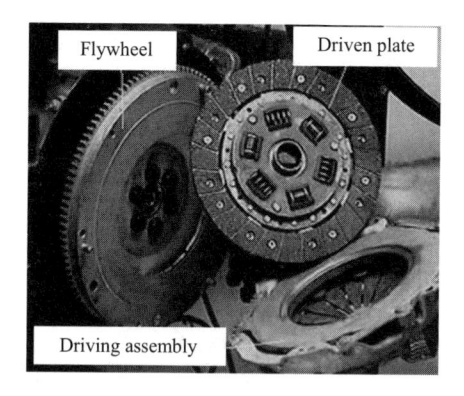

图 7.4　离合器安装位置

Fig.7.4　Position of clutch

飞轮是离合器的主要部件。其安装在发动机曲轴末端并将发动机转矩传递给离合器总成。当压盘将离合器从动盘压紧在飞轮上时，发动机的动力就会传递给变速器，如图 7.5 所示。

The flywheel is a major part of the clutch. The flywheel mounts to the engine's crankshaft and transmits engine torque to the clutch assembly. The flywheel, when coupled with the clutch disc and pressure plate makes the flow of power from engine to the transmission (Fig.7.5).

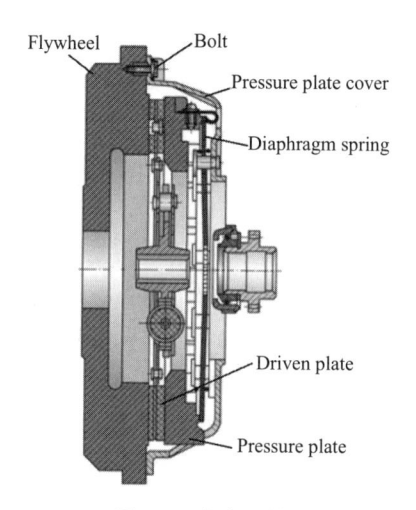

图 7.5　离合器的结构

Fig.7.5　Structure of clutch

飞轮也为离合器总成提供了安装位置。当离合器工作时，飞轮将发动机的转矩传递给离合器从动盘。飞轮因其自重较大，能使得发动机运行平稳。飞轮的外边缘装有大齿圈，当发动机启动时，起动机上的驱动齿轮与飞轮齿圈相啮合，如图 7.6 所示。

The flywheel provides a mounting location for the clutch assembly as well. When the clutch is applied, the flywheel transfers engine torque to the clutch disc. Because of its weight, the flywheel helps to smooth engine operation. The flywheel also has a large ring gear at its outer edge, which engages with a pinion gear on the starter motor during engine cranking (Fig.7.6).

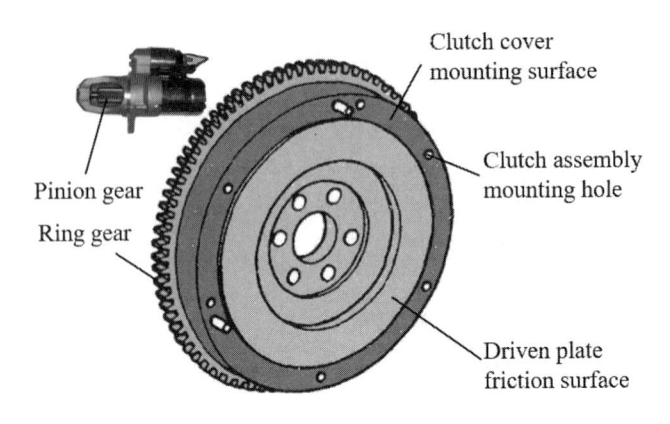

图 7.6　飞轮的结构

Fig.7.6　Structure of flywheel

从动盘包括花键毂、钢片、减震弹簧以及两侧摩擦衬片。所有的零部件通过铆钉连接在一起。从动盘安装在飞轮和压盘之间。从动盘中间的花键毂与变速器输入轴上的花键相匹配。输入轴上的花键长槽与从动盘花键配合在一起，使得从动盘可以在其上前后滑动并跟着输入轴等速转动，如图 7.7 所示。

Driven plate consists of spline hole/hub, steel sheet, anti-vibration spring and friction sheets. All parts combined together by rivets. It fits between the flywheel and the pressure plate. Driven plate has a splined hub that fits over splines on the transmission input shaft. A splined hub has grooves that match splines on the shaft. These splines fit in the grooves. Thus, the two parts held together and back-and-forth movement of the plate on the shaft is possible. Attached to the input shaft, the plate turns at the speed of the shaft (Fig.7.7).

压盘总成是安装在飞轮后表面上的主动部分，通常是由铸铁制成的圆形且和从动盘直径相同。压盘内侧加工成平滑的表面朝向飞轮并将从动盘压在飞轮上，外侧形状则便于安装压紧弹簧与操纵机构。压盘总成有两种主要的类型：螺旋弹簧式（图 7.8）和膜片弹簧式（图 7.9）。

Driving assembly is an active part and it is mounted on the back surface of flywheel. The clutch pressure plate is generally made of cast iron. It is round and about the same diameter as the clutch disc. One side of the pressure plate is machined smooth. This side will press the clutch disc facing against the flywheel. The outer side has shapes to facilitate attachment of spring and release mechanism. The two primary types of driving assemblies are coil spring assembly (Fig.7.8) and diaphragm spring (Fig.7.9).

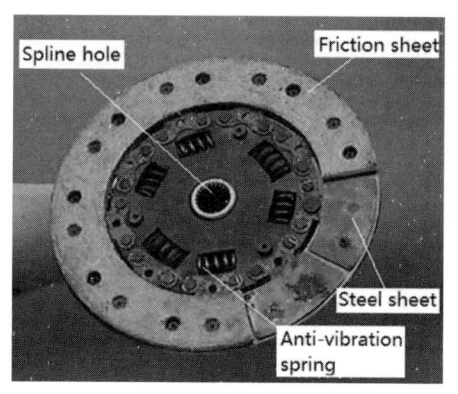

图 7.7　从动盘的结构

Fig.7.7　Structure of driven plate

图 7.8　周布螺旋弹簧式

Fig.7.8　Coil spring assembly

图 7.9　膜片弹簧式

Fig.7.9　Diaphragm spring assembly

膜片弹簧式离合器压盘总成包括离合器盖、膜片弹簧、传动片、压盘以及支撑簧，如图 7.10 所示。膜片弹簧的径向外侧连接压盘，中间位置通过支撑簧和铆钉铰接在离合器盖里面。其表面形状类似于圆盘添加一些径向的缝隙。膜片弹簧能够使得压盘将从动盘压紧到飞轮上。另外膜片弹簧工作时类似于杠杆。传动片连接离合器盖和压盘，将离合器盖驱动力传递给压盘并保证压盘可以前后移动。

Diaphragm spring driving assembly consists of clutch case, diaphragm spring, retainer rings, pressure plate and tension sheet (Fig.7.10). Outer end of diaphragm spring links pressure plate and the mid of it hanged inside clutch case by retainer ring and rivet. Diaphragm spring's appearance is like a dish with some radial gaps. It has the function of pressing pressure plate and driven plate against flywheel. It has another function which can act as a lever. Tension sheet links clutch case and pressure plate to ensure the pressure plate revolves with clutch case and moves close or away to clutch case.

离合器踏板踩下之前，分离叉不起作用，膜片弹簧将压盘压紧在飞轮表面。在膜片弹簧分离指与分离轴承之间有一个很小的间隙，如图 7.11 所示。此时发动机转矩和转速通过花键传递给变速器输入轴。从动盘跟着压盘和飞轮以同样的速度一块转动。此时为接合状态。

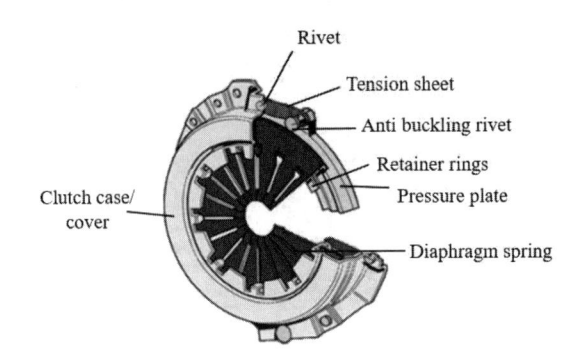

图 7.10　膜片弹簧离合器总成结构示意图

Fig.7.10　Structure of diaphragm spring assembly

Before putting down clutch pedal, release fork doesn't work. The diaphragm spring press driven plate to flywheel end surface through pressure plate. There is a small clearance between the inner end of diaphragm spring and separating bearing (Fig.7.11). In this case, the torque and rotation speed from engine is transmitted to input shaft of transmission by spline. Driven plate rotates at same speed with driving assembly and flywheel. It's an engaging situation.

离合器踏板是一个杠杆，当踩下离合器踏板时，踏板上端带动分离叉上端向右移动，而其下端朝左移动并且推动分离轴承向左移动。膜片弹簧也像杠杆一样，其内端分离指向左移动，外端拉动压盘向右移动，压盘两侧出现分离间隙，如图 7.12 所示。从动盘此时可自由移动，变速器动力中断。

The clutch pedal is a lever. When putting down clutch pedal, the upper end of pedal drags the upper end of release fork to move right, and the lower end moves left to push separating bearing to move left. Diaphragm spring works also as a lever, with its inner end moving left and outside end pulling pressure plate to move right, separate clearance appear on both sides of driven plate (Fig.7.12). Driven plate now is free and the power to transmission is broken completely.

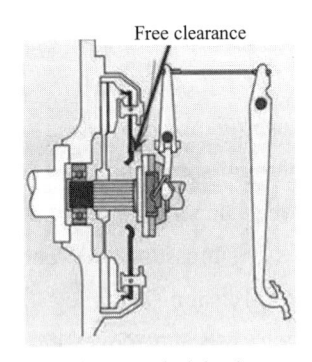

图 7.11　自由间隙　　　　　　　　　　　图 7.12　分离间隙

Fig.7.11　Free clearance　　　　　　　　Fig.7.12　Separate clearance

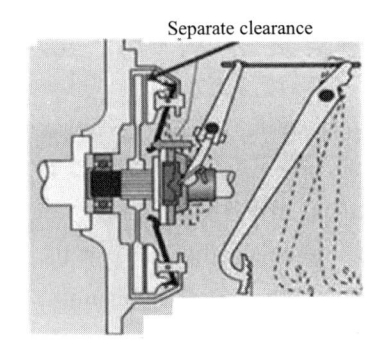

离合器连接杆件（操纵机构）（图 7.13）包括踏板、摇臂、摇臂轴以及到分离叉的中间一系

列杆件和分离轴承。分离轴承包括轴承和套筒，如图 7.14 所示。当分离叉推动分离轴承向左移动并接触膜片弹簧时，轴承会跟着膜片弹簧一块转动，而分离套筒保持静止，如图 7.15 所示。

The clutch pedal linkage (Fig.7.13) includes pedal, rocker arm, rocker arm shaft, and a series of linkage to release fork and separating bearing. Separating bearing consists of bearing and sleeve (Fig.7.14). When release fork pushes separating bearing to move left and touch diaphragm spring, bearing will revolve with diaphragm spring and the sleeve keep still (Fig.7.15).

图 7.13　离合器连接杆件

Fig.7.13　The clutch pedal linkage

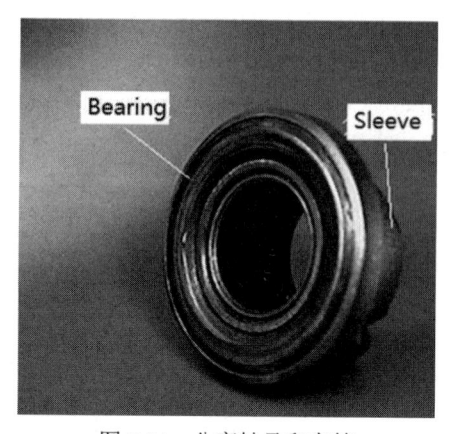

图 7.14　分离轴承和套筒

Fig.7.14　Separating bearing

图 7.15　分离轴承分离套筒的位置

Fig.7.15　The position of separating bearing

（2）手动变速器。变速器是汽车非常重要的部件，它可以改变传动比、改变转矩输出和转速输出，如图 7.16 所示。当爬坡时，汽车需要更大的扭矩，此时应选择低挡位；当高速行驶时，应挂入高挡位。变速器还可以改变转动方向以实现倒车。

Manual transmission. Transmission is very important to vehicle. It can change transmission ratio, and change torque output and rotation speed output (Fig.7.16). When climbing a slope, we need bigger torque, so we should select low gear. When we drive car running at a high speed, we should shift to high gear. It can also change rotation direction to reverse a car.

图 7.16　变速器结构

Fig.7.16　Components of transmission

手动变速器包括输入轴、输出轴、中间轴、多个齿轮副、同步器以及操纵系统。通常手动变速器被分为三轴手动变速器和两轴手动变速器两类。三轴手动变速器因其可以传递较大的动力常用在重型车辆上。其中三轴指的是输入轴、输出轴以及中间轴。

Manual transmission consists of input shaft, output shaft, counter shaft, a series of gear couples, synchronizer and handling system. Commonly it is divided into two types named three-shaft type transmission and two-shaft type transmission. Three-shaft type transmission can transmit large power, so it is usually used in heavy vehicles. There are input shaft, output shaft and counter shaft of three shafts.

同步器包括接合套、花键毂、同步锁环以及其他部件。接合套安装在花键毂外侧的花键上并且可以通过拨叉左右移动，如图 7.17 所示。

Synchronizer consists of connecting sleeve, hub with spline, synchronization lock ring and other parts. Connecting sleeve is mounted on hub with spline and can move left and right driven by fork (Fig.7.17).

花键毂通过花键以及支撑环固定在轴上。同步器保证花键毂和齿轮齿圈同步，此时接合套通过同步器在花键槽内左右移动以实现挂入不同的挡位。

Hub is fixed on shaft with spline but locked by retainer rings. Synchronizer ensure hub and gear ring have same rotation speed. In this case, connecting sleeve moves left through synchronizer to gear ring with spline to lock the gear to shaft.

两轴手动变速器（图 7.18）包括输入轴、输出轴以及多个齿轮副。其结构相较三轴手动变速器较为紧凑，通常应用在乘用车中。

Two-shaft type transmission (Fig.7.18) consists of input shaft, output shaft and some gear couples. The structure is more compact than three-shaft type transmission and it is usually used in passenger car.

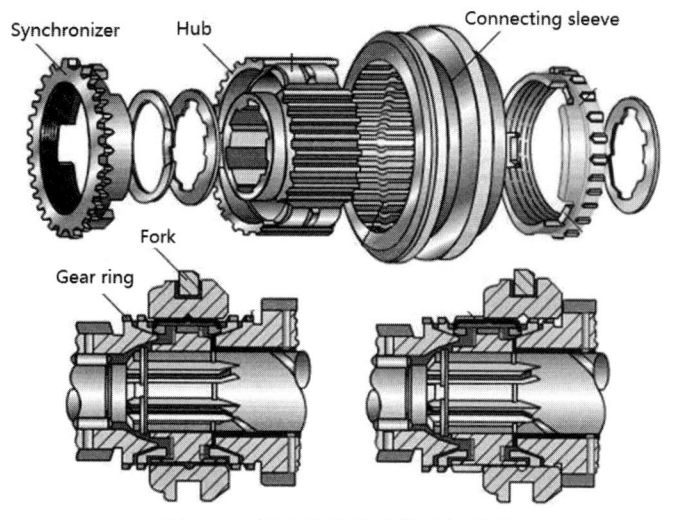

图 7.17 同步器的基本结构与原理

Fig.7.17 Basic structure and operating principle of synchronizer

图 7.18 两轴手动变速器

Fig.7.18 Two-shaft type transmission

两轴手动变速器的组成如图 7.19 所示。

The construction of two-shaft type transmission is shown in Fig.7.19.

操纵机构（图 7.20）中包含操纵杆、换挡轴、换挡拨叉等。通常换挡杆上有挡位标记，如图 7.21 所示换挡杆上标记显示共有 5 个前进挡和 1 个倒挡。

There are operating handle, shifting shafts, shifting forks on handling mechanism(Fig.7.20). Usually there is a mark on handle knob as following. Fig.7.21 shows there are 5 forward gears and one reverse gear.

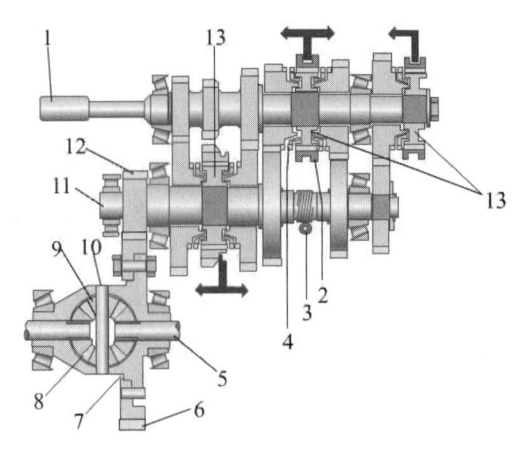

1—输入轴；2—接合套；3—里程表计数装置；4—同步器；5—半轴；6—从动锥齿轮；7—差速器壳；
8—半轴齿轮；9—行星齿轮；10—行星齿轮轴；11—输出轴；12—输出齿轮；13—花键毂

1-Input shaft; 2-Connecting sleeve; 3-Vss valve; 4-Synchronizer; 5-Axle shaft;
6-Final drive ring gear; 7-Differential housing; 8-Side gear; 9-Planetary pinions;
10-Pinion shaft; 11-Output shaft; 12-Output gear; 13-Hub

图 7.19　两轴手动变速器的组成

Fig.7.19　Construction of two-shaft type transmission

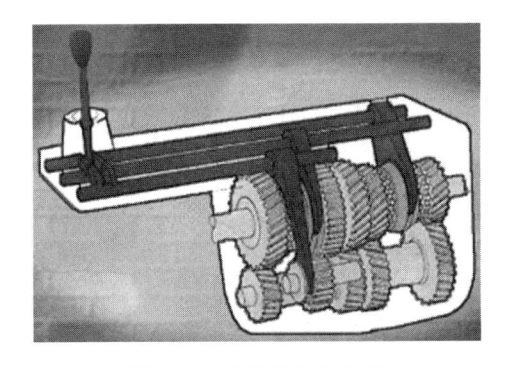

图 7.20　操纵机构的位置

Fig.7.20　The position of Handling mechanism

图 7.21　换挡杆

Fig.7.21　Shift knob

（3）自动变速器。自动变速器具有一些典型特点：

A. 根据节气门开度和汽车速度自动换挡。

B. 线性改变输出转速和转矩。

C. 当换挡时无需中断转速和转矩传递。

D. 比手动变速器容易操纵。

Automatic transmission. Automatic transmission has some typical features shown below:

A. Select gear automatically according to throttle opening and vehicle speed.

B. Shift output rotation speed and torque gradually (linearly).

C. Without rotation speed and torque break during gear shifting.

D. Easy handling than manual transmission.

常见的自动变速器有三种：无级变速器、液力自动变速器、双离合自动变速器。无级变速器包括液力变矩器、可移动锥轮、钢带和固定锥轮，如图 7.22 所示。

There are three common classifications of automatic transmission: stepless transmission, Hydraulic transmission, and dual clutches transmission. Stepless transmission consists of hydraulic torque convertor, movable bevel wheels, steel belt and stable bevel wheels (Fig.7.22).

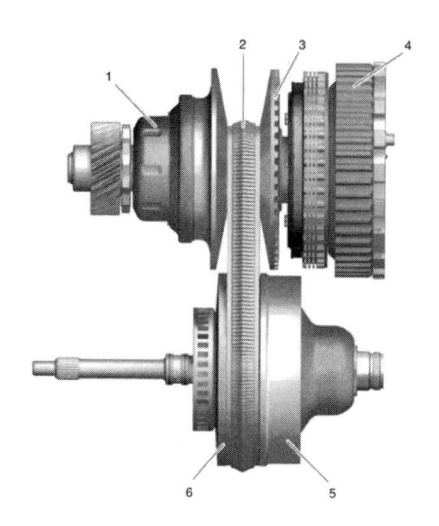

1—可移动锥轮；2—钢带；3—固定锥轮；4—输出轴；5—可移动锥轮；6—固定锥轮
1-Movable bevel wheel; 2-Steel belt; 3-Stable bevel wheel; 4-Output shaft;
5-Movable bevel wheel; 6-Stable bevel wheel

图 7.22 无级变速器

Fig.7.22 Stepless transmission

液力变矩器是一个液力转换装置，它包括泵轮、涡轮、导轮，如图 7.23 所示。泵轮固定在飞轮上，涡轮连接变速器输入轴，线性的传递动力。

Hydraulic torque convertor is a hydraulic transmitting mechanism. It consists of pump wheel, turbine wheel and guide wheel (Fig.7.23). The pump wheel is fixed on flywheel, and turbine wheel is connected to input shaft of transmission. It creates linear transmitting as well.

液力自动变速器包括液力变矩器、行星齿轮机构。液力变矩器与无级变速器中的部件相同。泵轮固定在飞轮上、涡轮连接行星齿轮机构的输入轴。

Hydraulic transmission consists of hydraulic torque convertor and planet gear mechanism. Hydraulic torque convertor is same as one on stepless transmission. Pump wheel is fixed on flywheel and turbine wheel is connected to input shaft of planet gear mechanism.

行星齿轮机构包括若干行星齿轮排和执行元件，能够产生若干挡位（4 挡、5 挡或 6 挡）。液力自动变速器中较为常用的有辛普森式自动变速器和拉威诺式自动变速器两类。

Planet gear mechanism consists of several planet gear units and executers and creates several gears (4, 5, or 6). This kind of transmission called Simpson automatic transmission and another called Ravigneaux automatic transmission are widely used.

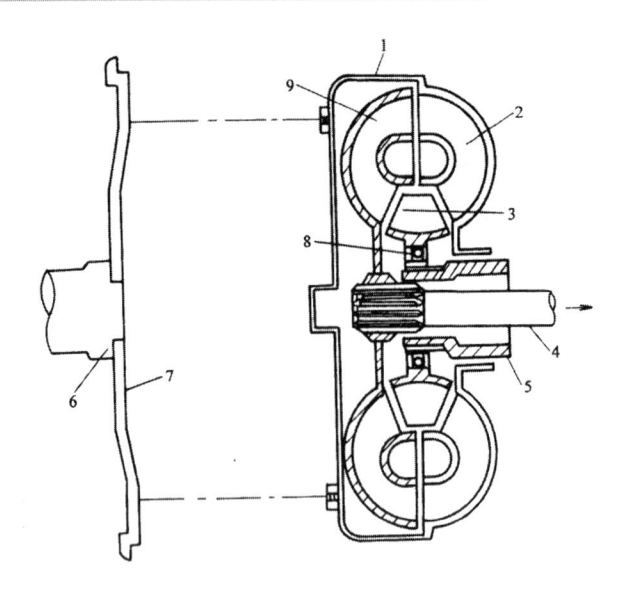

1—液力变矩器壳；2—泵轮；3—导轮；4—输出轴；5—导轮轴；6—输入轴；

7—飞轮；8—锁止离合器；9—涡轮

1-Hydraulic torque convertor case; 2-Pump wheel; 3-Guide wheel; 4-Output shaft;

5-Guide wheel shaft; 6-Input shaft; 7-Fly wheel; 8-Lockup clutch; 9-Turbine

图 7.23　液力变矩器

Fig.7.23　Hydraulic torque convertor

辛普森式自动变速器典型结构为两排行星齿轮排共用一个太阳轮，一排行星齿轮机构的行星架和另一个行星齿轮机构的齿圈分别与公用太阳轮连接，如图 7.24 所示，其结构简图如图 7.25 所示。有的加入了第三个行星齿轮机构称为超速排能够实现超速挡。

The typical structure of Simpson automatic transmission is that two planetary gear rows share a single sun wheel (Fig.7.24). The diagram of Simpson antomatic transmission is shown as Fig.7.25. The planetary frame of one planetary gear mechanism and the ring gear of another planetary gear mechanism are respectively connected with the common sun wheel. Some add a third planetary gear mechanism called overdrive planetary gear row to achieve overdrive gear.

图 7.24　辛普森式自动变速器

Fig.7.24　Simpson automatic transmission

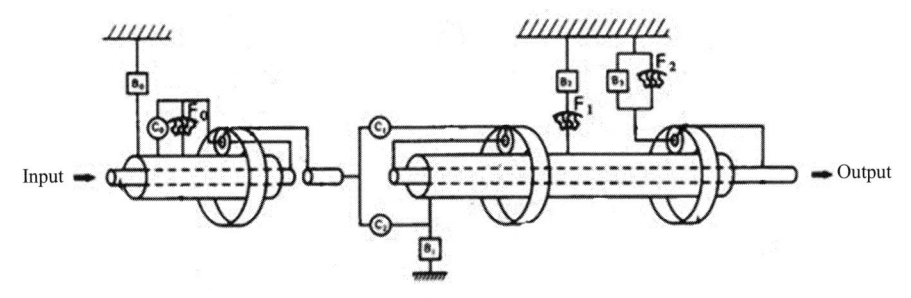

图 7.25　辛普森式自动变速器简图

Fig.7.25　Schematic diagram of Simpson automatic transmission

相比于辛普森式自动变速器，拉威诺式自动变速器结构紧凑，其典型结构为具备长短行星轮结构，如图 7.26 所示。它是由一个单行星排与一个双行星排组合而成的复合式行星机构，共用一行星架、长行星轮和齿圈。其中大太阳轮与长行星轮啮合，小太阳轮与短行星轮啮合。

Compared with Simpson automatic transmission, Ravigneaux automatic transmission has a compact structure, and its typical structure is with long and short planetary wheel structure (Fig.7.26). It is a compound planetary mechanism composed of a single planetary row and a double planetary row, which share a planetary rack, a long planetary wheel and a gear ring. The large sun wheel meshes with the long planetary wheel, and the small sun wheel meshes with the short planetary wheel.

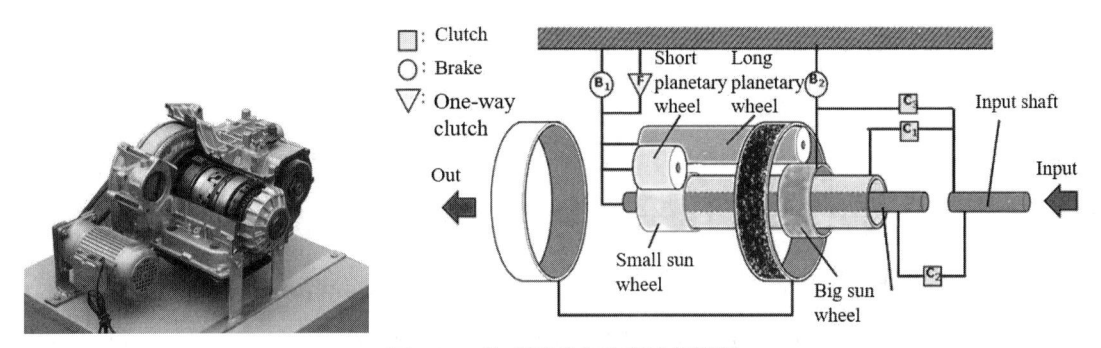

图 7.26　拉威诺式自动变速器简图

Fig.7.26　Ravigneaux automatic transmission

相比手动变速器，双离合式自动变速器有两套离合器、两个轴并且可以具备更多的挡位（8 挡或 9 挡）。其特点类似于手动变速器，其不使用离合器踏板，自动控制换挡，如图 7.27 所示。

Compared with manual transmission, dual clutch transmission has two clutches, two shafts and creates far more gears (8 or 9). The feature is like manual transmission but automatic shifting, without clutch pedal (Fig.7.27).

（4）传动轴。传动轴由万向节、传动轴管、滑动花键和法兰盘组成，如图 7.28 所示。

Propeller (driving) shaft. Components of Propeller (driving) shaft consists of universal joints, shaft tube, slide spline and flange (Fig.7.28).

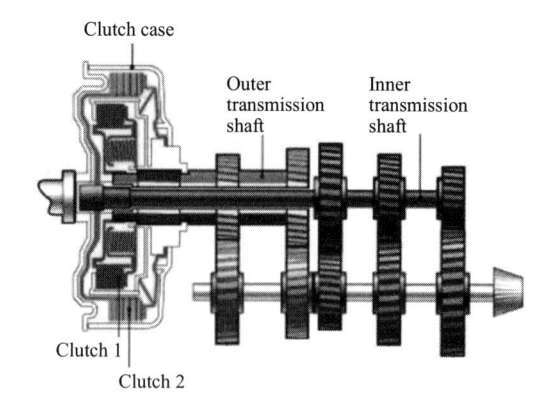

图 7.27 双离合式自动变速器

Fig.7.27 Dual clutch transmission

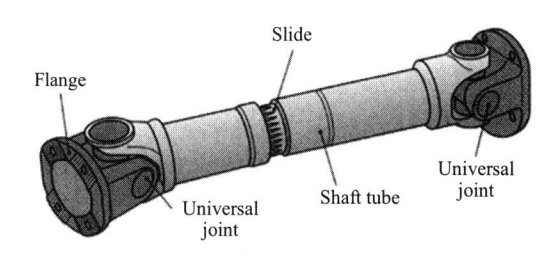

图 7.28 传动轴结构

Fig.7.28 Structure of a propeller (driving) shaft

传动轴有两个主要功能：将动力从变速器传递到驱动桥；万向节实现变速器和后桥不同的离地高度。当后桥上下跳动时，滑动花键实现传动轴的长度变化：当后桥向上跳动时传动轴变短，反之则变长，如图 7.29 所示。

There are two main functions of propeller (driving) shaft: Transmit power from transmission to driving axle, the universal joints fit different heights to ground between transmission and rear axle. Slide spline fits the length change when rear axle bumping up and down. When rear axle bumps up, the propeller shaft becomes short. On the contrary, it becomes long (Fig.7.29).

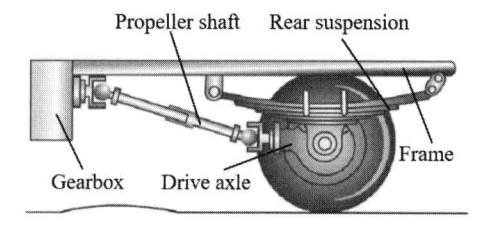

图 7.29 传动轴功能示意图

Fig.7.29 Functions diagram of propeller (driving) shaft

万向节有两种类型：球笼式万向节和十字轴式万向节。对于球笼式万向节，传递转矩和转速的稳定性更高，通常用于乘用车；对于十字轴式万向节，传递转矩和转速的能力较高，通常用于重型车辆，如图 7.30 所示。

There are two kinds of universal joints: ball cage type and cross shaft type. For ball cage type, the stability of transmitting torque and rotation speed is higher, it is usually used in passenger car. For cross shaft type, the ability of transmitting torque and rotation speed is higher, it is usually used in heavy vehicles (Fig.7.30).

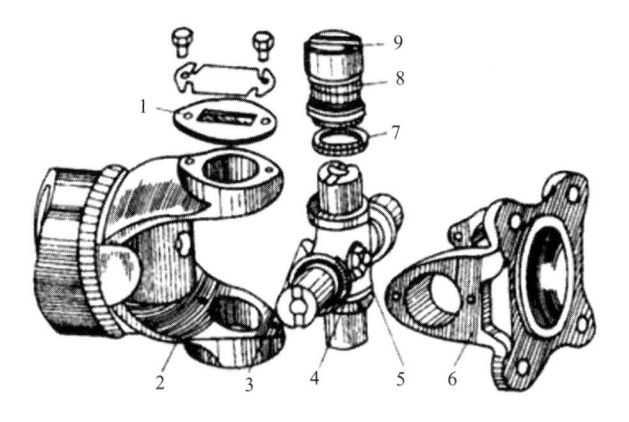

1—轴承盖；2—万向节叉（从动）；3—油嘴；4—十字轴；5—安全阀；

6—万向节叉（主动）；7—油封；8—滚针轴承；9—套筒

1-Bearing cover; 2-Driven fork; 3-Zerk; 4-Cross; 5-Valve; 6-Driving fork;

7-Oil seal; 8-Needle bearing; 9-Sleeve

图 7.30 十字轴式万向节

Fig.7.30 Cross and roller universal joint

（5）驱动桥总成。驱动桥（后驱类型）总成包括主减速器、差速器以及后桥壳。通常商用车后桥是中空的，前桥式是实心的，如图 7.31 所示。后桥总成位置如图 7.32 所示。

Drive axle assembly. Drive axle assembly consists of main reducer (main retarder), differential and rear axle box. Commonly, Rear axle on commercial vehicles is hollow and front axle is solid (Fig.7.31). The position rear axle assembly is shown as Fig.7.32.

图 7.31 前后桥

Fig.7.31 Front and rear axle

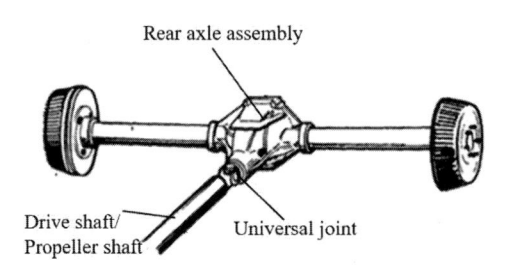

图 7.32　后桥总成的位置

Fig.7.32　Position of rear axle assembly

主减速器包括主动齿轮、从动齿轮，它们是圆锥齿轮，如图 7.33 所示。主减速器能够改变转矩和转速方向，也可以降速增距。主减速器传动比较大（大约 7 或 8），因此极大地减小了变速器的尺寸。

Main retarder includes driving pinion and ring pinion (driven pinion)(Fig.7.33). They are bevel gear type. Main retarder can change direction of torque and rotation speed. Also it can increase torque output and decrease rotation speed output. It has big transmitting ratio (about 7 or 8), so it largely reduces transmission size.

差速器（图 7.33）包括差速器壳、行星齿轮、半轴齿轮以及半轴。差速器壳通过螺栓安装在从动锥齿轮上。

Differential (Fig.7.33) includes differential case, planet gears, side gears and half shafts. Differential case is mounted on ring pinion by bolts.

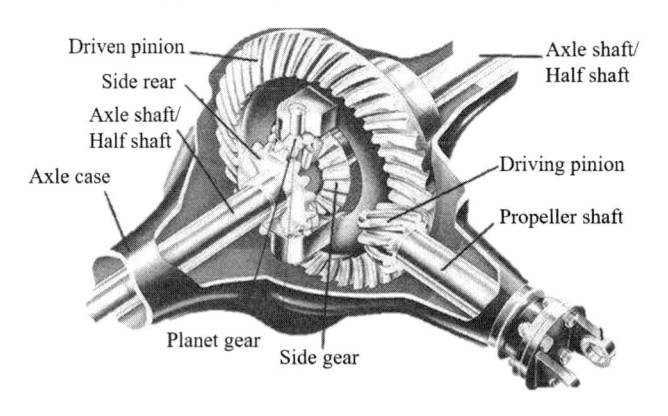

图 7.33　主减速器差速器结构

Fig.7.33　Structure of main retarder and differential

当转弯时，左半轴和右半轴转速不同，如图 7.34 所示。例如，差速器壳速度不变，当汽车左转时，左侧车轮转速为 110rpm，右侧车轮为 90rpm，此时两侧半轴齿轮转速不同，行星齿轮开始自转。

When turning, the left half shaft and right half shaft get different rotation speed. For example, differential case with invariable rotation speed, a vehicle turns right, left wheel gets rotation speed of 110rpm, right wheel gets 90rpm. In this case, both side gears get different rotation speed. There is a self-rotation on planet gears (Fig.7.34).

1—从动齿轮；2—行星齿轮；3—半轴
1-Driven gear; 2-Planetary gear; 3-Harf shaft

图 7.34　差速器功能示意图

Fig.7.34　The function diagram of differential

7.2　车身悬架系统

Frame and suspension system

悬架包括非独立悬架和独立悬架如图 7.35 所示。其中非独立悬架通常用于整体式车桥，独立悬架通常用于断开式车桥。悬架系统减小来自于不平路面的震动以提高乘客舒适性或防止货物损失。

The suspension system includes dependent suspension system and independent suspension (Fig.7.35). Dependent suspension system is used in one common bridge (axle); Independent suspension system is used in separate bridge (axle). Suspension system reduces vibration by rough road surface and avoids uncomfortableness to passenger and damage to cargo.

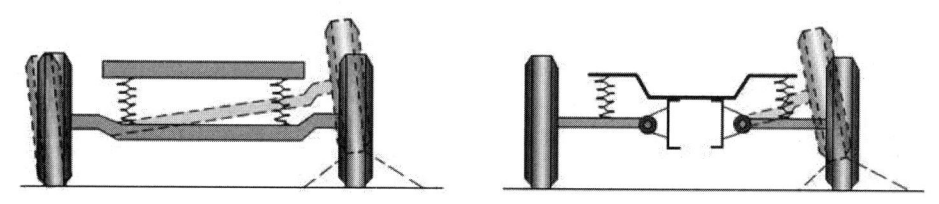

图 7.35　非独立悬架和独立悬架

Fig.7.35　Dependent suspension system and independent suspension system

非独立悬架通常用于货车以乘载重量，如图 7.36 所示。非独立悬架包括钢板弹簧以及减震器。钢板弹簧将跳动转化为弹性形变实现避震。减震器吸收振动能量能够快速减小震动，非独立悬架结构示意图 7.37 所示。

Dependent suspension system usually is used in trucks (Fig.7.36). It can bear heavy load. Dependent suspension system consists of leaf steel spring and absorber. Leaf steel spring transforms bump into elastic vibration to avoid shock. Absorber absorbs vibration energy and depletes vibration quickly Structure diagram of dependent suspension system is shown as Fig.7.37.

115

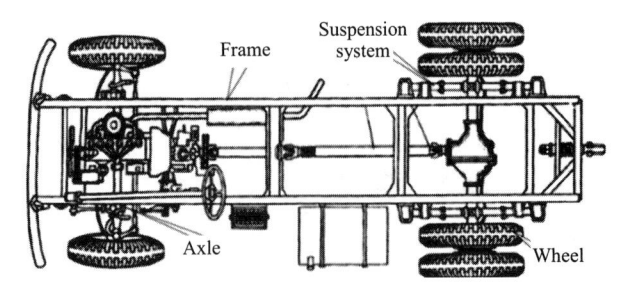

图 7.36　货车中的非独立悬架

Fig.7.36　Dependent suspension system used in trucks

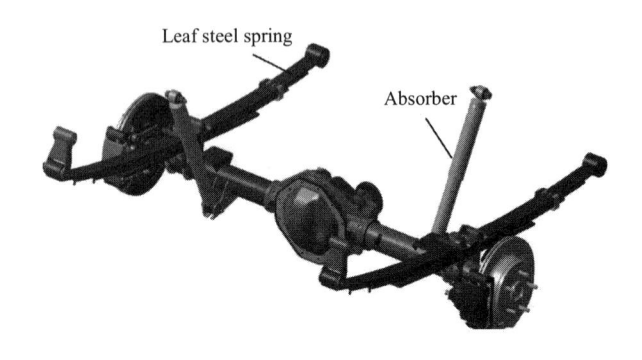

图 7.37　非独立悬架的结构示意图

Fig.7.37　Structure diagram of dependent suspension system

独立悬架（图 7.38）包括螺旋弹簧、减震器以及下摆臂等。下摆臂代替车桥并且可以绕车架上的轴销转动。独立悬架提高了舒适性，通常用于小型车辆上。

Independent suspension system (Fig.7.38) consists of coil spring, absorber and lower rocker arm. Lower rocker arm replaces bridge (axle) and can rock around pin on frame. It provides comfortable condition and is usually used in small car.

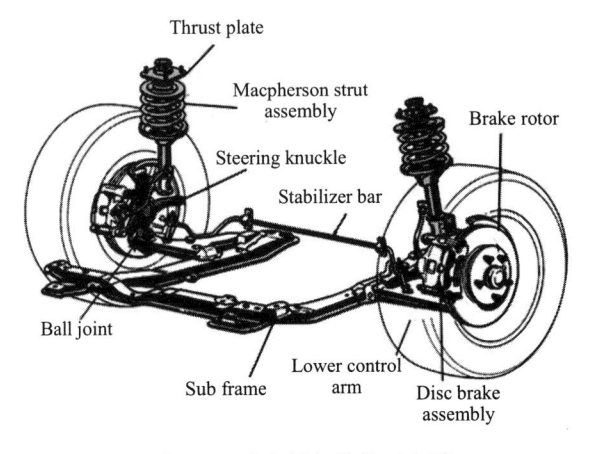

图 7.38　独立悬架结构示意图

Fig.7.38　Structure diagram of independent suspension system

7.3 转 向 系 统

Steering system

转向系统结构如图 7.39 所示。当转动方向盘时，扭矩通过转向柱、万向节、转向器、摇臂、直拉杆、转向节臂传递到转向节（前轮安装在转向节上）。转向器改变了来自于方向盘的转矩和转角，其提高了输出转矩、减小了输出转角。转向梯形臂包括前轴、梯形臂、球头和转向横拉杆。横拉杆使得内外轮一起转动但转角不同。

Structure of steering system is shown as Fig.7.39. When turning steering wheel, the revolution is transmitted to knuckle (front wheel is mounted on the knuckle) via steering column, universal joint, steering gear, rocker arm, pull rod and knuckle arm. Steering gear shifts revolution torque and revolution angle on steering wheel. It makes output torque bigger and output angular displacement smaller. Trapezoid mechanism is composed of front axle (shaft), trapezoid arm, ball joint and tie rod. The function is to fit different angle between outer wheel and inner wheel.

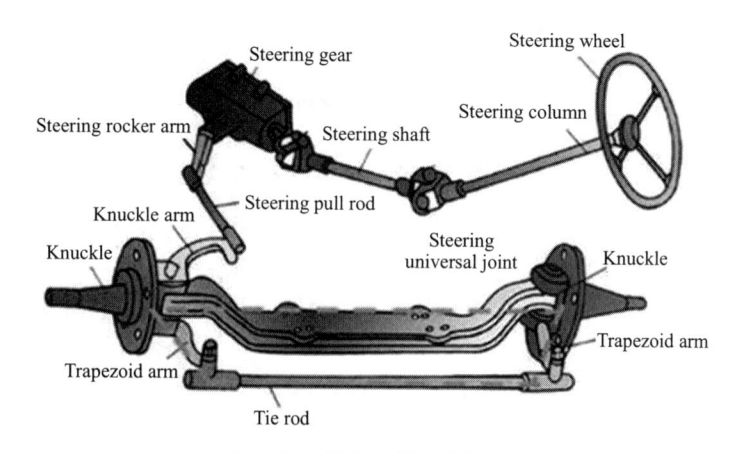

图 7.39　转向系统示意图

Fig.7.39　Structure diagram of steering system

随着转向系统的发展，出现了液压助力系统和电动助力系统以减小转向盘力矩，如图 7.40 所示。液压助力转向系统可以独立通过转向盘、中间杆件、转向器以及后续转向杆件实现转向。储液罐储存油液，油泵产生油压，它由发动机上的曲轴驱动。控制阀控制通往油缸的通道。油缸作为执行器可以根据转向需求推动转向杆件左右移动。

With the development of the steering system, hydraulic assisted system and electric power system are designed to release working strength on steering wheel (steering plate)(Fig.7.40). Steering system can work separately by steering wheel, some links, steering gear and steering rod to move left or right. Oil tank reserves oil. Oil pump creates oil pressure. It is driven by crankshaft on engine. Control valve controls the oil passage to oil cylinder. Oil cylinder is an executor. It works according to steering requirement to push steering rod moving left or right.

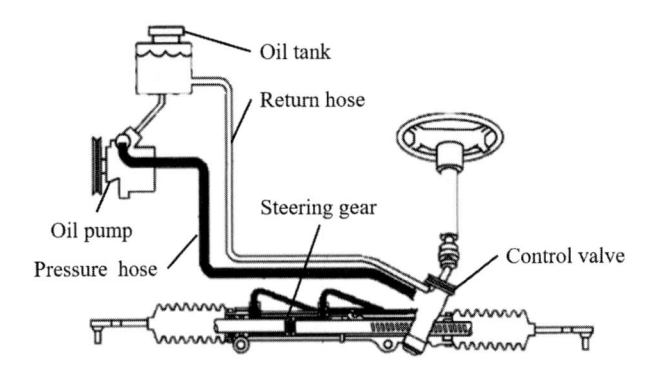

图 7.40　液压助力转向系统示意图

Fig.7.40　Structure diagram of hydraulic assisted steering system

与液压助力转向系统类似，电动助力转向系统通过电机、转角传感器等实现助力，如图 7.41 所示。

Like hydraulic assisted system, electric power system assists steering operating by motor, revolution angle sensor, as shown in Fig.7.41.

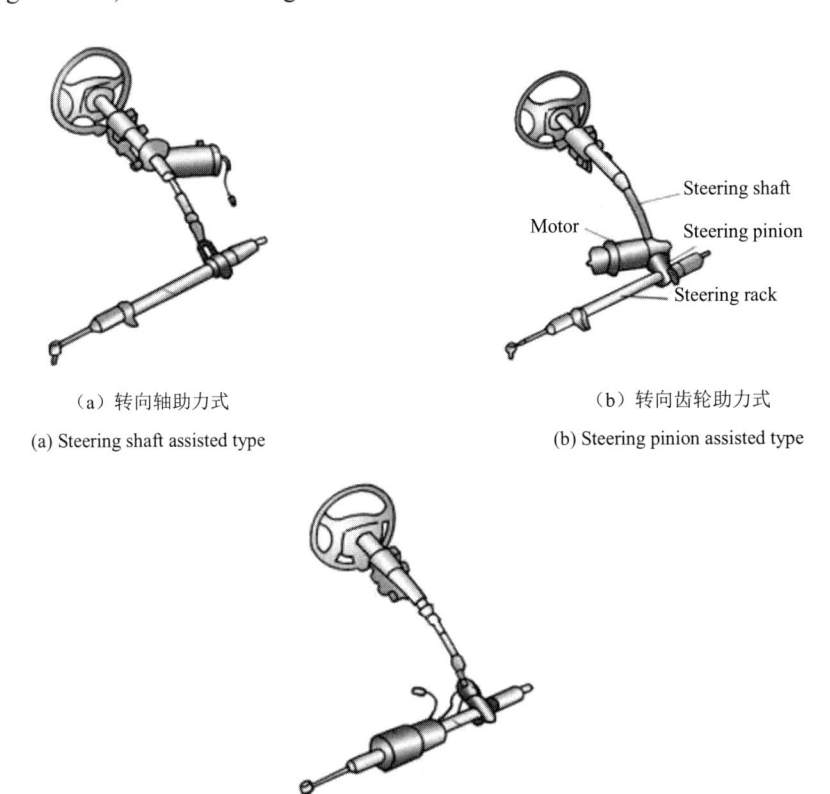

（a）转向轴助力式

(a) Steering shaft assisted type

（b）转向齿轮助力式

(b) Steering pinion assisted type

（c）转向齿条助力式

(c) Rack assisted type

图 7.41　电动助力转向系统

Fig.7.41　Electric power system

7.4 制动系统

Brake system

液压制动系统结构简单，通常应用于小型汽车，如图 7.42 所示。

Hydraulic brake system has simple construction. Usually it is used in small car, as shown in Fig.7.42.

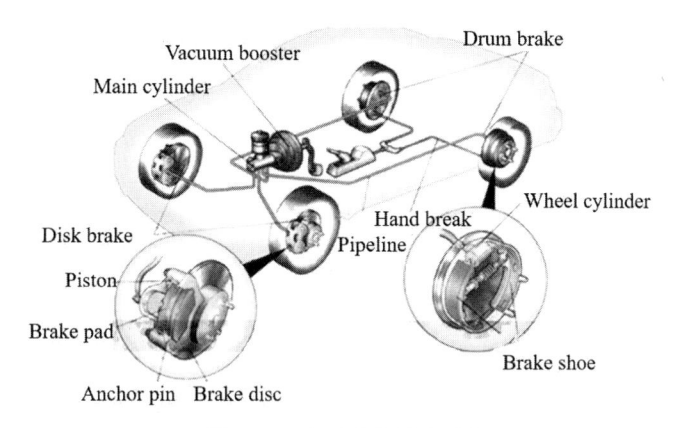

图 7.42　液压助力制动系统

Fig.7.42　Hydraulic brake system

液压制动系统包括制动踏板、推杆、助力器、主缸、制动控制阀以及制动器，如图 7.43 所示。助力器提供额外的制动力来辅助驾驶员使其制动更加便利。主缸内产生油压。通常制动系统采用双回路液压制动系统以保证当一条回路失效时汽车仍能保证安全。

Hydraulic brake system consists of brake pedal, push rod, booster, main cylinder, brake fluid control valve and breaker (Fig.7.43). Booster provides extra brake force and assists driver to operate easily. Main cylinder creates oil pressure. Usually there is a dual-circuit layout in hydraulic brake system in order to ensure security when one circuit is in failure.

液压控制阀产生变动的液压力以防止制动器抱死。在制动阶段，滑移率达到 15%～20%，制动力最大（当制动器完全抱死时，滑移率为 100%）。这种系统被称为防抱死制动系统。

Brake fluid control valve creates variable fluid pressure to avoid being locked on braker. In brake process, the slip ratio reaches 15%–20%, the brake force becomes the biggest (When braker is completely locked, the slip ratio is 100%). That is called anti-lock brake system.

制动器被分为两类：盘式制动器和鼓式制动器。鼓式制动器包括轮缸、制动蹄、制动鼓，如图 7.44 所示。当踩下制动踏板时，制动液进入轮缸，推动制动蹄张开产生摩擦力来使得车辆减速直至停止。

Braker is divided into two categories: disc brakes and drum brakes. Drum braker consists of wheel cylinder, brake shoes, brake drum. When press down brake pedal, brake fluid enters into wheel cylinder, push brake shoes stretch out, create friction force, and slow down the moving vehicle till to standstill (Fig.7.44).

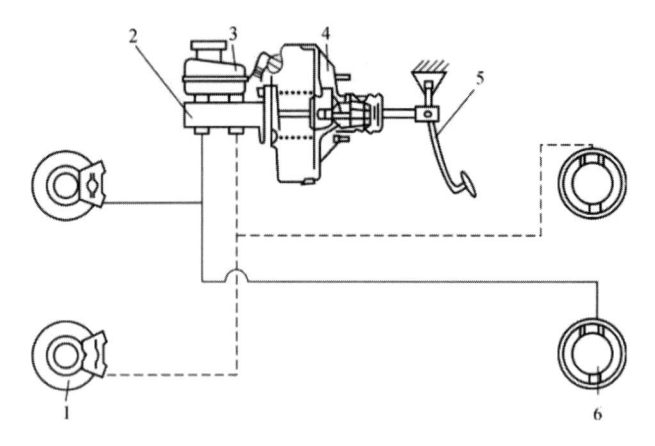

1—前制动器；2—制动主缸；3—储液罐；4—真空助力器；5—制动踏板；6—后制动器
1-Front brake; 2-Main cylinder; 3-Oil reservoir; 4- Vacuum booster; 5-Brake pedal; 6-Rear brake

图 7.43　液压助力制动系统原理

Fig.7.43　The principle of hydraulic brake system

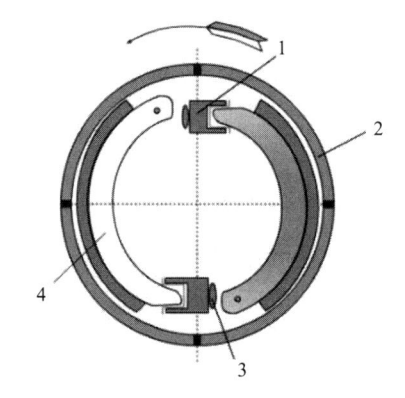

1—轮缸；2—制动鼓；3—支撑销；4—制动蹄
1-Wheel cylinder; 2-Brake drum; 3-Holding pin; 4-Brake toe

图 7.44　鼓式制动器结构与原理

Fig.7.44　The structure and principle of drum braker

盘式制动器包括制动盘、制动钳、制动活塞、制动块、摩擦片等，如图 7.45 所示。和鼓式制动器类似，盘式制动器的液压力作用在轮缸活塞上，使得卡钳两侧的摩擦片与制动盘进行摩擦产生制动。

Disc brake includes brake disc, brake caliper, brake piston, brake pad, friction plate and so on (Fig.7.45). Similar to the drum brake, the liquid pressure of the disc brake acts on the piston of the wheel cylinder, driving the friction plate on both sides of the caliper and the brake disc to create friction and to achieve the purpose of braking.

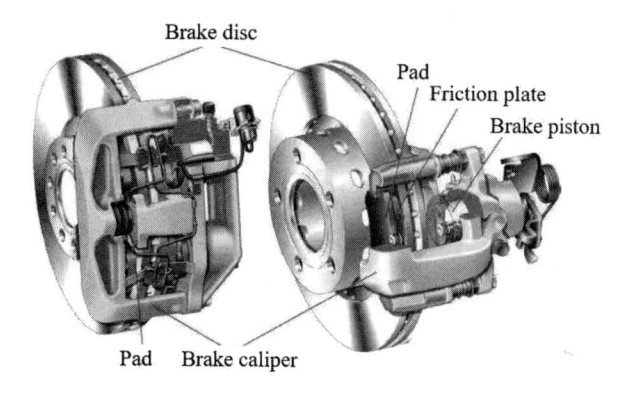

图 7.45 盘式制动器结构

Fig.7.45 The structure of disk brake

气压制动系统结构较为复杂，制动效能较高，一般用于重型车辆，如图 7.46 所示。气压制动系统主要包括空气压缩机、压缩空气回路、油水分离器、主制动阀、空气储存罐、制动气室、空气压力调节器以及空气压力表等。

Pneumatic brake system has complicated construction. It can get high braking efficiency and usually used in heavy vehicles (Fig.7.46). Pneumatic brake system is mainly composed of air compressor, compression air circuit, oil and water separator, main brake valve, air reserve tin, air brake house, air pressure regulator and air pressure gauge.

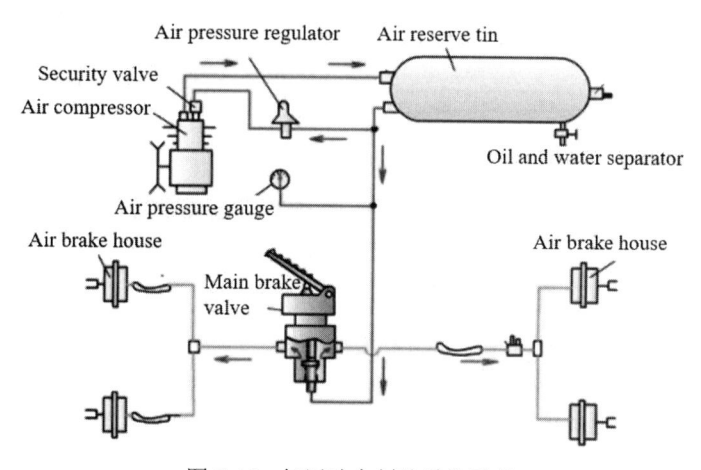

图 7.46 气压助力制动系统原理

Fig.7.46 Pneumatic brake system

习　题

一、选择题

1. 离合器踏板自由行程中消除了离合器中（　）与（　）之间的间隙。
   A．压盘与离合器盖　　　　　　　　　B．离合器盖与飞轮

C．分离指与分离轴承　　　　　　　D．分离轴承与分离套筒
2．以下哪项最有可能是手动挡轿车所采用的离合器类型（　　）。
　　A．膜片弹簧式离合器　　　　　　B．中央弹簧式离合器
　　C．斜置弹簧式离合器　　　　　　D．多片湿式离合器
3．当驾驶手动挡汽车爬坡度非常高的坡时应挂（　　），此时挡位传动比有可能（　　）。
　　A．5挡，小于1　　　　　　　　　B．1挡，大于1
　　C．5挡，大于1　　　　　　　　　D．1挡，小于1
4．直行时差速器行星齿轮为（　　），左转过程中行星齿轮为（　　）。
　　A．自转，公转　　　　　　　　　B．公转，公转
　　C．自转，自转　　　　　　　　　D．公转，自转
5．以下属于金属带式自动变速器简称的是（　　）。
　　A．DSG　　　　B．DCT　　　　C．CVT　　　　D．CRV
6．以下（　　）不属于独立悬架。
　　A．麦弗逊式　　B．五连杆式　　C．双叉臂式　　D．扭力梁式
7．汽车转向时外侧车轮转角（　　）内侧车轮的转角。
　　A．大于　　　　B．小于　　　　C．等于　　　　D．约等于
8．转弯半径是指由转向中心到（　　）。
　　A．内转向轮与地面接触点间的距离　　B．外转向轮与地面接触点间的距离
　　C．内转向轮之间的距离　　　　　　　D．外转向轮之间的距离
9．以下不属于汽车制动系统的是（　　）。
　　A．鼓式制动器　　　　　　　　　B．储液罐
　　C．通风盘式制动器　　　　　　　D．转向节
10．以下不属于汽车底盘组成的是（　　）
　　A．传动系统　　　　　　　　　　B．悬架与车架
　　C．转向与制动系统　　　　　　　D．曲轴

二、简答题

1．膜片弹簧离合器的组成有哪些？
2．自由间隙是如何定义的？
3．手动变速器由哪些部分组成？
4．常见的万向节有哪几种？
5．后驱动桥由哪几部分组成？说出其名称。
6．动力从发动机到车轮经过哪些部件？
7．悬架有哪些种类，分别应用在哪些车型上？
8．转向系统的分类有哪些？
9．助力转向系统有哪些分类？
10．制动系统有哪些分类，分别应用在哪些车型上？

第 8 章　汽车电气设备

Electric equipments

电气设备包括充电系统、起动系统、点火系统和照明系统。

Electric equipments consist of Charging System, Starting System, Ignition System and Lighting System.

8.1　充 电 系 统

Charging system

充电系统为蓄电池充电，并为电气设备供电，如火花塞、喇叭、灯、加热器、起动机等，如图 8.1 所示。

充电系统主要由铅酸蓄电池和发电机组成。电池储存电力。发电机发电并给电池充电。电池中的电量由发电机维持。

A charging system charges battery and supplies electricity for electrical equipments, such as spark plug, horn, lights, heater, starter and so on (Fig.8.1). Charging system mainly consists of lead-acid battery and generator. A battery stores electricity. A generator creates electricity and charge battery. The electricity level in battery is maintained by generator.

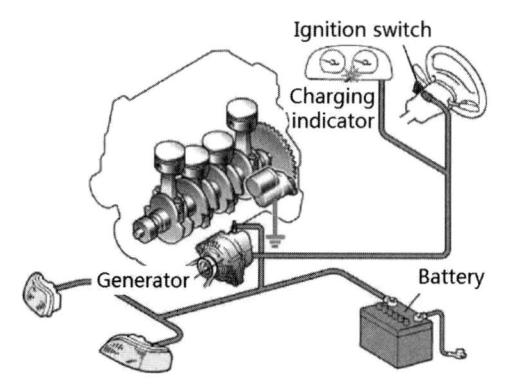

图 8.1　充电系统

Fig.8.1　Charging system

1. 铅酸蓄电池

　　Lead-acid battery

（1）铅酸蓄电池工作原理。铅酸蓄电池是一种产生电压和输出电流的电化学装置，如

图 8.2 所示。蓄电池是当今汽车所用的主要电能来源。当充电时，蓄电池将电能转变成化学能。当放电时，它将化学能转变成电能，从而产生电流。

Operating principle of lead-acid battery. A lead-acid battery is an electrochemical device (Fig.8.2). The battery is the primary "source" of electrical energy used in vehicles. When charging, the battery converts electricity into chemical energy, and when discharging, it converts chemical energy into electricity, producing a current.

图 8.2　铅酸蓄电池

Fig.8.2　Lead-acid Battery

必须对电路进行保护，以防电路短路（意外触地）而导致线路烧毁。还要对电气设备进行保护以防过载。在电路中，电路保护装置必须与所要保护的电气设备或线路串联连接。常见的电路保护装置有熔断器、易熔线和电路断电器，见表 8.1。

It is necessary to protect electrical circuit against shorting (accidentally touching ground) that could burn up the wiring. Electrical units must be protected against overloads also. In circuits, circuit protection devices must be installed in series with the electrical devices or wiring to be protected. The common types of circuit protection devices are fuse, fusible link and circuit breaker, see Table 8.1.

所有的汽车熔断器通常都装在一个被称为熔断器盒或继电器盒的支架上。一条电路可以用一个用作熔断器的特种导线来保护。这根线被称为易熔线。

All of the vehicle fuses are usually contained in a holder called fuse block or relay block. A circuit may be protected by a special wire that acts as a fuse. This wire is called a fusible link.

电路断电器通过双金属片和一组触点来为电路的其他部分供电。当电流超过断电器额定电流值时，双金属片就会发热并弯曲，从而将触点断开。一旦冷却下来，电路断电器会将电路重新闭合。

A circuit breaker feeds current through a bimetallic strip and a set of points to the remainder of the circuit. When the current exceeds the breaker's rating, the bimetallic strip heats and bends to separate the points. Once it cools, it will close the circuit.

继电器用来传导能使开关过热而损坏的大电流。继电器是一些能使电路触点闭合的电磁开关。大多数继电器通常都装在继电器盒或接线盒（J/B）内。

Relays are used to direct large current flows that might overheat and damage a switch, they are a type of solenoid switch that closes electrical contacts. Most of relays are usually contained in relay block and junction block (J/B).

表 8.1　丰田汽车电路图所用的电路保护装置

Table 8.1　Circuit protection devices used for Toyota automotive wiring diagrams

Illustration	Symbol	Name	Abbreviation
		Fuse	Fuse
		Medium current fuse	M-Fuse
		High current fuse	H-Fuse
		Fusible link	FL
		Circuit breaker	CB

蓄电池上有两个接线柱。一个是正极，另一个是负极。连接电线时，火线安装在正极接线柱上，接地线安装在负极接线柱上。否则，蓄电池将损坏。

There are two terminal posts on a battery. One is of positive and another is of negative. When connect wires, firewire is fitted on positive post and earth wire is fitted on negative post. Otherwise, the battery will be damaged.

如今，几乎所有的电池都是免费维护的。电池上有个孔。孔里有一个小球。如果小球的颜色是绿色，则表明电池状况良好。黄色代表电量不足。红色表示蓄电池损坏。

Nowadays, almost all batteries are of free maintenance. There is hole on battery and a small ball inside the hole. If the colour of small ball is green, the battery is in good condition. Yellow colour stands for electricity shortage. Red colour stands for battery damage.

（2）车辆蓄电池的特点：

①铅酸蓄电池输出直流电。（家用灯使用交流电，电路电压通常为220V。）

②铅酸蓄电池电压约为12V。通常汽油发动机车辆配备一个蓄电池，柴油发动机车辆配备

两个蓄电池（串联）。因此，汽油发动机车辆电路上的工作电压为12V，柴油发动机车辆电路上的工作电压为24V。

③电解液由硫酸和纯水组成。之前，电池需要保养（在电池中注入一些纯净水）。但现在所有的电池都是终身免维护的，如图8.3所示。

④硫酸是一种强腐蚀性化学物质。它可以烧毁人体以及除了玻璃和塑料外的一切，使土地硬化。因此，必须对蓄电池中的电解液进行特殊处理。（切勿用皮肤接触硫酸。）

Features of battery on vehicle:

①A lead-acid battery outputs direct current (DC). (Family light makes use of alternative current(AC). Circuit voltage is usually 220 Volts.)

②A lead-acid battery voltage is about 12 Volts. Usually petrol engine vehicle equips one battery, and diesel engine vehicle equips two batteries (series connection). So working voltage on petrol engine vehicle circuit is 12 Volts and 24 Volts on diesel engine vehicle circuit.

③ Electrolyte is composed of sulphuric acid and pure water. Before, battery needs maintenance (Fill some pure water in battery). But now all of batteries are of free maintenance over its all lifetime (Fig.8.3).

④Sulphuric acid is heavy corrosive chemical. It can burn out human body and everything except for glass and plastic, harden land. Hence electrolyte in battery has to be treated specially. (Never touch sulphuric acid with skin.)

图 8.3　蓄电池观察孔

Fig.8.3　Battery observation hole

2. 发电机

Generator

（1）发电机工作原理。发电机是现代汽车充电系统的主要组成部分，如图8.4所示，典型交流发电机的组成如图8.5所示。它由发动机驱动发电。电能为电池充电，同时为电气设备供电。

电力输出有一个正极。发电机外壳为接地端。正极与外壳绝缘。

Operating principle of generator. Generator is the main part of modern vehicle charging system

(Fig.8.4). Composition of a typical alternator is as shown in Fig.8.5. It is driven by engine to create electricity. The electricity charges the battery and at the same time provides power to electrical equipments.

There is a positive pole for electricity output. The shell of generator is earth end. The positive pole is insulated from the shell.

图 8.4 发电机

Fig.8.4 Generator

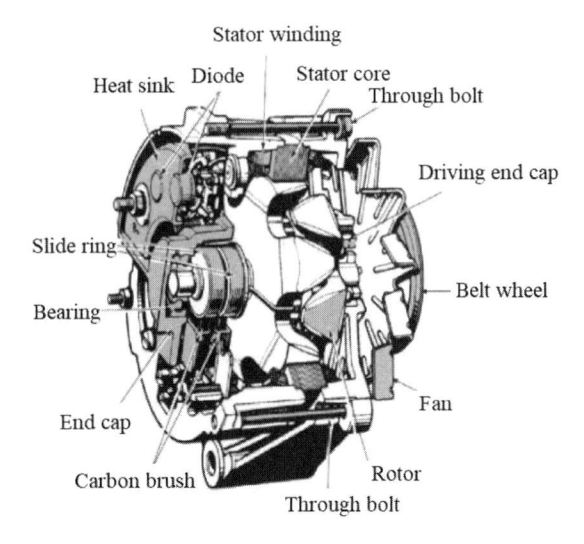

图 8.5 典型交流发电机的组成

Fig.8.5 Composition of a typical alternator

（2）发电机的特点。

①输出的电是直流电。无论发动机在低转速或高转速下工作，输出电压均稳定在 12～14V 左右。

②当发电机工作时，它会产生大量热量，这些热量应及时释放。切勿遮盖发电机周围的

任何物体。

③如果水进入发电机，会导致短路，发电机可能损坏。

Features of generator.

① The output of electricity is direct current. The output voltage is steady around 12-14V no matter engine works in a low or high revolution speed.

② When a generator works, it creates a large amount of heat which should release in time. Never cover anything around a generator.

③ If water enters generator, it causes short circuit, and generator maybe damaged.

8.2 起动系统

Starting system

起动系统的作用是将电池的动力通过起动机转化为机械能，再传递给发动机飞轮，使发动机运转，如图 8.6 所示。

The function of starting system is to transfer the power from the battery into mechanical energy through the starter, and then pass it to the engine flywheel, so that the engine is running (Fig.8.6).

（1）起动系统工作原理。现代内燃机是由电起动马达（或起动机）起动的。

Operating principle of starting system. Modern internal combustion engines are started by electric starting motor (or starter).

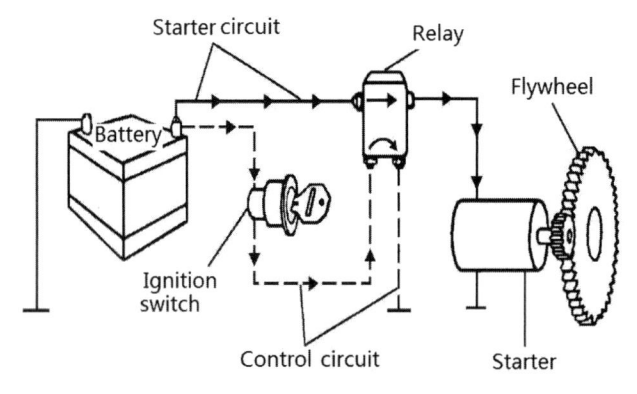

图 8.6 起动系统电路

Fig.8.6 Start system circuit

起动系统由蓄电池、点火开关和起动机组成。为了驱动起动机，将点火开关转到 START（点火开关有三个位置：OFF、ON 和 ST），这将闭合起动电路。起动机与飞轮上的齿圈啮合，从而驱动曲轴旋转，直到发动机自行工作。

起动机是一台电动机，它将电能转换为机械能，如图 8.7 所示。

A starting system consists of battery, ignition switch and starter. To drive the starter, the ignition switch is turned to START (There are three positions for a ignition switch: OFF, ON and ST), which closes a starting electrical circuit. The starter engages the ring gear on flywheel, which drives the crankshaft rotate till engine works by itself.

The starter is an electric motor. It converts electricity energy to mechanic energy (Fig.8.7).

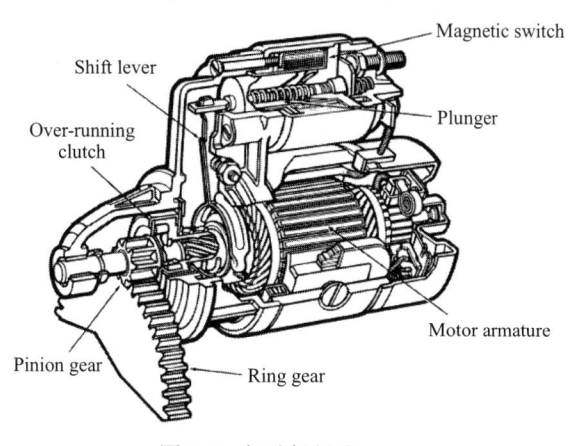

图 8.7　起动机组成

Fig.8.7　Starting motor components

（2）起动机的特点。

①起动时，电路电流很大。连续启动几次后，每隔一段时间（时段）从电池中回收电能。否则，蓄电池可能会因过度放电而损坏。

②起动机上的一些带电导线（火线）是裸露在外的（尽可能释放热量）。要远离任何杂质，以避免短路。

Features of starter.

①When starting, the circuit current is large. After starting several times continuously, take a time interval (time break) to recover electrical energy from battery. Otherwise, the battery maybe damaged due to over discharging.

②Some live wire (firewire) is bare on starter (releasing heat as much as possible). Keep away from any impurity to avoid short circuit.

8.3　点　火　系　统

Ignition system

点火系统的作用是产生点燃发动机缸内空气燃油混合气的火花。点火系统可分为两个部分：初级电路和次级电路。低压初级电路以蓄电池电压（12～14.5V）工作，其任务是在精确地时刻产生让火花塞跳火的信号并发出该信号给点火线圈。点火线圈的作用是将 12V 信号转变成 20000V 以上的高电压。电压升高后，高电压就会到达次级电路，然后再在适当的时刻到达正确的火花塞。

The purpose of the ignition system is to create a spark that will ignite the fuel-air mixture in the cylinder of an engine. The ignition system is divided into two sections, the primary circuit and the secondary circuit. The low-voltage primary circuit operates at battery voltage (12 to 14.5 Volts) and is responsible for generating the signal to fire the spark plug at the exact right time and sending that signal to the ignition coil. The ignition coil is the component that converts the 12 Volts signal into the high 20000+ Volt charge. Once the voltage is stepped up, it goes to the secondary circuit which then directs the charge to the correct spark plug at the right time.

点火系统有三种不同类型。传统式点火系统（图 8.8）是机械与电气设备相结合的系统，没有电子元件。电子式点火系统（图 8.9）在 20 世纪 70 年代初期期间才开始用于批量生产的汽车上，并且随着排放控制装置的出现，更精确的控制和可靠性的改善变得更为重要的时候，电子式点火系统才开始普及起来。最后，无分电器点火系统（图 8.10）在 20 世纪 80 年代才得到应用。该系统总是采用计算机控制并且不再含有运动零件，可靠性大大改善。

There are three distinct types of ignition systems. The conventional ignition system (Fig.8.8) was mechanical and electrical and used no electronics. The electronic ignition system (Fig.8.9) started finding its way to production vehicles during the early 1970s and became popular when better control and improved reliability became important with the advent of emission controls. Finally, the distributorless ignition system (Fig.8.10) became available in the mid 1980s. This system was always computer controlled and contained no moving parts, so reliability was greatly improved.

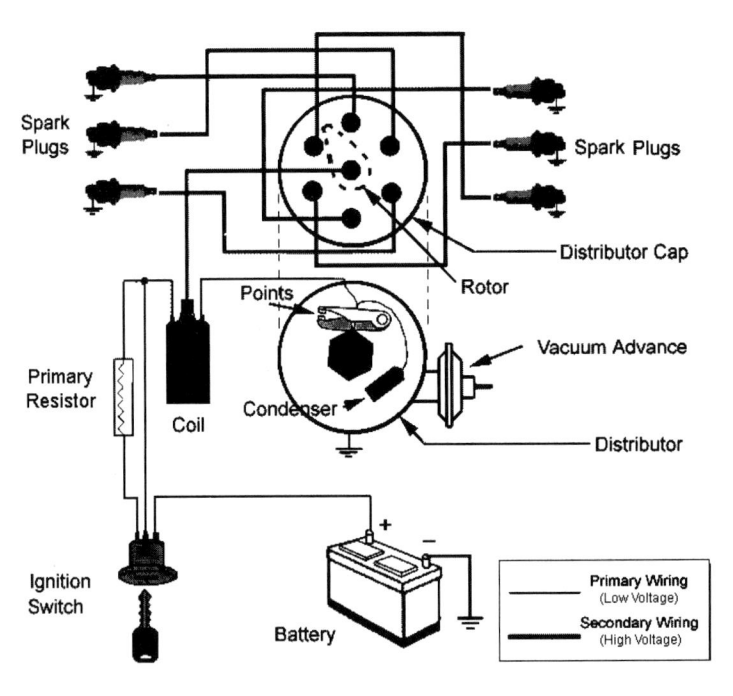

图 8.8　传统式点火系统

Fig.8.8　Conventional ignition system

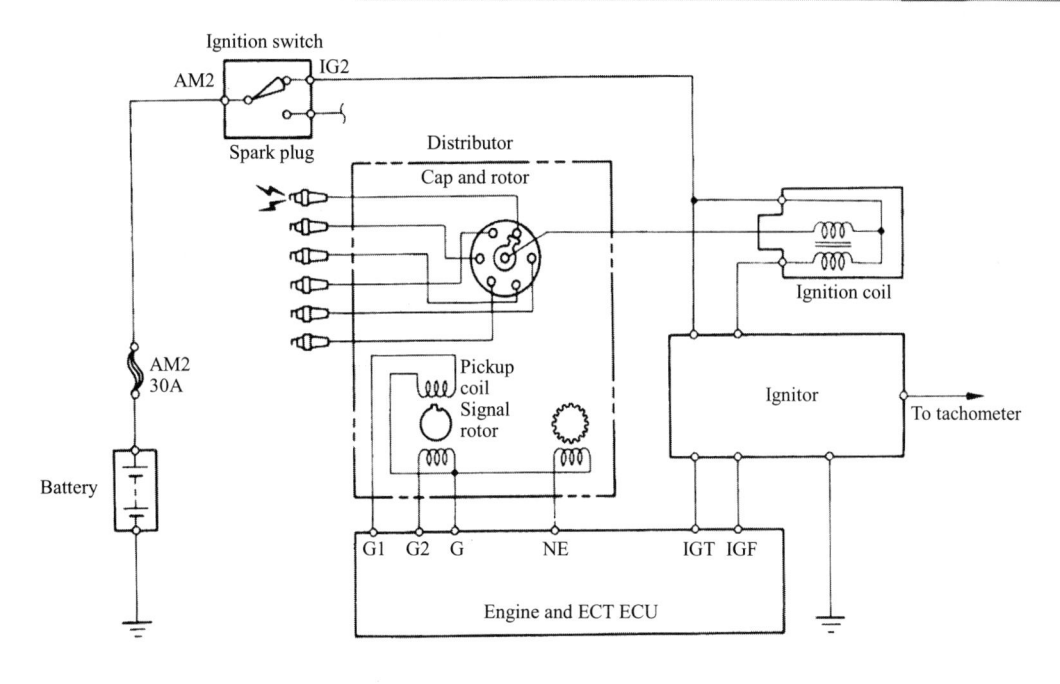

图 8.9　电子式点火系统

Fig.8.9　The electronic ignition system

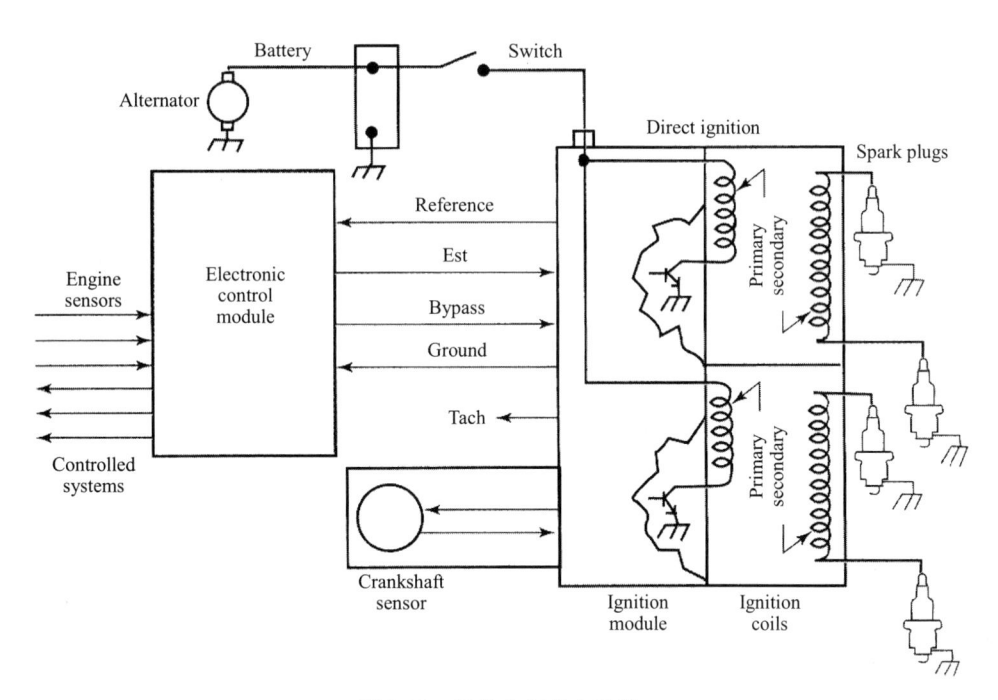

图 8.10　无分电器点火系统

Fig.8.10　The distributorless ignition system

（1）点火系统工作原理。发动机上有两种点火系统：火花点火和压燃。柴油机依靠燃烧室中的高温高压点燃空气—燃料混合物。它被称为压缩点火。在图 8.11 中，零件 2 代表向燃烧室喷射燃油的喷油器。

Operating Principle of Ignition System. There are two types of ignition systems on engine: spark ignition and compression ignition.

A diesel engine relies on the high temperature and high pressure in combustion chamber to ignite the air-fuel mixture. It is called compression ignition. In the Fig.8.11, part 2 stands for injector which sprays fuel to chamber.

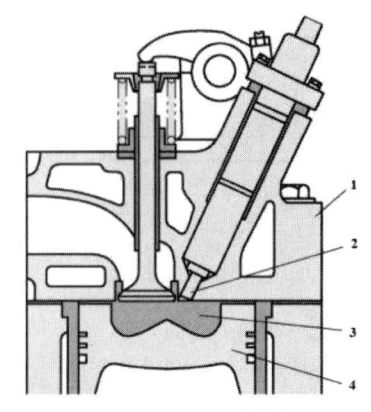

1—汽缸盖；2—喷油器；3—燃烧室；4—活塞
1-Cylinder head; 2-Injector; 3-Combustion chamber; 4-Piston
图 8.11　柴油发动机采用压燃方式

Fig.8.11　Diesel engines make use of compression ignition type

新型汽车的点火系统完全由车载计算机进行控制。一台典型的四缸发动机在一个线圈"包"内将两个线圈装在一起。在有些汽车上，每个气缸都有一个独立的点火线圈，这些线圈直接安装在火花塞的顶部（图 8.12）。对于将点火模块集成到每个线圈总成内的独立点火系统，点火线圈总成的初级侧连接有四个导线（图 8.13）。这四个导线分别是蓄电池正极接线、搭铁线、点火正时信号线和点火确认信号线。PCM 利用点火确认信号来判定点火线圈是否工作。这些点火线圈的初级电路不能用欧姆表进行检测。

The ignition systems on newer automobiles are completely controlled by the on-board computer. A typical 4-cylinder engine has 2 coils that are mounted together in a coil "pack".

On some vehicles, there is an individual coil for each cylinder mounted directly on top of the spark plug (Fig.8.12). The independent ignition system with integrated ignition modules into each coil assembly typically use four wires connected to the primary side of the assembly (Fig.8.13). The four wires consist of battery positive, ground, ignition timing signal, and ignition confirmation signal. The PCM uses the ignition confirmation signal to determine if a coil is not operating. The primary circuits of these coils cannot be tested with an ohmmeter.

这种设计完全消除了高压火花塞线，获得了更好的可靠性。这些系统大多数使用设计寿命超过 10000 英里的火花塞，这就降低了维护成本。

This design completely eliminates the high tension spark plug wires for even better reliability.

Most of these systems use spark plugs that are designed to last over 100000 miles, which cuts down on maintenance costs.

图 8.12　空气—燃料混合物由电火花点燃

Fig.8.12　The air-fuel mixture is ignited by an electrical spark

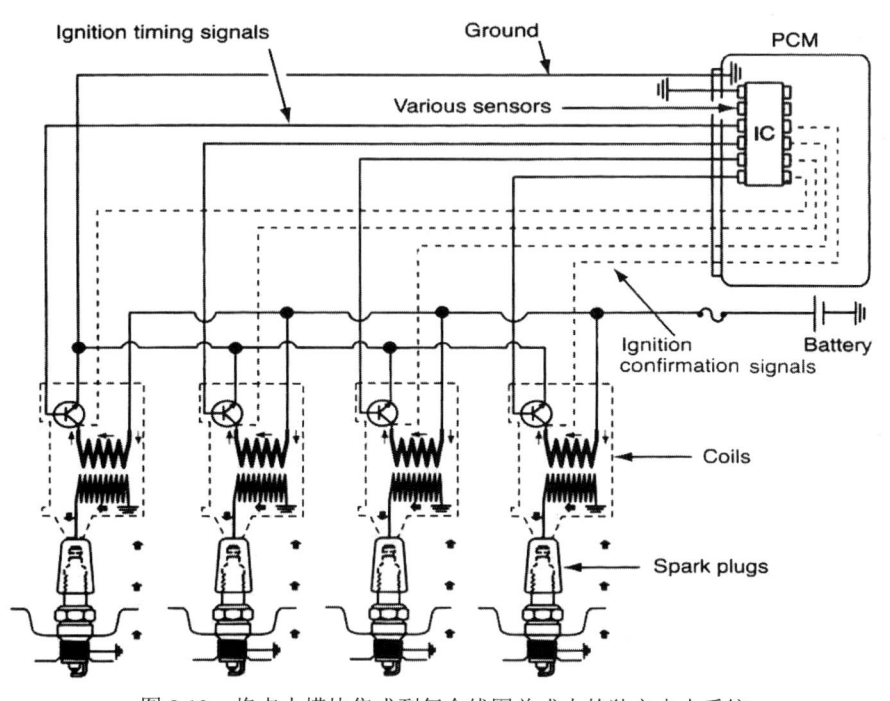

图 8.13　将点火模块集成到每个线圈总成内的独立点火系统

Fig.8.13　A independent ignition system that integrates the ignition module into each coil assembly

点火系统分为两部分，一次电路和二次电路。主电路在蓄电池电压（12V）下工作。它由蓄电池、火线、初级线圈、三极管、地线、点火正时信号线和点火确认信号线组成。二次电路在高压下工作（瞬时电压超过 30000V）。它由线圈、火花塞组成。点火线圈是将 12V 电压转换为高压电压的部件。一旦初级电路被三极管断开，次级电路就会被点火线圈感应到高电压。高压使火花塞产生火花。

The ignition system is divided into two sections, the primary circuit and the secondary circuit.

The primary circuit operates at battery voltage (12V). It consists of battery, fire wire, primary coil, triode, ground wire, ignition timing signal wire and ignition confirmation signal wire.

The secondary circuit operates at high voltage (the instant voltage is more than 30000V). It consists of coil, spark plug. The ignition coil is the component that converts 12V into high volts. Once the primary circuit breaks by triode, the secondary circuit is induced high voltage by ignition coil. The high voltage makes spark plug creates spark.

（2）点火系统特点：

①对于四缸发动机，通常有四个火花塞和四个线圈。

②每个线圈包括两个线圈，第一个线圈的转数更少，第二个线圈的转数更多。

③对于每个火花塞，主电路有四根导线。它们是蓄电池正极、接地、点火正时信号和点火确认信号的导线。

④动力系统控制模块利用点火确认信号来了解线圈是否工作。

⑤瞬时高压可能会让维修人员感到不舒服，但不会导致死亡风险（测试时，通常戴上绝缘手套）。

The feature of ignition system:

①For four-cylinder engine, there are usually four spark plugs and four coils.

②Every coil includes two coils, the primary one with fewer revolutions and the second with much more revolutions.

③For every spark plug, the primary circuit has four wires. They are wires of battery positive, ground, ignition timing signal, and ignition confirmation signal.

④The PCM makes use of the ignition confirmation signal to know if a coil is operating.

⑤The instant high voltage may make a repair worker uncomfortable, but never causes death risk (When testing, usually wear insulating gloves).

8.4 照 明 系 统

Lighting system

（1）照明系统的功能。

①在黑夜驾驶车辆或通过长隧道时照明。

②当驾驶员操作时，例如转弯、制动或倒车时，向驾驶员发出警告信号。

③在异常工况下，如燃油不足、润滑系统压力低，向驾驶员发出报警信号。

④在紧急情况下，例如在高速公路上停车时，向他人发出警告信号。

The function of lighting system:

①Give light when driving vehicle at dark night or pass through long tunnels.

②Give driver a caution signal when driver operates, such as turning, braking or reversing car.

③Give driver an alarm signal in abnormal working condition, such as lack of fuel, low pressure on lubrication system.

④Give other person caution signal in emergency, such as parking on highway.

（2）前照灯和尾灯如图 8.14 所示。在夜间或黑暗的白天驾驶车辆或通过长隧道时，前照灯向道路发出光束。

前照灯上有两个光束。一个是近光束，另一个是远光束。当我们在城市道路上开车时，我们应该使用短光束，以避免照射到对面的司机。

Headlight and taillight is shown as Fig.8.14. Headlights give light beam to the road when driving vehicle at night or in dark day or pass through long tunnels. There are two light beams on a headlight. One is near light beam, another is far light beam. When we drive a car on city road, we should use short light beam to avoid shining opposite driver. When we drive vehicle on highway, we should use far light beam to shine farther distance on road.

当我们在公路上开车时，我们应该用远光束在公路上照更远的距离。当我们打开大灯开关时，尾灯会提醒我们后面的司机，让司机注意到我们，并与我们保持足够的距离。该操作非常重要，尤其是在隧道运行中。

When we turn on headlight switch, the taillight works to remind drivers behind us, let the driver notice us and keep enough distance with us. The operation is very important especially in tunnel running.

图 8.14 前照灯与尾灯

Fig.8.14 Headlight and taillight

（3）转向信号和危险警示灯如图 8.15 所示。转向信号灯向其他驾驶员或车外人员提供转向指示。紧急情况下使用危险警示灯。例如，我们开车时遇到一些麻烦。我们必须在紧急通道上停车。在这种情况下，我们必须打开危险警示灯开关。所有转向灯都以高频闪烁，以提醒其他驾驶员。

Turn signal and hazard warning light is shown as Fig.8.15. Turn signal light gives turning indication to other drivers or person out of the vehicle.

Hazard warning light is used in emergency. For example, we get some trouble when we are driving a car. We have to stop the car on emergency passage. In this case, we must turn on hazard warning light switch. All the four turning lights glitter at a high frequency to remind other drivers.

雾天使用雾灯。它发出黄色光束，帮助驾驶员清楚地看到路面。

Fog light is used in foggy day. It gives out yellow colour beam to assist driver to see road surface clearly.

图 8.15 转向信号和危险警示灯

Fig.8.15 Turn light and hazard warning light

（4）刹车灯和倒车灯如图 8.16 所示。刹车灯（制动灯）在制动时发出信号。红灯亮起是为了提醒我们后面的司机。倒车时，倒车灯发出信号。这些灯是白色的。

Stop light and back up light is shown as Fig.8.16. Stop light (brake light) gives signal when braking. The lights work in red color to remind drivers behind us. Back up light gives signal when reversing car. The lights work in white color.

图 8.16 刹车灯和倒车灯

Fig.8.16 Stop light and back up light

（5）指示灯系统如图 8.17 所示。指示板上有许多指示灯和仪表。指示灯提醒驾驶员照明系统是否工作，如转向灯、前照灯或是否存在缺油等警告。仪表显示工作参数，如发动机转速表、车速、行驶距离、冷却温度和燃油量。

Indicator light system is shown as Fig.8.17. There are many indication lights and gauges on indication board. Indication lights remind driver if the light system works, such as turning lights, headlights or if there is something caution such as fuel tortage.The gauges show working parameters, such as revolution speed gauge of engine, vehicle speed, driving distance, cooling temperature and fuel amount.

当点火开关转到 on 位置时，一些信号灯将闪烁一段时间，然后熄灭。如果出现故障，信号灯将一直亮起，显示相关故障，如预热器故障、发动机故障、电路电压低、润滑故障、安全带解锁、手制动器工作、燃油短缺等。

When the ignition switch is turned to the on position, some signal lights will flash for a period of time and then go out. If a fault occurs, the signal signal light will remain on to indicate a fault, such as pre-heater fault, engine fault, low circuit voltage, lubrication fault, safety safety belt unlock, hand brake operation, fuel shortage, etc.

图 8.17　指示灯系统

Fig.8.17　Indicator light system

指示板上符号的含义如表 8.2 所示。

The meaning of the symbols on the indicator board are shown in Table 8.2.

表 8.2　指示板上符号的含义

Table 8.2　The meaning of symbols on indication board

车门打开（关闭不完全） car door open (closed incompletely)	冷却系统指示 cooling system indicator
驻车（手）制动工作 parking (hand) brake working	安全气囊故障 air bag fault
电力故障 electricity fault	防抱死制动系统故障 anti-lock brake system fault
制动器故障 brake fault	示廓指示 outline indicator

续表

	 润滑系统故障 lubrication system fault		 燃料量指标 fuel amount indicator
	 风挡玻璃清洁水 windshield glass cleaning water		 安全带指示 safety belt indicator
	 前后雾灯指示 front, rear fog light indicator		 超速挡位指示器 overspeed gear indicator
	 转向灯指示器 turning light indicator		 内循环指标 inner circulation indicator
	 远光灯指示器 far headlight indicator		 近光灯指示器 near headlight indicator

习　　题

一、选择题

1. 蓄电池观察孔红色表示（　　）。
   A．电池状况良好　　　　　　　　B．电量不足
   C．损坏　　　　　　　　　　　　D．充满电
2. 蓄电池在充电时将化学能转化为（　　）。
   A．化学能　　　B．电能　　　C．太阳能　　　D．风能
3. 下列不属于起动系统的是（　　）。
   A．蓄电池　　　B．点火开关　　　C．起动机　　　D．发电机

4. （　　）是机械与电气设备相结合的系统，没有电子元件。
   A．传统点火系统　　　　　　　　B．电子点火系统
   C．微机点火系统　　　　　　　　D．独立点火系统
5. 制动灯是（　　）色。
   A．白色　　　　B．黄色　　　　C．红色　　　　D．橙色
6. 倒车灯是（　　）色。
   A．白色　　　　B．黄色　　　　C．红色　　　　D．橙色

二、简答题

1．汽车电气系统包括哪些部分？
2．简述铅酸蓄电池的工作原理。
3．简述车辆蓄电池的特点。
4．简述发电机的特点。
5．简述点火系统的特点。
6．简述照明系统的功能。

第 9 章　新能源汽车

New energy vehicles

新能源汽车在节能环保方面具有巨大优势，目前得到迅猛发展。新能源汽车主要包括纯电动汽车，混合动力电动汽车和燃料电池车。

New energy vehicles are thriving now with huge advantages in energy saving and environment protection. New energy vehicles contains pure electric vehicles (EVs), hybrid electric vehicles (HEVs) and fuel cell vehicles (FCVs).

9.1　新能源汽车优缺点

Advantages and disadvantages of new energy vehicles

1. 新能源汽车优点

   Advantages of new energy vehicles

（1）新能源汽车，如混合动力汽车，比汽油机或柴油机车辆产生更少的二氧化碳气体。二氧化碳气体诱发了温室效应。

It produces less carbon dioxide (CO_2) which induces "greenhouse effect" than petrol or diesel engine vehicles, such as hybrid electric vehicles.

（2）当使用新能源时（比如氢燃料，这种车辆被称为燃料电池车），新能源汽车不产生碳排放。因此新能源汽车减少了诸如二氧化碳和一氧化碳的温室气体和有毒气体的排放，对环境保护有利。

It produces no carbon emissions when using renewable energy (such as hydrogen fuel. This kind of vehicle is called as fuel cell vehicle). Hence it reduces greenhouse gas and poisonous gas emissions such as carbon dioxide (CO_2) and carbon monoxide (CO). It is a profit for the environment.

（3）使用新能源汽车便宜，因为：
①制造成本低。
②电比汽油或柴油价格低。

It is cheaper to run because:
①Manufacture cost is low.
②The price of electricity is cheaper than petrol or diesel.

（4）新能源汽车降低了噪声污染。

It reduces noise pollution.

（5）新能源汽车在整个生命周期（生产、使用和报废后处理）对环境的影响小。

It takes less environmental impacts across their life-cycle (manufacture, use and disposal after discard).

2. 新能源汽车缺点

Disadvantages of new energy vehicles

（1）蓄电池，特别是新型蓄电池（如锂基电池）没有足够的储存容量，所以车辆运行的续驶里程短。

Batteries, especially new kinds of battery (such as lithium-based battery) have not enough storage capacity. So the vehicle runs in short range.

（2）蓄电池的使用寿命短。工作两三年后，电池充电能力下降。

Batteries have short life time. After working 2 or 3 years, the charging ability descends largely.

9.2 纯电动汽车构造及工作原理

Structure and operation control principle of pure electric vehicles

1. 纯电动汽车控制原理

Operation control principle of electric vehicles

以前，从现有的内燃机车辆变换为电动汽车，主要是应用电动机驱动装置和蓄电池组件替代内燃机和燃油箱，而保留所有其他组件。但一些缺陷比如重量大、灵活性低以及车辆性能下降等已导致这类型式电动汽车的逐渐消失。在此领域，基于原来的车身和车架设计，现代电动汽车已按诉求制造出来。它满足只有电动汽车才有的结构要求，并利用了电驱动的灵活性。

Previously, the EV was mainly converted from the existing ICEV by replacing the IC engine and fuel tank with an electric motor drive and battery pack while retaining all the other components. Drawbacks such as its heavy weight, lower flexibility, and performance degradation have caused the use of this type of EV to fade out. In its place, the modern EV is purposely built, based on original body and frame designs. This satisfies the structure requirements unique to EVs and makes use of the greater flexibility of electric propulsion.

现代电驱动系统如图 9.1 所示。该电驱动系由三个主要的子系统组成：电动机驱动子系统、能源子系统和辅助子系统。电动机驱动子系统由车辆控制器、电力逆变器、电动机、机械传动装置和驱动轮组成；能源子系统包含能源、能量管理单元和能量的燃料续供单元；辅助子系统由功率控制单元、车内温度控制单元和附加的供给单元。

A modern electric drive train is conceptually illustrated in Fig.9.1. The drive train consists of three major subsystems: electric motor propulsion, energy source, and auxiliary. The electric propulsion sub-system is comprised of the vehicle controller, the power electronic converter, the electric motor, mechanical transmission, and driving wheels. The energy source sub-system involves the energy source, the energy management unit, and the energy refueling unit. The auxiliary sub-system consists of the power steering unit, the hotel climate control unit, and the auxiliary supply unit.

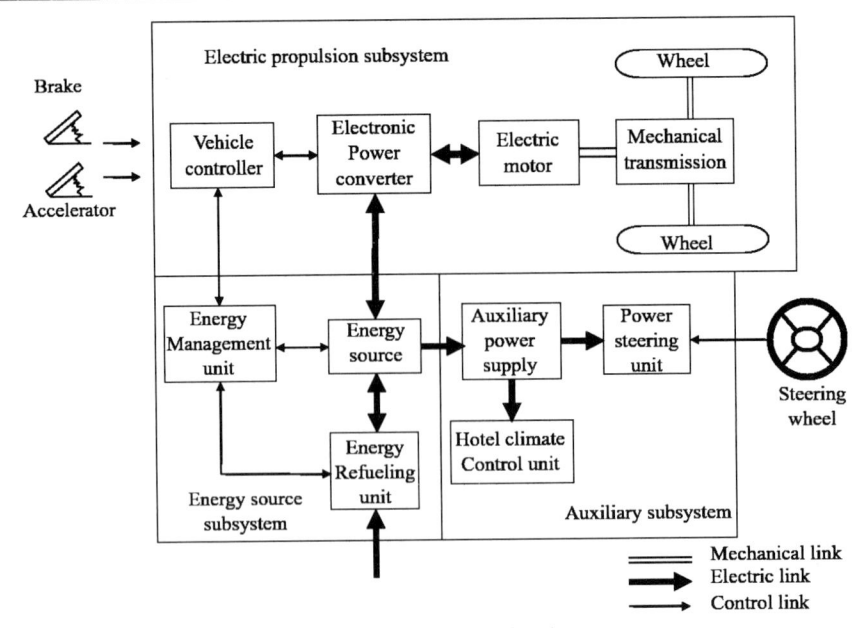

图 9.1　电动汽车结构图解

Fig.9.1　Conceptual illustration of a general EV configuration

2. 纯电动汽车构造和工作原理

Structure and operation principle of EVs

纯电动汽车（通常称为 BEVs 或 EVs，B 代表蓄电池）组成如图 9.2 所示。

Pure electric vehicles (usually called BEVs or EVs, B from battery) shows in Fig.9.2.

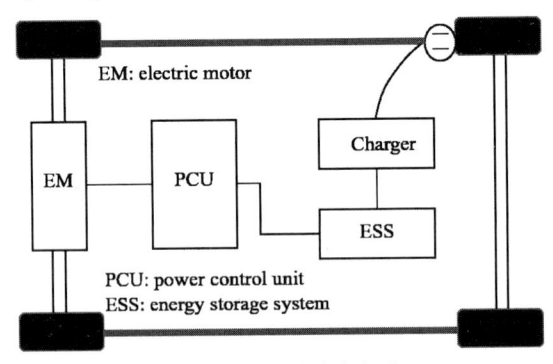

图 9.2　纯电动汽车组成

Fig.9.2　Components of BEVs

纯电动汽车结构及工作原理：

充电器是用于充电的装置。

能量储存系统用于储存电能，主要装置是电池，它通常决定了汽车的性能和行驶里程。

能量控制单元控制从能量储存到电动机的电力。

电动机驱动车辆运行。

In construction and operation of BEVs:

Charger is a charging system.

Energy storage system (ESS) stores electric energy. The main device is battery which generally determines the performance and operating range of the vehicle.

Power control unit (PCU) controls electric power from battery to EM.

Electric motor (EM) drives vehicle.

（1）电池种类。纯电动汽车上有三种电池：铅酸蓄电池、镍基电池和锂基电池。铅酸蓄电池比镍基电池和锂基电池便宜，在低速车辆上应用较多。镍基电池和锂基电池逐渐用在电动汽车，特别是豪华轿车，得益于其较高的能量和功率密度，以及较长的使用寿命。

Types of batteries. There are three types of batteries available in pure electric vehicles: lead-acid battery, nickel-based battery, and lithium battery. The lead-acid battery is less expensive than the other two types and is widely used in low-speed vehicles.

The nickel-based battery and lithium battery are increasingly being used in electric road vehicles especially in luxurious vehicles because of its higher energy and power density, and longer service life.

（2）电动机种类。电动汽车上通常用两种电动机：直流电动机和交流电动机。直流电动机结构简单，尺寸小，通常作动力源使用，如油泵、玻璃升降电机、雨刷电机等。交流电动机能产生大的驱动力，主要用于驱动电动汽车运行。

The types of motors. Two types of electric motors are commonly used in electric vehicles: direct current (DC) motor and alternative current (AC) motor. DC motor has simple configuration and small size. It is widely used as power source such as fuel pump, glass lifting motor, rain brusher motor and so on. AC motor can create big driving force, so it is mainly used as power source in EVs driving.

（3）纯电动汽车特点。

①纯电动汽车重量轻，制造成本低，维护费用低。

②无论硬件还是软件，动力控制单元很复杂，很多研究工作还在继续。

③一旦电池技术难关被克服，纯电动汽车将完全取代内燃机车辆。

Characteristics of EVs.

①EVs weighs light and manufacture cost is low. The running and maintenance cost is low.

②Power control unit (PCU) is a complicated system on either software or hardware. Some research work on it is continuous.

③Once the technology hurdle on battery is overcome, EVs will replace IC engine vehicles completely.

9.3　混合动力电动汽车构造及工作原理
Structure and operation control principle of HEVs

1. 混合动力电动汽车组成

   Components of hybrid electric vehicles

以内燃机作为动力源，电动力是另一个动力源，这种车辆被称为混合动力电动汽车，目前已批量生产并得到实际应用。有些混合动力电动汽车（如燃料电池混合动力汽车，称为

FCHEVs）没有内燃机，但是同时有蓄电池和燃料电池，由电动机驱动，这种结构目前少用。

Vehicles with hybrid drives, consisting of an IC engine as one power source and electric motors as the other one, are called hybrid electric vehicles (HEVs). They are currently mass-produced and in practice use. Some hybrid cars (such as fuel cell hybrid electric vehicles, namely FCHEVs) have no IC, but have both batteries and fuel cells, and are driven by electric traction motor. It is seldom used by now.

2. 混合动力电动汽车常用的工作状态

General operation states of hybrid electric cars

混合动力电动汽车的内燃机和电动机有可能以不同状态共同工作，以实现最好的燃油经济性和最佳排放。共有四种状态（或环境）：

The hybrid cars possess the possibility of the internal combustion engine and electric motors working together in different states to give the best economic performance and the best exhaust emission. There are 4 kinds of states (or circumstances):

（1）汽车起步，并加速至15mph，车辆通常仅由电动机驱动，使用蓄电池供电。

When driving away and up to 15mph, the vehicle often uses only electric motor to power the car, drawing on the battery for the energy source.

（2）在很高的加速阶段，内燃机和电动机都工作以增大车轮驱动力。当电动机消耗蓄电池电能时，汽油机还要驱动发动机发电。

During heavy acceleration, both the engine and electric motors work to increase power to the wheels. The petrol engine also powers the generator while the electric motor uses electricity from the battery.

（3）一般巡航速度行驶时，汽油机单独工作，以最高效能运行。

When cruising normally, the petrol engine is used solely and it operates most efficiently.

（4）当减速行驶或制动时，混合动力电动汽车可通过再生制动系统捕获汽车行驶动能，转变成电能储存于蓄电池中，以备后用。

When slowing or braking, hybrid cars can capture the energy of vehicle motion by regenerative braking system. In this case, the revolving wheels power the generator which produces electricity and stores it in the battery for later use.

3. 混合动力电动汽车结构及工作原理

Construction and operation of hybrid electric vehicles

混合动力电动汽车包括串联、并联和混联三种结构类型。

The types of hybrid electric vehicles (HEVs) include series, parallel, and series-parallel (or mixed) designs.

（1）串联式混合动力电动汽车结构及工作原理。在串联式混合动力系统中，电动机提供唯一驱动力，蓄电池电能从其他能量源如内燃机获得，如图9.3所示。

Construction and operation of series-hybrid design. In a series-hybrid design(Fig.9.3), sole propulsion is by a battery-powered electric motor, but the electric energy for the batteries comes from another energy source, such as an internal combustion engine.

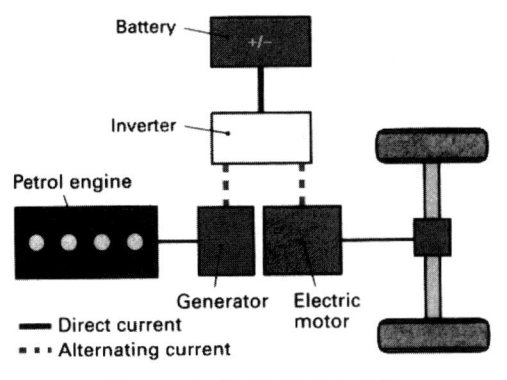

图 9.3 串联式混合动力系统

Fig.9.3 Series-hybrid design

在串联混合动力系统中，发动机驱动发电机，发电机既可为蓄电池充电，又可为电动机提供电能。发动机从不直接驱动车辆运行，所以汽车运行时，发动机可能工作，也可能不工作。逆变器可以将交流电转换成直流电，为蓄电池充电，也可以将直流电转换成交流电，为电动机供电。

In this design, the engine drives a generator and the generator can either charge the batteries or power an electric motor. The engine never powers the vehicle directly. Therefore, the vehicle could be moving with or without the internal combustion engine running. Inverter can either convert alternating current to direct current for charging battery or convert direct current to alternating current for powering electric motor.

串联混合动力系统优点：结构简单，发动机是否工作取决于蓄电池电能是否够用。

Advantage of series-hybrid design: The hybrid control system is simple. Engine's work or not depends on whether the electricity in battery is full or not.

串联混合动力系统缺点：发动机产生机械能，由发电机转变成电能。而蓄电池的电能由电动机转变成机械能，所以从发动机到驱动轮的机械效率太低。

Disadvantage of series-hybrid design: Mechanical energy from engine is converted to electric energy by generator and electric energy from battery is converted to mechanical energy by electric motor. Thus the power transmitting efficiency from engine to driving wheel is too low.

（2）并联式混合动力电动汽车结构及工作原理。在并联式混合动力系统中，有两条传力路线，一条是由发动机驱动，另一条是由电动机驱动。发动机和电动机都连到驱动轮上，如图 9.4 所示。

Construction and operation of parallel-hybrid design. In a parallel-hybrid design, there are two propulsion sources, one is internal combustion engine, and another is electric motor. In this design, the electric motor and engine are both connected to the driving wheels (Fig.9.4).

并联式混合动力电动汽车可以由内燃机单独驱动，也可以由电动机单独驱动，或者由两者结合起来同时驱动。跟传统内燃机车辆一样，由发动机驱动发电机发电，为蓄电池充电。这种并联式混合动力系统称为弱混合动力。大多数情况下，电动机用以辅助内燃机工作。

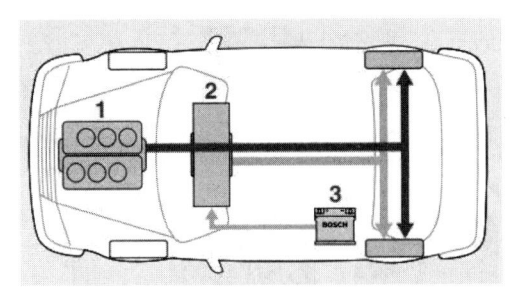

1—内燃机；2—电动机；3—蓄电池
1-Internal combustion engine; 2-Electric motor; 3-Battery

图 9.4　并联式混合动力系统

Fig.9.4　Parallel-hybrid design

The vehicle using a parallel-hybrid design can be powered by the internal combustion engine alone, by the electric motor alone, or by a combination of engine and electric motor propulsion. The battery is usually charged by generator driven by engine just like traditional construction. This kind of parallel-hybrid is called light hybrid. In most cases, the electric motor is used to assist the internal combustion engine.

并联式混合动力系统优点之一是有电动机辅助，内燃机就可以比正常需求尺寸小些，可以改善燃油经济性和废气排放。但这是有限的，反而是汽车结构更复杂，生产成本更高。

One of the advantages of using a parallel-hybrid design is that by using an electric motor to assist the internal combustion engine, the engine itself can be smaller than would normally be needed. There are some improvements on fuel economy and exhaust emission, but it is too limited. However, the construction is too complicated. The cost of manufacture is too high.

（3）混联式混合动力电动汽车结构及工作原理。混联式混合动力系统串联和并联两种结构的优点。在混联式混合动力系统中，有发电机 MG1 和电动机 MG2，行星齿轮机构，逆变器和蓄电池等部件，如图 9.5 所示。

Construction and operation of series-parallel hybrid design. Series-parallel hybrids combine the functions of both a series and a parallel design. There are engine, MG1 (generator), MG2 (electric motor), planetary gear unit, inverter and battery on series-parallel hybrids (Fig.9.5).

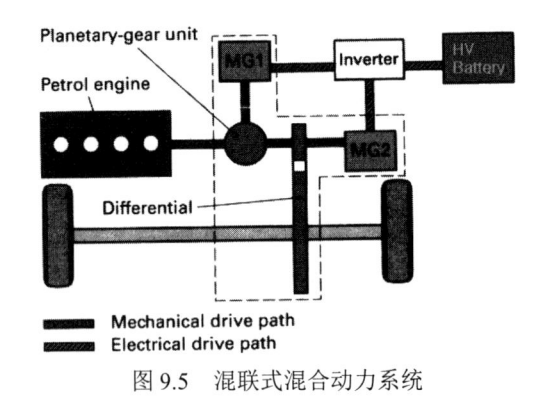

图 9.5　混联式混合动力系统

Fig.9.5　Series-parallel hybrid

与并联式混合动力系统相比，混联式混合动力系统增加了两个装置：发电机 MG1 和行星齿轮机构。从发动机—行星齿轮机构—发动机 MG1—逆变器—电动机 MG2—差速器（和驱动轮），该线路与串联式混合动力系统相似。从发动机—行星齿轮机构—差速器（和驱动轮）和蓄电池—逆变器—电动机 MG2—差速器（和驱动轮），有两条传力路线，该线路与并联式混合动力系统相似。

Comparing with parallel hybrid design, mixed hybrid design adds two devices: MG1 and planetary gear unit. By engine-planetary-MG1-inverter-MG2-differential (and driving wheel), it seems like series hybrid; by engine-planetary-differential (and driving wheel), and battery-inverter-MG2-differential (and driving wheel), there are two propulsion sources, it seems like parallel hybrid.

行星齿轮机构包含齿圈、行星齿轮和行星齿轮架、太阳轮，如图 9.6 所示。其连接方式：齿圈连接驱动轴；星齿轮和行星齿轮架连接发动机；太阳轮连接发电机。

Planetary gear unit consists of internal gear, planetary gears and holder and sun gear (Fig.9.6).

1-Internal gear: drives the vehicle's powered axle; 2-planetary gears and holder: driven by engine; 3-Sun gear: drives the generator.

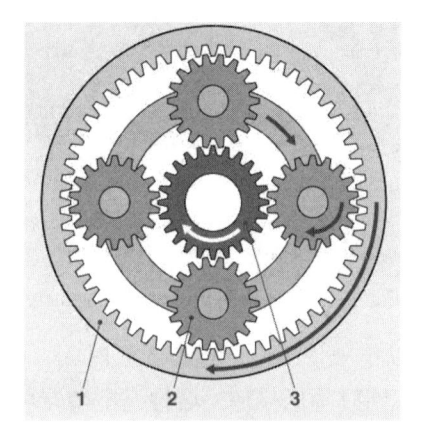

1—齿圈；2—行星齿轮和行星齿轮架；3—太阳轮

1-Internal gear; 2-planetary gears and holder; 3-Sun gear

图 9.6 行星齿轮机构

Fig.9.6 Planetary gear unit

如果电控单元检测到蓄电池需要充电，即便车辆停止运行，内燃机可能依然工作。通过混联是混合动力系统，车辆可实现重度混合或全混合模式，发动机起到辅助作用，车辆主要由电动机驱动。因此，车辆获得最佳经济性、最好的动力性和最佳废气排放。目前这种结构得到广泛应用。

The internal combustion engine may be operating even though the vehicle is stopped if the electronic controller has detected that the batteries need to be charged. By the mixed hybrid design, it can get heavy or full hybrid mode. The engine acts an assistant role, the vehicle is driven mostly by electric motor. So the vehicle gets the best economic performance, best power ability and best exhaust emission. It is widely used in nowadays transportation.

9.4 插电式汽车基本工作原理
General operation principle of plug-in hybrid electric vehicle

插电式汽车（PHEV）是在混合动力电动汽车上安装充电口，通过电缆连接到电源插座，在晚上或空余时间为车上的蓄电池充电，如图 9.7 所示。

A plug-in hybrid electric vehicle (PHEV) is a hybrid electric vehicle that is designed to be plugged into a charging cable which connects to electrical outlet at night or any spare time to charge the batteries (Fig.9.7).

图 9.7　插电式混合动力电动汽车

Fig.9.7　Plug-in hybrid electric vehicle

给蓄电池充电后，车辆可以单独使用电能运行很长时间，因此减少了发动机的运行时间。发动机运行时间越少，越省油，同时降低排放。这种充电装置可以安装在纯电动汽车上，也可以安装在混合动力电动汽车上。

By charging the batteries in the vehicle, it can operate using electric power alone for a longer time, thereby reducing the use of the internal combustion (IC) engine. The less the IC is operating, the less fuel is consumed and the lower the emissions. The charging device maybe equped either on pure electric vehicle or on hybrid electric vehicle.

9.5 燃料电池汽车
Fuel cell electric vehicles (FCEVs)

燃料电池汽车动力驱动系统与纯电动汽车相似，但它的能量源是一个燃料电池反应堆，如图 9.8 所示。

As shown in Fig.9.8, fuel cell electric vehicles (FCEVs) have similar power trains like BEV but its energy source is a fuel cell stack.

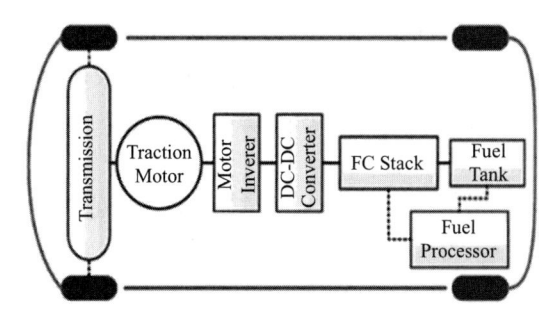

图 9.8　燃料电池车

Fig.9.8　Fuel cell electric vehicles

（1）燃料电池汽车工作原理。

①燃料电池汽车以氢气作能源，仅产生水和热量，没有废气污染。燃料电池汽车被看作零污染车辆。

②直流电/直流电转换器将低压直流电转换成高压直流电，以降低电力传输损失。

③电动机逆变器将直流电转换成交流电。

④必要时燃料罐可加注燃料（如氢气）。

Operating principle of an FCEV.

①A FCEV uses hydrogen as energy source producing only water and heat, hence there is no exhaust pollutant, thus it's recognized as zero emission vehicle.

②DC/DC Converter converts low voltage direct current to high voltage direct current to lessen the electricity loss in delivery.

③Motor Inverter converts direct current to alternative current (AC).

④Fuel Tank can be filled in with fuel (such as hydrogen) when necessary.

（2）燃料电池的主要特性。燃料电池的主要特性，其一是在燃料电池堆发生化学反应，但参加反应的燃料从外部直接输送，燃料反应堆没有电力负担，反应过程由燃料处理器控制，不发生反应，就没有电力。就蓄电池来讲，反应发生在蓄电池内，电力储存也在蓄电池内，蓄电池使用寿命短。

Main characteristics of fuel cells. One of the main characteristics of fuel cells is that the chemical reaction happens in fuel cell stack, but fuel for reaction are fed directly from external sources. There is no electricity burden on fuel cell stack. The reaction is controlled by fuel processor. Without reaction, without electricity. For batteries, chemical reaction happens in battery, electricity is stored in battery as well. Battery has short life time.

习　　题

一、选择题

1．纯电动汽车通常表示为（　　）。

　　A．BEVs　　　　　B．PEVs　　　　　C．HEVs　　　　　D．PHEVs

2. 电动汽车与传统内燃机车辆相比（　　）。
   A．噪声大，污染轻　　　　　　　　B．噪声大，污染重
   C．噪声小，污染轻　　　　　　　　D．噪声小，污染重
3. 逆变器的作用是（　　）。
   A．直流电流转换　　　　　　　　　B．交流电流转换
   C．直流电流与交流电转换　　　　　D．不确定
4. 在串联式混合动力系统中，（　　）提供驱动力。
   A．内燃机唯一　　　　　　　　　　B．电动机唯一
   C．发电机唯一　　　　　　　　　　D．电动机和内燃机
5. 行星齿轮机构用在（　　）。
   A．纯电动汽车　　　　　　　　　　B．串联式混合动力汽车
   C．并联式混合动力汽车　　　　　　D．混联式混合动力汽车

二、简答题

1. 简述新能源汽车的优缺点。
2. 简述现代电驱动系统的组成。
3. 简述纯电动汽车的特点。
4. 简述混合动力电动汽车常用的工作状态。
5. 简述串联式混合动力电动汽车的工作原理。
6. 简述混联式混合动力电动汽车的工作原理。
7. 简述插电式混合动力汽车的结构及工作原理。
8. 简述燃料电池汽车的结构及工作原理。

第10章　未来汽车技术

Future car technologies

未来潜在的汽车技术包括智能交通系统（ITS）、新构造技术、新材料和新能源。汽车正在以各种方式向前发展。

Potential future car technologies include intelligent transportation system (ITS), new construction technologies, new materials and energy sources. Cars are being developed in many different ways.

1. 先进的控制技术

   Advanced control

（1）无人驾驶汽车。无人驾驶汽车，或称自动驾驶汽车，就像人对传统车辆运输操控一样，是一款能够实现自主驾驶的车辆。作为自动化车辆，它能感受到周围环境并自动驾驶。人可以选择目的地并按下智能控制开关，但不需要对车辆有任何机械操作。

Driverless car. A driverless car, also known as self-driving car, is an autonomous vehicle capable of fulfilling the human transportation capabilities of a traditional car. As an autonomous vehicle, it is capable of sensing its environment and driving on its own. A human may choose a destination and open the intelligence control switch, but is not required to perform any mechanical operation of the vehicle.

自动驾驶车辆通过雷达、GPS 和计算机视野感受周围世界。先进的控制系统收发信息验证确切的行驶路径，所遇障碍和道路标志。

Autonomous vehicles sense the world with such techniques as radar, GPS and computer vision. Advanced control systems send and receive information to identify exact running paths, as well as obstacles and relevant signage on road.

世界上已有几个相关项目法规出现。2011 年 6 月，美国内华达州率先就自动驾驶车辆成功地通过了一项法律，该法律于 2012 年 3 月 1 日生效。2012 年 5 月内华达州机动车管理部门颁发了第一个自动驾驶车辆的驾驶证。到 2012 年 9 月，美国已有三个州通过法律允许自动驾驶车辆运行，分别是内华达州、佛罗里达州和加利福尼亚州。

There have been several programs around the world. In June 2011 the state of Nevada was the first succeeder in the United States to pass a law about the operation of autonomous cars. The Nevada law went into effect on March 1, 2012, and the Nevada Department of Motor Vehicles issued the first license for a self-driven car in May 2012. Three U.S. states have passed laws permitting driverless cars, as of September 2012: Nevada, Florida and California.

自动驾驶是超级先进的工程。它包含很多学科，如先进的信息传输系统、完善的道路标志、精准的标志识别设施和复杂的自动操作机械装置。自动驾驶工程刚刚开始，还有很长的路要走，但显然其发展前景是广阔的。

Self-driving is a super advanced engineering. It involves many subjects, such as advanced signal transmission system, perfect road signage, exact signage identification facilities and complicated self-operating machinery. It is only a beginning on self-driving project. There is a long way to go. But obviously there is a broad development prospect.

（2）编队技术。通常，信号灯转成绿色后，前面的驾驶员首先动作，后面的驾驶员依次动作，后面驾驶员的操作时间滞后了。把车辆编成一队是提高路面通过能力的一种方法。自动化高速公路控制系统对编队行驶来讲是可行的技术。

Platoon technology. Usually, after a traffic light changes to green, the front drivers react and operate first, the rear drivers react and operate one by one. The time for operating of rear drivers is delayed. Grouping vehicles into platoons is a method of increasing the capacity of roads. An automated highway system is a proposed technology for doing this.

编队行驶具有如下特点：

①编队车辆由领队车辆管控。

②编队技术通过电子控制系统减少了前后两车之间的距离，能允许很多车辆同时加速或制动，并消除了驾驶员反应时间。同步化的汽车编队如同一辆车在行驶，使通行能力得到很大提升。

编队技术需要购买配备智能系统的新车。驾驶员需要有特殊的驾驶证，能满足驾驶技能要求，特别是领队车辆驾驶要求。

The features of platoons are as follows:

①Platoons of cars are controlled by the lcad car.

②Platoons decrease the distances between cars using electronic control system. This capability would allow many cars to accelerate or brake at the same time and eliminate reacting time. Synchronized platoon would move as one, allowing up to a high increase in traffic throughput.

Platoon capability might require buying new cars with intelligence system. Drivers would probably need a special license with the new skills required in driving, especially in the lead vehicle driving.

（3）车辆基础设施整合。车辆基础设施整合（VII）是一项新技术，它直接连接路面车辆和它们真实的周边环境，首先且最重要的是为了行车安全。保证行车安全能提高总体效率。车辆基础设施整合的目标是提高行车安全和行驶效率。车辆基础设施整合所需技术涉及几个信息通信技术，包括车辆至网络通信技术，车辆至车辆通信技术，车辆至行人通信技术，车辆至基础设施通信技术，如图 10.1 所示。这种技术需要因特网工程、电子工程、汽车工程和计算机科学等的支持。

Vehicle infrastructure integration. Vehicle Infrastructure Integration (VII) is a new technology directly linking road vehicles to their real surroundings, first and foremost in order to improve road safety. Improving the safety of a roadway can enhance overall efficiency. VII targets improvements in both safety and efficiency.

The technology draws on several communications, including Vehicle-to-Network, Vehicle-to-Vehicle, Vehicle-to-Pedestrian, Vehicle-to-Infrastructure communication (Fig.10.1). It gets support from internet engineering, electrical engineering, automotive engineering, and computer science.

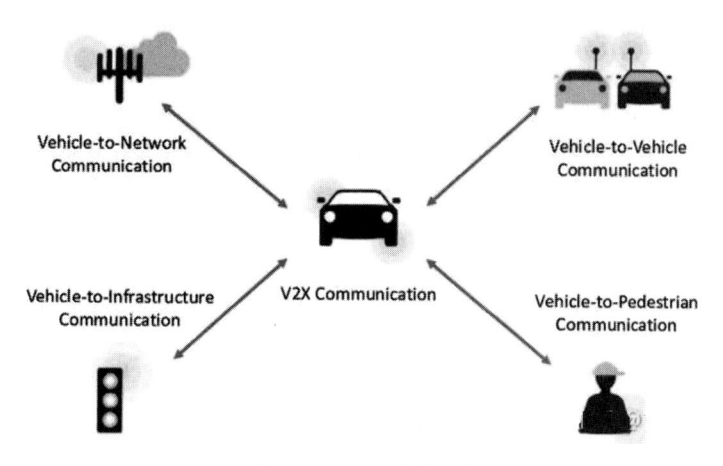

图 10.1 汽车通信网络

Fig.10.1 Vehicle communication network

2. 能源

Energy sources

要开发出清洁、高效、低排放的汽车，其中一个主要问题是用于驱动发动机运转的能源来源问题。目前，替换燃油的各种能源车辆已被建议或已被使用，这些车辆包括电动汽车、氢燃料汽车、压缩空气汽车和液氮汽车。

One major problem in developing cleaner, highly efficient and lower-emission automobiles is the source of energy to drive the engine. At present, a variety of alternative fuel vehicles have been proposed or used, including electric cars, hydrogen cars, compressed-air cars and liquid nitrogen cars.

混合动力电动汽车目前已被广泛应用。在改进汽车行驶性能的一次试验中，一种新型电池被（如锂基电池）安装在两辆不同充电类型的汽车上。其中一辆车由内燃机带动发动机充电，另一辆车（插电式混合动力电动汽车）通过电缆在车外墙上的插座充电。

Hybrid electric vehicle is widely used at present. In one experiment done to improve the running performance of cars, a new kind of battery (such as Lithium based battery) was installed cars that can be recharged in two different types. First, by a generator integrated with the IC and second by external outlet on the wall via cable (Plug-in HEV).

结论如下。第一辆车效能低，因为电能来自内燃机驱动的发电机，内燃机效能低；第二辆车是插电式混合动力电动汽车，来自车外电源插座的电能可能是水力发电、热力发电或核能发电。第二辆车效能高。

There is a conclusion. The first type in which electricity comes from generator driven by IC engine has lower efficiency because engine operates at low efficiency. The second type is a Plug-in HEV in which some of electricity comes from external outlet. Electricity maybe generated by water hydropower generation, thermal power generation or nuclear power generation. It has higher efficiency.

氢燃料汽车、压缩空气汽车和液氮汽车可能具有更高的效能，但因其技术难题目前处于研发阶段。

Hydrogen cars, compressed-air cars and liquid nitrogen cars may have higher efficiency, but because of their technological hurdles they are in researching range now.

3. 未来汽车用的新材料

Some new materials for future cars

（1）铝合金。这种材料是铝材料中融入了铜、锰等元素。铝合金比钢材轻很多，但比纯铝强度更高。伴随着严重的空气污染和能源危机，汽车研究人员将环境保护作为主要责任。研究表明：汽车车身大量使用铝合金材料，降低汽车重量，因而明显降低燃油消耗和废气排放。图 10.2 所示为全铝合金框架。

Aluminum alloy. This material is aluminum fused with copper, manganese and so on. It is much lighter than steel but has greater strength than pure aluminum. With the serious air pollution and energy crisis, automobile researcher takes the environmental protection as their major duty. The research shows: a large amount of aluminum alloy in use on vehicle body reduces the weight of car, so it lowers the fuel consumption and exhaust emission obviously. Fig.10.2 shows full aluminum space frame.

图 10.2　铝合金车身

Fig.10.2　Car body of aluminum alloy

（2）纤维玻璃。纤维玻璃是一种塑料，是在塑料中加入微量的玻璃的材料。目前这种材料在赛车中使用。质量轻、强度高使得该材料满足燃油消耗的高标准要求。纤维玻璃价格高了些，但质量轻和强度高使其成为 21 世纪汽车工程领域中越来越受欢迎的材料。

Fiberglass. Fiberglass is a form of plastic reinforced with a trace of glass. It is commonly used for sports cars now. The material's light weight and significant strength make it ideal for helping meet high fuel efficiency standards. Fiberglass is relatively expensive, but its strength and light weight have made it increasingly popular with 21st century automotive engineers.

（3）碳纳米管。纳米管是仅有几个原子构成薄壁的一种管子（1 纳米等于十亿分之一米），代表着新的构造技术发展方向。与上述材料相比，碳纳米管具有惊人的强度和轻质，目前不太受重视，但在将来的 21 世纪中叶，轿车、货车、飞机、轮船甚至宇宙飞船上，构造使用的碳纳米管材料将像塑料一样普及。

Carbon nanotubes. Nanotubes, which is a tube with thin wall just a few atoms thick (one nanometer is equal to one billionth of a meter), represent the newest trend in construction technology. Amazingly strong and light than any of the other materials discussed above, carbon nanotubes may be not much concerned today, but they are likely to become as common as plastic in the construction of cars, trucks, aircraft, ships and even spacecraft by the mid-21st century.

4. 悬车

Suspended bus

伴随着城市交通运输业的不断发展，交通问题越来越严重，交通堵塞是首要问题。许多城市正在建造悬车以缓解交通压力。人们可能想象不到，它在空中悬挂在一根单梁上，如图 10.3 所示。这种车首先在德国开发并投入商业运营，逐渐引入中国，并得到巨大发展。重要的是悬车电驱动、零污染、低噪声、不占路面空间，并且效率很高。

With the development of city transportation, the traffic condition is becoming more and more serious. Traffic block is the major concern. Many cities are building suspended bus to release the traffic pressure. Unlike people's image, it is suspended against a single rail in the sky (Fig.10.3). This kind of bus is launched to commercial operation which was earlier developed in Germany. It is gradually introduced to China and got huge development. What's the important is that the bus is an electric-drive vehicle with zero pollution, low noise, non-space occupy of road and high efficiency.

与地铁相比，同等条件下，一个车厢，地铁耗电 5～6kW，悬车耗电 2～3kW；制造成本，地铁每公里 150 万元人民币，是悬车的 5 倍；建造周期，地铁每 100 公里需要大约 3～5 年，比悬车多大约 1 年。悬车比地铁优越很多，在城市交通中越来越受欢迎。

Comparing with subway (metro), in normal situation, a compartment of subway consumes electricity of 5-6kW than 2-3kW on suspended bus. For subway, the costs of building is 15 million yuan RMB every 1km, 5 times cost of suspended bus. Building period on subway is about 3-5 years every 100km, is longer than suspended bus by about 1 year.

图 10.3　悬车

Fig.10.3　Suspended bus

Suspended bus is much superior than subway. It becomes more and more popular in city traffic.

习 题

一、选择题

1. 下列汽车中，不属于新能源汽车的是（　　）。
   A．氢燃料汽车　　　　　　　　　　B．压缩空气汽车
   C．液氮汽车　　　　　　　　　　　D．乙醇燃料汽车
2. 再生制动技术不能用在（　　）。
   A．传统内燃机车辆　　　　　　　　B．纯电动汽车
   C．混合动力电动汽车　　　　　　　D．燃料电池车
3. 纤维玻璃是一种（　　）。
   A．橡胶　　　　　B．塑料　　　　　C．玻璃　　　　　D．纤维
4. 碳纳米材料具有良好的（　　）。
   A．硬度　　　　　B．强度　　　　　C．铸造性能　　　D．焊接性能
5. 悬车跟地铁相比（　　）。
   A．造价高，生产周期长，运行成本高　　B．造价低，生产周期高，运行成本高
   C．造价低，生产周期短，运行成本高　　D．造价低，生产周期短，运行成本低

二、简答题

1. 简述无人驾驶在美国的应用情况。
2. 简述编队行驶的特点及技术要求。
3. 简述基础设施整合的技术特点。
4. 简述铝合金材料的性能特点。
5. 简述悬车结构的特点。

附录　生词与短语

New words and expressions

第 1 章

hydrocarbon	/ˌhaɪdrəˈkɑːbən/	n.碳氢化合物，烃
photosynthesis	/ˌfəʊtəʊˈsɪnθəsɪs/	n.光合作用，光能合成
nitrogen	/ˈnaɪtrədʒən/	n.〈化〉氮，氮气
dioxide	/daɪˈɒksaɪd/	n.〈化〉二氧化物
monoxide	/mɒˈnɒksaɪd/	n.一氧化物
nitric acid		n.硝酸
phenomenon	/fəˈnɒmɪnən/	n.现象，事件；奇迹；非凡的人
hemoglobin	/ˌhiːməʊˈgləʊbɪn/	n.血红素；血红蛋白
sulfur	/ˈsʌlfə/	n.硫黄；硫黄色
		vt.用硫黄处理
sulfuric acid		n.硫酸
methane	/ˈmiːθeɪn/	n.〈化〉甲烷，沼气
inundation	/ˌɪnʌnˈdeɪʃn/	n.淹没；洪水；（洪水般的）扑来；压倒
coastal	/ˈkəʊstl/	adj.临海的，沿海的；海岸的；沿岸
digest	/daɪˈdʒest/	vt&vi.消化；整理
		vt.吸收；领悟；玩味
		vi.消化；吸收食物；〈化〉加热
		n.文摘；摘要；法律汇编；罗马法典
fossil	/ˈfɒsl/	n.化石；僵化的事物；老顽固，食古不化的人；习语中保存的旧词
geological	/ˌdʒiːəˈlɒdʒɪkl/	adj.地质（学）的
sediment	/ˈsedɪmənt/	n.〈地〉沉淀物；沉积物，沉渣
finite	/ˈfaɪnaɪt/	adj.有限的；〈语〉限定的；〈数〉有穷的，有限的
corrosion	/kəˈrəʊʒn/	n.腐蚀，侵蚀，锈蚀；受腐蚀的部位；衰败
hurricane	/ˈhʌrɪkən/	n.飓风，十二级风；飓风般猛烈的东西；（感情等的）爆发；〈英〉飓风式战斗驱逐机
commercialization	/kəˌmɜːʃəlaɪˈzeɪʃn/	n.商业化，商品化
hurdle	/ˈhɜːdl/	n.障碍，困难；跳栏；障碍赛跑；〈史〉囚笼，囚车

		*vi.*克服困难；越过障碍；参加跨栏赛跑
		*vt.*跳过障碍；跳栏；用疏篱围住；克服困难
assume	/əˈsjuːm/	*v.*假定，认为；承担；装出；呈现
strategy	/ˈstrætədʒi/	*n.*策略，战略；战略学
scenario	/səˈnɑːriəʊ/	*n.*设想；可能发生的情况；剧情梗概
reveal	/rɪˈviːl/	*vt.*显露；揭露；泄露

第 2 章

mobility	/məʊˈbɪləti/	*n.*流动性；移动性；〈社〉流动；机动性
Sumerians		*n.*苏美尔人（Sumerian 的复数）
buggy	/ˈbʌɡi/	*n.*婴儿车，童车；〈俚〉旧汽车；小机动车；轻便马车
inconsiderate	/ˌɪnkənˈsɪdərət/	*adj.*不替别人着想的；不体谅别人的；轻率的；考虑不周的
motorist	/ˈməʊtərɪst/	*n.*汽车驾驶员；乘汽车旅行的人
acquisition	/ˌækwɪˈzɪʃn/	*n.*获得；购置物；获得物；收购
nonexistent	/ˌnɒnɪɡˈzɪstənt/	*adj.*不存在的
blacksmith	/ˈblækˌsmɪθ/	*n.*铁匠，锻工；打铁工人；装蹄工；蹄铁
prevail	/prɪˈveɪl/	*vi.*流行，盛行；获胜，占优势；说服，劝说
motorize	/ˈməʊtəraɪz/	*vt.*给（车辆）装上发动机；使机动化；用机动车装配（部队等）；使（部队等）机动化
pneumatic	/njuːˈmætɪk/	*adj.*充气的；气动的；装满空气的；有气胎的
mushroom	/ˈmʌʃrʊm/	*n.*蘑菇；蘑菇状物，蘑菇形物体；（女用）蘑菇形草帽；暴发户
		*vi.*迅速增长；采蘑菇；迅速增加；（火）猛然的扩大
impetus	/ˈɪmpɪtəs/	*n.*动力；促进；势头；声势
individual	/ˌɪndɪˈvɪdʒuəl/	*adj.*个人的；独特的；个别的
		*n.*个人；个体
juncture	/ˈdʒʌŋktʃə(r)/	*n.*时刻，关键时刻；接合点
acceptance	/əkˈseptəns/	*n.*接受，接纳；〈金融〉承兑；无怨接受（逆境、困境等）；赞成
marketplace	/ˈmɑːkɪtpleɪs/	*n.*市场，集市；商业界
consideration	/kənˌsɪdəˈreɪʃn/	*n.*考虑，考察；照顾，关心；报酬；尊敬
integrated	/ˈɪntɪɡreɪtɪd/	*adj.*完整的；整体的；结合的；（各组成部分）和谐的
beetle	/ˈbiːtl/	*n.*甲壳虫

recuperate /rɪˈkuːpəreɪt/	vi.恢复，复原；弥补
	vt.使恢复；〈化〉同流换热
counterpart /ˈkaʊntəpɑːt/	n.配对物；副本；相对物；极相似的人或物
rheostat /ˈriːəˌstæt/	n.〈电〉变阻器；〈电〉可变电阻
trigger /ˈtrɪɡə(r)/	n.（枪）扳机；起动装置，扳柄；引发其他事件的一件事；〈电子学〉触发器，触发电器
	vt.引发，触发；扣……的扳机；发射或使爆炸（武器或爆炸性弹药）
obstacle /ˈɒbstəkl/	n.障碍（物）；障碍物（绊脚石，障碍栅栏）
culminate /ˈkʌlmɪneɪt/	vt.&vi.达到极点
context /ˈkɒntekst/	n.上下文；背景；环境；语境
undoubtedly /ʌnˈdaʊtɪdli/	adv.毋庸置疑地，的确地；显然；必定；无疑
hazard /ˈhæzəd/	vt.冒险；使遭受危险
	n.危险；冒险的事；机会；双骰子游戏
attribute /əˈtrɪbjuːt/	vt.认为……是；把……归于；把……品质归于某人认为某事（物）属于某人（物）
	n.属性；性质；特征
witness /ˈwɪtnəs/	n.目击者，见证人；〈法〉证人；证据
	vt.出席或知道；作记录；提供或作为……的证据
	vi.做证人；见证
cumulative /ˈkjuːmjələtɪv/	adj.累积的；渐增的；追加的；（判刑等）加重的
lineup /ˈlaɪnʌp/	n.行列；人（或物）的列队；选手阵容；电视节目时间表
outsource /ˈaʊtsɔːs/	vt.外购（指从外国供应商等处获得货物或服务）；外包（工程）
advent /ˈædvent/	n.出现，到来，问世
supplementary /ˌsʌplɪˈmentri/	adj.增补的，追加的
incompatible /ˌɪnkəmˈpætəbl/	adj.不相容；矛盾，不能同时成立的；（与某物）不匹配；〈医〉配伍禁忌的
quash /kwɒʃ/	vt.〈法〉废除，使无效；捣碎，压碎；平息，镇压
alkaline /ˈælkəlaɪn/	adj.碱性的，碱的；含碱的
nickel /ˈnɪkl/	n.〈化〉镍；五分镍币
catalyst /ˈkætəlɪst/	n.〈化〉触媒，催化剂；〈比喻〉触发因素；促进因素；〈口〉有感染力的人
substantial /səbˈstænʃl/	adj.大量的；结实的，牢固的；重大的
compact /ˈkɑːmpækt; kəmˈpækt/	v.把……压实
	adj.小型的；坚实的；矮壮的
	n.化妆粉盒；协定

proven /ˈpruːvn/   adj.经过验证或证实的
v.证明（prove 的过去分词）；检验，试验

第 3 章

armament /ˈɑːməmənt/   n.军备；武器装备；〈复〉军事力量；军队
humanitarian /hjuːˌmænɪˈteəriən/   adj.人道主义的；博爱的；慈善的
compel /kəmˈpel/   vt.强迫，迫使；强制发生，使不得不
remembrance /rɪˈmembrəns/   n.回想，回忆；纪念品；记忆，记忆力
standardise /ˈstændədaɪz/   vt.使合乎规格，使标准化
legitimate /lɪˈdʒɪtɪmət/   adj.合法的，合理的；正规的；合法婚姻所生的；真正的，真实的

heir /eə(r)/   n.继承人；后嗣，嗣子
robot /ˈrəʊbɒt/   n.机器人；遥控装置；自动机；机械呆板的人
acronym /ˈækrənɪm/   n.首字母缩略词
headquarter /ˈhedˈkwɔːtə/   vi.设总部
vt.将……的总部设在；把……放在总部里

scheme /skiːm/   v.密谋，图谋；认为
n.计划；方案；阴谋；体系

reference /ˈrefrəns/   n.参考；参考书；提及，涉及；证明人，介绍人
v.引用；参照

displacement /dɪsˈpleɪsmənt/   n.取代，替代；免职，停职；〈船〉排水量；〈化〉置换

roadster /ˈrəʊdstə(r)/   n.跑车，敞篷车
depression /dɪˈpreʃn/   n.萎靡不振，沮丧；下陷处，坑；衰弱；减缓
motorsport   n.赛车运动；摩托车运动
rally /ˈræli/   vt.召集，集合；重整；重振，恢复
vi.聚集；集合；反弹，反败为胜；恢复（元气等）
n.集合；重新集合；重整的信号；反败为胜

roomy /ˈruːmi/   adj.宽敞的，宽大的
brilliant /ˈbrɪliənt/   adj.明亮的；〈非正式〉美好的；闪耀的；才华横溢的

falter /ˈfɔːltə(r)/   vi.（嗓音）颤抖；支吾其词；蹒跚；摇晃
foreshadow /fɔːˈʃædəʊ/   vt.预示，是……的先兆
investor /ɪnˈvestə(r)/   n.投资者；出资者；包围者，围攻者
refinement /rɪˈfaɪnmənt/   n.精炼，提纯，净化；改良品；细微的改良，极致；优雅，高贵的动作

soar /sɔː(r)/   vi.高飞；飞腾；猛增，剧增；高耸，屹立

		vt.高飞越过；飞升到
junk	/dʒʌŋk/	n.废旧物品，破烂物；中国式平底帆船；便宜货，假货；废话，哄骗
		vt.丢弃，废弃；把……分成块
downgrade	/ˌdaʊnˈgreɪd/	v.使降低；使降职；贬低；低估
grid	/grɪd/	n.格子，非实质的；地图上的坐标方格；（输电线路、天然气管道等的）系统网络
demonstration	/ˌdemənˈstreɪʃn/	n.游行示威；示范；证明；表露
fleet	/fliːt/	n.舰队；船队；车队；港湾，小河
		adj.快速的，敏捷的；转瞬即逝的
sustainability	/səsˌteɪnəˈbɪlɪti/	n.持续性，能维持性，永续性
multiplied	/ˈmʌltɪplaɪd/	v.乘（multiply 的过去式和过去分词）；（使）相乘；（使）增加；（使）繁殖
ignorance	/ˈɪgnərəns/	n.无知，愚昧
Substantial	/səbˈstænʃl/	adj.大量的；结实的，牢固的；重大的
marque	/mɑːk/	n.（尤指汽车的）商品型号；捕拿特许；有捕拿特许证的船
subcompact	/sʌbˈkɑmˌpækt/	n.微型小客车，微型汽车
stability	/stəˈbɪləti/	n.稳定（性），稳固；坚定，恒心
distinction	/dɪˈstɪŋkʃn/	n.区别；荣誉；特质；卓越
bankruptcy	/ˈbæŋkrʌptsi/	n.破产，倒闭；彻底失败；（勇气）完全丧失
cripple	/ˈkrɪpl/	vt.使跛；受伤致残；严重削弱；使陷于瘫痪
		n.跛子，瘸子；瘫子，残疾；〈美方〉杂木丛生的沼地；脚蹬

第 4 章

pioneer	/ˌpaɪəˈnər/	n.先驱；开拓者
		v.开创
onward	/ˈɑnwərd/	adj.向前的，前进的
formulate	/ˈfɔːrmjuleɪt/	vt.构想出，规划；确切地阐述；用公式表示
demonstrate	/ˈdemənstreɪt/	v.证明；说明；（游行）示威；演示
superiority	/suːpɪriˈɔːrəti/	n.优越（性），优等；傲慢
trial	/ˈtraɪəl/	v.测试
		n.审讯；试验；试用期；磨难；预赛；比赛
systematic	/ˌsɪstəˈmætɪk/	adj.有系统的，有规则的；有条不紊的；有步骤的；一贯的，惯常的
apprenticeship	/əˈprɛntɪʃɪp/	n.学徒制；学徒期

revise	/rɪˈvaɪz/	vt.修订；改变；修正；复习
		vt.& vi.复习
		vi.修订，校订
carburetor	/ˈkɑbəˌreɪtə/	n.〈机〉汽化器，化油器
contemporary	/kənˈtempəreri/	adj.当代的；同时发生的
		n.同时期的人
inventor	/ɪnˈventər/	n.发明家；创造者；发明者
Mannheim	/ˈmænhaim; ˈmɑːn-/	曼海姆（德意志联邦共和国西南部城市）
pursue	/pərˈsuː/	vt.继续；追求；进行；追捕
		vi.追，追赶；继续进行
null	/nʌl/	adj.〈术〉零值的；等于零的；（协议）无法律效力；失效的
precondition	/ˈprikənˈdɪʃən/	n.前提，先决条件
Dearborn	/ˈdɪrbən/	n.迪尔伯恩马车（一种小型四轮马车），迪尔伯恩（美国一城市）
segment	/ˈsegmənt; segˈment/	n.部分，段落；环节；〈计算机〉（字符等的）分段；〈动物学〉节片
		v.分割；划分
stationary	/ˈsteɪʃəneri/	adj.不动的，固定的；静止的，不变的；常备军的；定居的
marine	/məˈriːn/	adj.海洋的；海产的；海军的；海船的
		n.海军陆战队士兵
utilization	/ˌjuːtəlɔˈzeɪʃn/	n.利用，使用，效用
license	/ˈlaɪsns/	vt.同意；发许可证
		n.执照，许可证；特许
scrutiny	/ˈskruːtəni/	n.细看，细阅；仔细的观察；监督
enterprise	/ˈentərpraɪz/	n.公司，企（事）业单位；事业；创业，企业发展；事业心，创业精神
merchandise	/ˈmɜːrtʃəndaɪs; -daɪz/	n.商品；货物
		vt.买卖；销售
		vi.经商
magneto	/mægˈnitoʊ/	n.磁发电机
breakthrough	/ˈbreɪkθruː/	n.重大进展；突破
purposefulness	/ˈpɜpəsflnəs/	n.果断，意志坚定
ignite	/ɪgˈnaɪt/	vt.点燃；使燃烧；使激动；使灼热
		vi.点火；燃烧
headlamp	/ˈhɛdˌlæmp/	n.（矿工）头上戴的小型照明灯
semaphore	/ˈseməfɔːr/	n.臂板信号系统，（铁道）臂板信号装置

		vt.& vi.发出信号，打旗语
motorist	/ˈmoʊtərɪst/	n.汽车驾驶员；乘汽车旅行的人
trademark	/ˈtreɪdmɑːrk/	n.（注册）商标；（人的行为或衣着的）特征，标记
ambition	/æmˈbɪʃn/	n.追求，理想；雄心，野心
implement	/ˈɪmplɪment; ˈɪmplɪmənt/	vt.实施，执行；使生效，实现；落实（政策）；把……填满
		n.工具，器械；家具；手段；〈法〉履行（契约等）
compensate	/ˈkɑːmpenseɪt/	v.补偿，赔偿；弥补；抵消
reichsmark	/ˈraɪkˌsmɑːk/	n.马克（德国货币单位）
pension	/ˈpenʃn/	n.养老金
handicapped	/ˈhændikæpt/	adj.残疾的；有生理缺陷的；智力低下的
inauguration	/ɪˌnɔːgjəˈreɪʃn/	n.就职；就职典礼；开始；开创
confiscated	/ˈkɑːnfɪskeɪt/	vt.没收；充公；查抄；征用
unyielding	/ʌnˈjiːldɪŋ/	adj.坚硬的，不能弯曲的，不屈的；刚强；不屈服；倔强
mourn	/mɔːrn/	v.悼念；为失去……而悲哀
zeitgeist	/ˈtsaɪtgaɪst/	n.（尤指文学、哲学和政治中表现出的）时代精神，时代思潮
diligence	/ˈdɪlɪdʒəns/	n.勤奋，用功
inaugurate	/ɪˈnɔːgjəreɪt/	vt.开创；创始；举行开幕典礼；举行就职典礼
sponsor	/ˈspɑːnsər/	n.发起者，主办者；担保者；倡议者，提案人；后援组织
		vt.赞助
welfare	/ˈwelfer/	n.幸福，安全与健康；福利
		adj.福利的

第 5 章

distinguish	/dɪˈstɪŋgwɪʃ/	vi.区分，辨别，分清；辨别是非
		vt.区分，辨别，分清；辨别出，识别；引人注目，有别于；使杰出，使著名
emblem	/ˈembləm/	n.象征，标记；纹章，徽章；标记，典型；〈古〉寓意画
symbolize	/ˈsɪmbəlaɪz/	vt.象征；用符号表现
		vi.使用符号；采用象征；作为……的象征
dimensional	/dɪˈmenʃənəl/	adj.尺寸的；〈物〉量纲的；〈数〉因次的；维的
ancestral	/ænˈsestrəl/	adj.祖先的；与祖先有关的；祖宗传下的
overhaul	/ˌoʊvəˈhɔːl/	vt.彻底检查；翻修，检修

		n.检查；彻底检修；详细检查；大修
patriotic	/ˌpeɪtriˈɒtɪk/	adj.爱国的，有爱国心的；爱国主义的
motif	/məʊˈtiːf/	n.（文艺作品等的）主题；（音乐的）乐旨，动机；基本图案
tore	/tɔː(r)/	v.撕（tear 的过去式）；（使）分裂；撕碎；扯破
inverted	/ɪnˈvɜːtɪd/	adj.反向的，倒转的
		v.使倒置，使反转（invert 的过去式和过去分词）
prance	/prɑːns/	vi.（马）腾跃
legendary	/ˈledʒəndri/	adj.传说的；传奇的；极其著名的
victorious	/vɪkˈtɔːriəs/	adj.胜利的；得胜的；凯
duel	/ˈdjuːəl/	n.决斗；竞争，斗争
wizard	/ˈwɪzəd/	n.男巫；行家；奇才；向导（程序）
oval	/ˈəʊvl/	adj.椭圆形的；卵形的
		n.椭圆形；椭圆运动场（等）；椭圆，美式足球用球；〈物〉卵形线
jaguar	/ˈdʒægjuə(r)/	n.〈动〉（中、南美洲的）美洲虎
bull	/bʊl/	n.公牛；雄性动物；（预期证券价格上升的）买空者；胡说
evoke	/ɪˈvəʊk/	vt.产生，引起；唤起
creativity	/ˌkriːeɪˈtɪvəti/	n.创造性，创造力，创作能力
vitality	/vaɪˈtæləti/	n.活力；生气；生命力；持久性
flexibility	/ˌfleksəˈbɪləti/	n.柔韧性，机动性，灵活性；伸缩性；可塑度；柔度
clause	/klɔːz/	n.从句，分句；条款，款项
ellipse	/ɪˈlɪps/	n.椭圆
interpretation	/ɪnˌtɜːprɪˈteɪʃn/	n.解释，说明；翻译；表演，演绎；理解
interlock	/ˌɪntəˈlɒk/	v.互锁；连锁
abundance	/əˈbʌndəns/	n.丰富，充裕；大量，极多；盈余；丰度
diagonally	/daɪˈægənəli/	adv.对角线地，斜线地
lithium	/ˈlɪθiəm/	n.〈化〉锂
undertake	/ˌʌndəˈteɪk/	v.承担；承诺
internation	/ˌɪntəˈnæʃn/	n.〈计〉国际；〈医〉拘禁，禁闭（如精神病人）
abdomen	/ˈæbdəmən/	n.腹部；〈虫〉腹部；下腹；腹腔
impressive	/ɪmˈpresɪv/	adj.给人印象深刻的，感人的；引人注目的；可观的；显赫
hantom	/ˈfæntəm/	n.幻影；幽灵；错觉；恐惧的事物
		adj.幽灵似的；幻影的，虚幻的；虚构的
jubilee	/ˈdʒuːbɪliː/	n.周年纪念；欢乐，欢乐的节日

revive /rɪˈvaɪv/	vt.使复活，使恢复；使振奋，复原；使再生，使重新流行；唤醒，唤起
	vi.复苏，恢复；振作，恢复；再生，重新流行；再生效力
configuration /kənˌfɪgəˈreɪʃn/	n.布局，构造；配置；〈化〉（分子中原子的）组态，排列；〈物〉位形，组态

第 6 章

principle /ˈprɪnsəpl/	n.道德原则；法则；观念；理由；定律
shaft /ʃɑːft/	n.柄，轴；矛，箭；〈非〉嘲笑；光线
	vt.给……装上杆柄；〈俚〉苛刻的对待
chamber /ˈtʃeɪmbər/	n.（作特殊用途的）议会；（人体、植物或机器内部的）腔；私人房间
convert /kənˈvɜːrt; ˈkɑːnvɜːrt/	v.（使）转变；改造；换算；（使）改变信仰；使……迷上
	n.刚迷上……的人
combustion /kəmˈbʌstʃən/	n.燃烧；烧毁；氧化；骚动
radiator /ˈreɪdieɪtər/	n.暖气片，散热器；（汽车引擎的）冷却器；辐射体；冰箱
gasoline /ˈgæsəliːn; gæsəˈliːn/	n.汽油
diagram /ˈdaɪəgræm/	n.图表，示意图
	v.用图表表示
stroke /stroʊk/	n.中风；（铅笔等的）笔画；划水动作；游法；钟声；击球；一件（幸运的）事；（灵感）突发
	v.抚摩；轻拭
spark /spɑːrk/	n.燃烧的颗粒；火星；火花；余火；（金属的）发光的颗粒；电火花
	vi.发出火星；发出闪光；热烈赞同；正常运转
	vt.发动；触发；激起运动；鼓舞
classification /ˌklæsɪfɪˈkeɪʃn/	n.分类，类别；分类法；分类系统
compress /kəmˈpres; ˈkɑːmpres/	v.（使）压缩；精简
	n.敷布；压布
cylinder /ˈsɪlɪndər/	n.圆柱体；圆筒状物；（发动机）汽缸
plug /plʌg/	n.塞子；插头；消防栓；（内燃机的）火花塞
	vt.& vi.插上插头
	vt.以（塞子）塞住；插入；〈俚〉枪击；殴打
	vi.填塞，堵；〈俚〉勤苦工作，用功

165

单词	音标	释义
layout	/'leɪaʊt/	n.布局，安排，设计；布置图，规划图
diesel	/'diːzl/	n.柴油；柴油机机车（或船等）
inject	/ɪn'dʒekt/	vt.（给……）注射（药物等）；（给……）注射（液体）；（给……）添加；（给……）投入（资金）
sufficiently	/sə'fɪʃ(ə)ntli/	adv.足够地；充分地；十分；相当
distribute	/dɪ'strɪbjuːt/	v.分发；配销；分配；分散；撒，播
ignite	/ɪg'naɪt/	vt.点燃，使燃烧；使激动；使灼热 vi.点火；燃烧
piston	/'pɪstən/	n.〈机〉活塞
cycle	/'saɪkl/	v.骑自行车 n.自行车；摩托车；整套；循环；组诗
inlet	/'ɪnlet/	n.进口；〈电〉引入；插入物；水湾
swept	/swɛpt/	v.扫（sweep 的过去式和过去分词）；扫视；蜿蜒；步态轻盈地走
crankshaft	/'kræŋkʃæft/	n.机轴
exhaust	/ɪg'zɔːst/	v.耗尽；使精疲力竭；详尽地讨论 n.废气；排气管
capacity	/kə'pæsəti/	n.容量；才能；职责；生产能力；载客量 adj.座无虚席的
valve	/vælv/	n.阀；真空管；（管乐器的）活栓；（心脏的）瓣膜
suction	/'sʌkʃn/	n.吸；抽吸；吸出；相吸
schematic	/skiˈmætɪk; skɪ-/	adj.纲要的；示意的；严谨的；有章法的
revolution	/ˌrevə'luːʃn/	n.革命；变革；旋转
axle	/'æksəl/	n.轮轴；车轴；轴端
induction	/ɪn'dʌkʃn/	n.归纳（法）；（电或磁的）感应；诱发；就职，就职典礼
manufacturer	/ˌmænju'fæktʃərər/	n.制造商，制造厂；厂主；〈经〉厂商
sequence	/'siːkwəns/	n.〈数〉数列，序列；顺序；连续；片断插曲 vt.使按顺序排列，安排顺序；〈生化〉确定……的顺序，确定……的化学结构序列
propel	/prə'pel/	vt.推进；推动；驱动；驱使
block	/blɑːk/	n.一块，一批；立方体；大楼；街区；一片土地；障碍（物），拦截 v.堵塞，挡住；妨碍；拦截
preliminary	/prɪ'lɪmɪneri/	adj.初步的，初级的；预备的；开端的；序言的 n.准备工作；预赛；初步措施；（对学生等的）预考
rod	/rɑːd/	n.杆，拉杆；惩罚，体罚；（责打人用的）棍棒；手枪

词	音标	释义
kinetic	/kɪˈnɛtɪk; kaɪ-/	*adj.* 运动的，活跃的，能动的，有力的；〈物〉动力（学）的，运动的
part	/pɑːrt/	*n.* 部分；零件；角色；成员；部位；区域；集；参与；声部；等份；分缝 *v.* 离开；分离；解散；梳成分头 *adv.* 部分地
reciprocate	/rɪˈsɪprəˌket/	*vt.* 互换，互给；回报 *vi.* 往复运动；互换；回报；互给
component	/kəmˈpoʊnənt/	*n.* 组成部分；成分 *adj.* 组成的；构成的
accessory	/əkˈsesəri/	*n.* 附件，配件；配饰；从犯，同谋 *adj.* 辅助的；副的
circular	/ˈsɜːrkjələr/	*adj.* 圆形的；环形的 *n.* （同时发送给多人的）印刷品广告
swivel	/ˈswɪvl/	*n.* 转节；转环；旋轴；旋转接头 *vt. & vi.* （使）旋转；在枢轴上转动；（把身子或脸等）转向另一方；转身
gudgeon	/ˈɡʌdʒən/	*n.* 易骗的人；舵枢；枢轴
pan	/pæn/	*n.* 平底锅；盘状的器皿；淘盘子，金盘，秤盘 *vt.* 淘金；在浅锅中烹调（食物）；〈非正式用语〉严厉的批评 *vi.* 淘金；在淘洗中收获金子
pin	/pin/	*n.* 钉；别针，扣针，饰针；大头针；没价值的东西 *vt.* 压住；（用钉等）钉住，钉住，别住，扣住；用障壁等围住，关住；〈军〉牵制
rotate	/ˈroʊteɪt/	*vt. & vi.* （使某物）旋转；使转动；使轮流，轮换；交替
coupling	/ˈkʌplɪŋ/	*n.* 〈电〉耦合；联结；〈机〉管箍；（火车的）车钩 *v.* 连接（couple 的现在分词）
crankpin	/ˈkræŋkpɪn/	*n.* 曲柄针，曲柄梢
formula	/ˈfɔːrmjələ/	*n.* 公式，方程式；方案，方法；惯用词语；配方（奶）
simultaneously	/ˌsaɪməlˈteɪniəsli/	*adv.* 同时地；一齐
bearing	/ˈberɪŋ/	*n.* 关系，影响；举止；方位；轴承
plate	/pleɪt/	*n.* 盘子，盆子；金属板；均匀厚度的片状硬物体；〈摄〉底片，感光板 *vt.* 镀，在……上覆盖金属板；覆盖；电镀；〈印〉给……制铅板
offset	/ˈɔːfset/	*vt.* 抵消；补偿；（为了比较的目的而）把……并列

（或并置）；为（管道等）装支管
vi. 形成分支，长出分枝；装支管
adj. 分支的；偏（离中）心的；抵消的；开端的

词	音标	释义
retainer	/rɪˈteɪnə/	*n.* 〈机〉承盘，挡板；家臣，侍从；〈牙科〉牙架；保持着
crankcase	/ˈkræŋkˌkeɪs/	*n.* 曲轴箱
seal	/siːl/	*v.* 封上；密封；覆盖表面；确定；关闭 *n.* 印章；保证；密封处/物/垫；封条/蜡；海豹
gasket	/ˈɡæskɪt/	*n.* 束帆索；垫圈；衬垫
timing	/ˈtaɪmɪŋ/	*n.* 时机掌握；配光；记时；定时
pump	/pʌmp/	*n.* 泵；加油泵；帆布鞋；女士浅口鞋；抽吸 *v.* 输送；涌出；快速摇动；快速运动；不停地追问
toothed	/tuːθt/	*adj.* 有齿的，锯齿状的
pulley	/ˈpʊli/	*n.* 滑轮（组），滑车；皮带轮
carburetor	/ˈkɑbəˌreɪtə/	*n.* 〈机〉汽化器，化油器
drain	/dreɪn/	*v.* 排出；（使）流干；喝光；使……耗尽 *n.* 下水道；排水管
fuelling	/ˈfjuəlɪŋ/	*n.* 加燃料，加油
bolt	/boʊlt/	*n.* 螺栓；闩；一道（闪电）；一匹（布） *v.* 用螺栓固定；闩上；（因受惊吓）迅速逃跑；狼吞虎咽；逃窜
regulator	/ˈreɡjuleɪtər/	*n.* 校准者，〈机〉调整器，校准器，调节器，〈化〉调节剂，〈无线〉稳定器，调节基因，（钟表的）整时器，标准钟
crush	/krʌʃ/	*v.* 挤；压坏，捣碎；镇压；使消沉 *n.* 拥挤的人群；迷恋，爱慕
spray	/spreɪ/	*n.* 水花；喷剂；喷水器；喷雾；小树枝；花簇 *v.* 喷；使飞溅；往……上撒扫射（子弹）；在……上喷涂料；喷农药；撒尿
ring	/rɪŋ/	*n.* 戒指；环状物；圆形（表演场）；炉口；帮派；铃声；清晰的响声；特性 *v.* 包围，给……戴上金属环；画圈；打电话；铃响，按铃；回响；充满
throttle	/ˈθrɑtl/	*n.* （汽车、飞机的）节流阀，油门杆，油门踏板；功率，马力；风门（杆） *v.* 扼杀，压制；勒死，使窒息；使节流；（用节汽阀等）调节
filter	/ˈfɪltər/	*n.* 过滤器；筛选（过滤）程序；分流信号/指示灯

	v.过滤；渗透；泄露；仅可左转行驶
gauge /geɪdʒ/	n.测量的标准或范围；尺度，标准；测量仪器；评估
	vt.(用仪器)测量；确定容量，体积或内容；评估，判断；采用
manifold /ˈmænɪfoʊld/	adj.多种多样的；多方面的；有多种形式的；有多种用途的
	n.具有多种形式的东西；多支管；歧管（汽车引擎用于进气或排气）
volume /ˈvɑːljəm/	n.体积；音量；一卷；合订本
radius /ˈreɪdiəs/	n.半径（距离）；用半径度量的圆形面积；半径范围；桡骨
diameter /daɪˈæmɪtər/	n.直径；放大倍数
displacement /dɪsˈpleɪsmənt/	n.取代；免职；迫使迁徙；〈船〉排水量；〈化〉置换
torque /tɔrk/	n.（尤指机器的）扭转力；转（力）矩；〈史〉（古高卢人、布立吞人戴的）金属项圈；金属颈环
clearance /ˈklɪrəns/	n.清除，清理；(官方)许可；间距
circulate /ˈsɜːrkjəleɪt/	v.传递；传阅；流传；循环；传播；往来应酬
friction /ˈfrɪkʃn/	n.摩擦；冲突，不和；摩擦力
lubricant /ˈluːbrɪkənt/	n.润滑剂，润滑油；能减少摩擦的东西；〈俚〉奶油，黄油
minimize /ˈmɪnɪmaɪz/	vt.把……减至最低数量；对（某事物）作最低估计，极力贬低（某事物）的价值；极度
wear /wer/	v.穿，戴；蓄留；流露（表情）；磨损，用旧；耐用
	n.(特定时候或场合穿的)服装；穿戴；耐用性，使用率；磨损
overhaul /ˈoʊvərhɔːl; oʊvərˈhɔːl/	n.全面检修；(系统、体制等的)全面修改；修订
	vt.彻底检修；全面改革（制度、方法等）；赶上（赛跑对手）
jacket /ˈdʒækɪt/	n.短上衣，夹克；土豆皮；书籍的护封；文件套，公文夹
splash /splæʃ/	v.(使)溅起；戏水；以醒目方式刊登；引人注目
	n.溅泼声；扑通声；一片鲜艳颜色；洒泼上去的一点儿
impeller /ɪmˈpelə/	n.推进者；叶轮
hose /hoʊz/	n.（橡胶或塑料制的）水管，软管；袜类（包括连裤袜、长筒袜、短袜）；（旧时的）男式紧身裤
	v.用水管冲洗（或浇灌）

droplet /ˈdrɑːplət/	n.小滴，微滴；小水珠
mist /mɪst/	n.薄雾；视线模糊不清；液体喷雾
	vt.（使）蒙上薄雾；（使）模糊
	vi.下雾；变模糊
surround /səˈraʊnd/	v.围绕；包围；与……密切相关；喜欢结交
	n.边饰；环境
gallery /ˈɡæləri/	n.画廊，走廊；（教堂，议院等的）边座；旁听席；大批观众
exchanger /ɪksˈtʃeɪndʒə/	n.交换器，换热器
strainer /ˈstreɪnə/	n.滤器；滤盆、滤网
flatten /ˈflætn/	vt.& vi.变平，使（某物）变平；打倒，击倒；使失去光泽
quantificationally /ˌkwɒntɪfɪˈkeɪʃənəlɪ/	adv.定量（化）地
aluminum /əˈlumənəm/	n.铝
grease /ɡriːs/	n.动物油脂；油膏，润滑油；〈俚〉贿赂
	vt.涂油脂于，用油脂润滑；贿赂

第 7 章

chassis /ˈʃæsi/	n.（车辆的）底盘
assembly /əˈsembli/	n.集会装配；总成
vehicle /ˈviːəkl/	n.车辆，交通工具；手段，工具
power train	传动系
frame /freɪm/	n.框架，构架；体系；眼镜框
	v.给……装/做框；表达制定；诬陷
suspension /səˈspenʃn/	n.悬浮；暂停，暂缓；悬架；悬浮液
steering /ˈstɪərɪŋ/	n.转向装置
brake /breɪk/	n.制动器；刹车；抑制因素；阻力；障碍
	v.刹车；减速
clutch /klʌtʃ/	n.紧抓；控制；离合器；紧要关头
gearbox /ˈɡɪəbɒks/	n.变速箱；变速器；齿轮箱
drive shaft	（机器的）传动轴，驱动轴
final drive	最终传动
differential /ˌdɪfəˈrenʃl/	adj.差别的；特意的
	n.〈机〉差速器
automobile /ˈɔːtəməbiːl/	n.汽车
unitized body	承载式车身
torque /tɔːk/	n.（尤指机器的）扭转力；转（力）矩

rotation /rəʊˈteɪʃn/	n.旋转，转动；轮流，循环
reducer /rɪˈdjuːsə/	n.减速器
flywheel /ˈflaɪwiːl/	n.飞轮
driven plate	从动盘
pressure plate	压盘
spring /sprɪŋ/	n.弹簧
mounted /ˈmaʊntɪd/	adj.安装好的；裱好的
bolt /bəʊlt/	n.螺栓
overload /ˌəʊvəˈləʊd/	v.使负担太重；使超载；使过载；给……增加负担
ring /rɪŋ/	n.戒指；环状物
engage with	交战；接洽，处理
spline /splaɪn/	n.花键
	vt.用花键联接，开键槽
hub /hʌb/	n.轮轴；中心，焦点
friction /ˈfrɪkʃn/	n.摩擦；冲突，不和；摩擦力
rivet /ˈrɪvɪt/	n.铆钉
	v.铆接
cast iron	铸铁，生铁
coil /kɔɪl/	n.卷，圈；线圈；盘管
	v.卷，盘绕
diaphragm spring	膜片弹簧
revolve /rɪˈvɒlv/	v.（使）旋转
pedal /ˈpedl/	n.踏板
fork /fɔːk/	n.餐叉；岔口
separating /ˈsepəreɪt/	adj.分开的
	v.分开；（使）分离；区分；隔开
lever /ˈliːvə(r)/	n.杠杆；操作杆；工具
	vt.用杠杆撬动
sleeve /sliːv/	n.〈机〉套筒，套管
ratio /ˈreɪʃiəʊ/	n.比，比率；比例；系数
reverse /rɪˈvɜːs/	vt.& vi.（使）反转；（使）颠倒；掉换，交换
	adj.颠倒的；倒开的
	n.倒转，反向
manual /ˈmænjuəl/	adj.用手的；手工的；体力的；手动的
synchronize /ˈsɪŋkrənaɪz/	vt.使同步；使同时
	vi.同时发生；共同行动
couple /ˈkʌpl/	n.一对；一双
planetary /ˈplænətri/	adj.行星的；行星齿轮的

automatic /ˌɔːtəˈmætɪk/	adj.自动的
stepless /ˈstepləs/	adj.平滑，无级的，不分级的
hydraulic /haɪˈdrɔːlɪk/	adj.水力的，水压的；用水发动的
convertor /kənˈvɜːtə/	n.变换器，变流器
bevel /ˈbevl/	n.斜边和斜面
belt /belt/	n.腰带；区域；传送带；带状物
turbine /ˈtɜːbaɪn/	n.涡轮机；汽轮机
propeller /prəˈpelə(r)/	n.螺旋桨，推进器
axle /ˈæksl/	n.轮轴；车轴；轴端
universal joint	万向节
cage /keɪdʒ/	n.笼子
Zerk /zɜːk/	n.加油嘴
seal /siːl/	v.封上；密封
	n.密封处/物/垫
retarder /rɪˈtɑːdə/	n.阻滞剂，减速器
hollow /ˈhɒləʊ/	adj.空的；空洞的；虚伪的；空腹的
solid /ˈsɒlɪd/	adj.固体的；坚硬的；实心的
invariable /ɪnˈveəriəbl/	adj.恒定的，不变的，始终如一的
independent suspension	独立悬挂
cargo /ˈkɑːɡəʊ/	n.（船或飞机装载的）货物
absorber /əbˈsɔːbə/	n.吸收者，减震器；减振器
elastic /ɪˈlæstɪk/	adj.有弹力的；可伸缩的；灵活的
	n.松紧带，橡皮圈
knuckle /ˈnʌkl/	n.节，肘；铰结
trapezoid /ˈtræpəzɔɪd/	n.梯形，不等边四边形
assist /əˈsɪst/	v.帮助；协助；援助；促进
reserve /rɪˈzɜːvz/	n.储量，储备；
executor /ɪɡˈzekjətə(r)/	n.执行者；执行元件
booster /ˈbuːstə(r)/	n.（电器的）增压机；助推器
main cylinder	主缸
slave cylinder	从动缸，工作缸
pneumatic /njuːˈmætɪk/	adj.充气的；气动的
compressor /kəmˈpresə(r)/	n.压气机，压缩机

第 8 章

current /ˈkʌrənt/	adj.现在的；最近的；流行的；流传的； n.趋势；电流；水流；涌流

burn up		烧起来，烧掉，发怒；毁；烧毁
wire	/'waɪə(r)/	n.金属丝；电线；电报；（木偶的）牵线，操纵绳，背后操纵的势力，秘密引线，秘密策略
		vi.拍电报
		vt.拍电报；给……装电线
fusible	/'fjuːzəbl/	adj.熔解的，可熔的；易熔
exceed	/ɪk'siːd/	vt.超过；超越；胜过；越过……的界限
		vi.突出，领先
solenoid	/'səʊlənɔɪd/	n.螺线管；线包
junction	/'dʒʌŋkʃn/	n.连接，接合；会合点，接合点；（公路或铁路的）交叉路口；（电缆等的）主结点
terminal	/'tɜːmɪnl/	adj.末期的；晚期的；定期的；末端的
		n.终端；终点站；航空站；（电路的）端子
maintenance	/'meɪntənəns/	n.维持，保持；保养，保管；维护；维修
alternative	/ɔːl'tɜːnətɪv/	adj.替代的；备选的；其他的；另类的
		n.可供选择的事物
petrol	/'petrəl/	n.汽油
sulphuric	/sʌl'fjʊərɪk/	adj.硫黄的，含多量硫黄的
acid	/'æsɪd/	n.酸
		adj.酸（性）的；尖酸的，刻薄的
corrosive	/kə'rəʊsɪv/	adj.腐蚀性的；侵蚀性的；（对社会、个人情感等）有害的；（语言）激烈的
pole	/pəʊl/	n.〈物〉极点，顶点；地极；杆；两极端
		vt&vi.用篙撑船，摆船
		vt.〈航海〉用一根杆来推动；以杆推进；以杆支撑（植物）；用杆子击打、戳或搅拌
		vi.用滑雪杖加速
shell	/ʃel/	n.（贝、卵、坚果等的）壳；外壳；炮弹；（人的）表面性格
		vt.去壳，脱落；炮击
		vi.剥皮；炮轰
revolution	/ˌrevə'luːʃn/	n.革命；彻底改变；旋转；运行，公转
combustion	/kəm'bʌstʃən/	n.燃烧，烧毁；氧化；骚动
cylinder	/'sɪlɪndə(r)/	n.圆筒，圆柱；汽缸；（尤指用作容器的）圆筒状物
emission	/i'mɪʃn/	n.排放，辐射；排放物，散发物（尤指气体）；（书刊）发行，发布（通知）
diesel	/'diːzl/	n.柴油机；柴油机机车（或船等）
individual	/ˌɪndɪ'vɪdʒuəl/	adj.个人的；独特的；个别的

	*n.*个人；个体
assembly /ə'sembli/	*n.*立法机构；议会；集会；装配
coil /kɔɪl/	*n.*卷，圈；线圈；盘管
	*v.*卷，盘绕
confirmation /ˌkɒnfə'meɪʃn/	*n.*证实，确认书
voltage /'vəʊltɪdʒ/	*n.*电压，伏特数
alarm /ə'lɑːm/	*n.*惊恐；警报；闹铃；动员令
	*vt.*使惊恐；警告；给（门等）安装警报器
distance /'dɪstəns/	*n.*距离，路程；远处；疏远；（时间的）间隔，长久
	*vt.*把……远远甩在后面；疏远；与……保持距离
hazard /'hæzəd/	*vt.*冒险；使遭受危险
	*n.*危险；冒险的事；机会；双骰子游戏
beam /biːm/	*n.*梁，栋梁；束；光线；（电波的）波束
	*vi.*发出光与热；面露喜色
	*vt.*播送；以梁支撑；用……照射；流露
	*vt&vi.*笑容满面，眉开眼笑；发射电波，播送；放出束状的光（或热）
caution /'kɔːʃn/	*n.*小心；警告；〈英〉担保；〈口〉须警惕的事或人
	*vt.*警告；提醒

第 9 章

thrive /θraɪv/	*vi.*兴盛，兴隆；长得健壮；茁壮成长
subsystem /'sʌb'sɪstəm/	*n.*子系统，分系统
lithium /'lɪθiəm/	*n.*〈化〉锂
hybrid /'haɪbrɪd/	*n.*杂种；杂交生成的生物体；混合物；混合词
series /'sɪəriːz/	*n.*系列，连续；串联；（广播或电视上题材或角色相同的）系列节目；级数
parallel /'pærəlel/	*adj.*平行的；相同的，类似的；〈电〉并联的；〈计〉并行的
	*n.*平行线（面）；相似物；类比；纬线
planetary /'plænətri/	*adj.*行星的；俗世的，现世的；流浪的，飘忽不定的；〈机〉行星齿轮的
	*vt.*使平行；与……媲美；与……相比；与……相似

第 10 章

autonomous /ɔː'tɒnəməs/	*adj.*自治的；有自主权的；〈生，植〉自发的

fulfill	/fʊlˈfil/	vt. 履行（诺言等）；执行（命令等）；达到（目的）；使结束
capability	/ˌkeɪpəˈbɪləti/	n. 才能，能力；容量；性能；生产率
platoon	/pləˈtuːn/	n.〈军〉排，团；一群，一组；〈美〉警察队
synchronize	/ˈsɪŋkrənaɪz/	vt. 使同步；使同时； vi. 同时发生；共同行动
surrounding	/səˈraʊndɪŋ/	adj. 周围的，附近的 v. 包围（surround 的现在分词）；与……紧密相关；围绕；喜欢结交（某类人）
pedestrian	/pəˈdestriən/	n. 步行者；行人 adj. 徒步的；平淡无奇的；一般的
aluminum	/əˈljuːmɪnəm/	n.〈化〉铝
reinforce	/ˌriːɪnˈfɔːs/	vt. 加固；强化；增援 vi. 求援；得到增援；给予更多的支持
nanotube	/ˈneɪnəʊtjʊb/	n. 碳纳米管
visibility	/ˌvɪzəˈbɪləti/	n. 能见度；可见性；可见距离；清晰度

参 考 文 献

[1] REIF K, HOCHSCHULE BADEN-WURTTEMBERG D, FRIEDRICHSHAFEN. Fundamentals of Automotive and Engine Technology[M]. Konrad Reif Editor, 2014.

[2] 《汽车英语》教材编写组. 汽车英语[M]. 北京：高等教育出版社，2008.

[3] MARTINEZ I. The Future of the Automotive Industry[M]. Inma Martinez, 2021.

[4] SCHAFER H. The Automotive Development Process[M].Springer Dordrecht Heidelberg London, 2006.

[5] 尉庆国，张红光，杨翠芬. 汽车文化概论[M]. 北京：国防工业出版社，2013.

[6] 宋进桂，徐永亮. 新能源汽车专业英语[M]. 北京：机械工业出版社，2020.

[7] 宋进桂. 汽车专业英语[M]. 北京：机械工业出版社，2013.

[8] 李清民. 汽车技术[M]. 北京：清华大学出版社，2013.

[9] 帅石金. 汽车文化[M]. 2版. 北京：清华大学出版社，2007.

[10] 王云霞，张书诚. 汽车文化[M]. 合肥：中国科学技术大学出版社，2015.

[11] DESERT P. Electric, Hybrid, and Fuel Cell Vehicles[M]. Argonne National Laboratory Argonne, IL, USA, September 2021.

[12] YIMIN GAO E. Modern Electric, Hybrid Electric and Fuel cell Vehicles-Fundamentals, Theory, and Design[M]. Second Edition. Springer Science Business Media, 2010.